Classical Social Theory

DATE DUE

FEB 2 8 2018	

21St-CENTURY SOCIOLOGY

SERIES EDITOR: Steven Seidman, State University of New York at Albany

The *21st-Century Sociology* series provides instructors and students with key texts in sociology that speak with a distinct sociological voice and offer thoughtful and original perspectives. The texts reflect current discussions in and beyond sociology, avoiding standard textbook definitions to engage students in critical thinking and new ideas. Prominent scholars in various fields of social inquiry combine theoretical perspectives with the latest research to present accessible syntheses for students as we move further into the new millennium amidst rapid social change.

CLASSICAL SOCIAL THEORY
A Contemporary Approach

KENNETH H. TUCKER, JR.

Blackwell
Publishing

BLACKWELL PUBLISHING
350 Main Street, Malden, MA 02148-5020, USA
9600 Garsington Road, Oxford OX4 2DQ, UK
550 Swanston Street, Carlton, Victoria 3053, Australia

The right of Kenneth H. Tucker, Jr. to be identified as Author of this Work has been
asserted in accordance with the Copyright, Designs and Patents Act 1988.

First published 2002

2   2005

Library of Congress Cataloging-in-Publication Data

Tucker, Kenneth H.
  Classical social theory : a contemporary approach / Kenneth H. Tucker, Jr.
      p. cm. — (21st-century sociology)
  Includes bibliographical references and index.
  ISBN 0-631-21164-0 (alk. paper) — ISBN 0-631-21165-9 (pb. : alk. paper)
  1. Sociology—History. 2. Sociology—Philosophy. I. Title. II. Series.

  HM435 .T83 2001
  301'.01—dc21
                                                                2001025198

ISBN-13: 978-0-631-21164-8 (alk. paper) — ISBN-13: 978-0-631-21165-5 (pb. : alk. paper)

A catalogue record for this title is available from the British Library.

The publisher's policy is to use permanent paper from mills that operate a sustainable
forestry policy, and which has been manufactured from pulp processed using acid-
free and elementary chlorine-free practices. Furthermore, the publisher ensures that
the text paper and cover board used have met acceptable environmental accreditation
standards.

For further information on
Blackwell Publishing, visit our website:
www.blackwellpublishing.com

To the memory of my parents

Contents

Acknowledgments

There are many people who helped me throughout the writing of this book. Steven Seidman suggested and supported the project, and made valuable comments on the manuscript at an important stage in its development. Several anonymous readers recommended helpful revisions during the initial stages of the writing when I was formulating my ideas. Ken Provencher, commissioning editor at Blackwell Publishers, and copyeditor Jack Messenger were invaluable resources for me. Robert Antonio, Robert Dunn, Elizabeth Long, and Sherry Silveus Tucker read most or all of the manuscript. They often disagreed with me, and their critical comments vastly improved the book. I was unable to incorporate all of their suggestions, and any inaccuracies and/or misinterpretations are entirely attributable to me. The Sociology/Anthropology department and Critical Thought Program of Mount Holyoke College provide an interdisciplinary intellectual environment conducive to innovation in the teaching of social theory. Professors Joan Cocks and Harold Garrett-Goodyear and the students in various Critical Social Thought seminars made excellent comments on the Marx chapter. Finally, I wish to thank Sherry for her intellect, compassion, strength, and support. She has taught me far more than she realizes.

Introduction

As an undergraduate in the 1970s, I took a course on social theory during my sophomore year at the University of California, Santa Barbara. This class turned out to be a pivotal moment in my intellectual life. The professor discussed the critical Marxist social theory of a German group of philosophers and sociologists known as the Frankfurt School, including Max Horkheimer, Theodor Adorno, Herbert Marcuse, Jürgen Habermas, and its roots in the thought of Karl Marx, Max Weber, and Sigmund Freud. These authors began writing in the 1930s, and became popular in the 1960s. They criticized the conformity and standardization of modern societies, in which corporate capitalism, uncontrolled technology, and the mass culture industry reduced the scope of freedom and critical thinking. The professor's informal style of presentation and the course material intersected with the activist mood of the times (though it was waning in the 1970s) and my personal biography to generate what the sociologist Lillian Rubin calls, rather prosaically, an "aha experience," where public and private concerns intersect. Like many others at the time, I had questions about the structure of American social and cultural power in the wake of Vietnam. Like many young adults, my thoughts on these questions tended to be rather self-absorbed. I sensed that social and cultural power was tied to philosophical and personal issues. I wondered if there were connections between the reasons why people so often acted out of self-interest, treated each other as disposable means, and placed such great faith in technical solutions to social problems.

Social theory spoke to me regarding these questions, for it connected personal and social issues in a profound way. My fascination with Marxism was soon complemented by an interest in Weber and Emile Durkheim, early twentieth-century social theorists who struck me as addressing the same questions from different angles. As a graduate student at UC Berkeley, I moved from an interest in labor movements to a concern with the new social movements of the 1960s, 1970s, and 1980s, which centered around issues of civil rights, gender, sexual orientation, the environment, and the decolonization of the European nineteenth- and twentieth-century empires. These movements challenged not only entrenched social power, but the assumptions that informed understandings of society and history. They raised novel issues for social theory, including the role of colonization, gender, race, and sexual orientation in structuring social stratification and personal identity, how different social groups develop varied culturally based knowledges, and how to understand such differences in an egalitarian, non-hierarchical manner. Progress and science were not seen as objective processes guaranteeing truth, but critiqued as ideologies justifying elite power. The new movements also questioned the substance and preconditions of democratic practices, and the limitations of parliamentary versions of democracy.

These new issues challenge the viability of classical sociological traditions to understand contemporary issues and events. In the wake of the new social movements, much criticism has been directed at the sociological canon, especially the triumvirate of Marx, Weber, and Durkheim. They are accused of marginalizing race, gender, and colonialism in their theories, and their relevance to today's issues is questioned. It is time to write an undergraduate text that reviews the accomplishments of the classics while pointing to their theoretical limitations. This book summarizes the major themes of the classical sociological theory of Marx, Weber, and Durkheim. It also interprets their thought through the lens of new theoretical concerns, from the role of Empire in shaping sociological theory to the prospects and limitations for democracy in each theorist's perspective. The text examines other nineteenth- and early twentieth-century theorists who open up new perspectives on these issues in ways not adequately addressed by Marx, Durkheim, and Weber. These theorists include Freud, Georg Simmel, G. H. Mead, W. E. B. Du Bois, and Charlotte Perkins Gilman, who raise issues of colonialism, race, gender, and the complexity of cultural and personal identity.

I will closely read the texts of these theorists, drawing out their major themes and internal contradictions. I think the best criticism intensively examines the arguments of the thinkers under study. I will also place their thought in the historical circumstances of their time, so that their ideas are presented in the context of the social problems and intellectual debates they addressed. But such internal or "immanent" criticism is not enough. We always interpret thinkers of the past with contemporary themes in mind. I will be led by my own interpretation of the major issues of social theory today, and whether the classical theorists can contribute to an understanding of them. I will defend and criticize the classical theorists where appropriate, assessing their significance for our time. While some of their viewpoints are indeed dated, others can help to puncture the conventional wisdom of current social theory.

The Canon and Its Problems

In most colleges and universities, sociology students who study social theory read texts by Marx, Weber, and Durkheim. These three nineteenth-century European social theorists are considered to have formulated many of the fundamental themes of sociology. They achieved several of sociology's most distinctive approaches and central concepts. Each of these thinkers was contributing to a common intellectual enterprise, what Collins and Makowsky refer to as the discovery of society.[1] They responded in divergent ways to a shared historical context, which included the rise and transformation of Western society in the nineteenth and early twentieth centuries. The aftermath of the French Revolution, the industrial revolution, the emergence of the market, and European colonialism opened up social, economic, and cultural opportunities and problems previously unimaginable, from the possibilities of more complex types of social organization (capitalism and socialism) to a novel type of culture based on rationality, social participation, and individualism rather than tradition.

These theorists recognized that these new societies differed in dramatic ways from those that preceded them. They were involved in explaining modernity, the rise of new institutions associated with democracy and industrial capitalism, and an emerging culture of constant innovation and widespread rationality.[2] They faced a cultural crisis, where old values and orientations no longer seemed to make sense of this new world. This new society called for a revised social science, which attempted to answer fundamental philosophical and moral questions, such as the scope of reason and the nature of liberty, from a sociological angle. Marx, Weber, and Durkheim see the possibilities for human freedom embodied in the rationality, industry, and democracy arising in the nineteenth and twentieth centuries, and each also recognizes dilemmas inherent in these societies, exemplified in Marx's criticisms of alienation, Weber's view of the loss of meaning in the iron cage of bureaucratic rationality, and Durkheim's analysis of anomie. They contend that religion can no longer provide a basis for social solidarity and ethics, and turn to variants of democratic and republican traditions to provide social integration and meaning in the modern world.

These are powerful insights which can help illuminate many social processes today, in my view. Yet these theorists' arguments reflected many taken-for-granted assumptions that they did not interrogate in any depth. There is no doubt that sociological theory was to some degree a collective product of nineteenth-century European society, heavily influenced by colonialism, which these thinkers sometimes ignored.[3] Despite many differences, Marx, Durkheim, and Weber agree that modern societies are largely industrial societies, consisting of increasing rationality, specialization, economic growth, and social complexity. These theorists share a belief in the efficacy of social scientific explanation, which they think can grasp the forces determining human behavior by plumbing the depths behind the surfaces of social life. They argue that the use of reason is the best means to achieve social progress, and they tend to accept European societies as the model for the rest of the world. They rarely questioned the privileges associated with being European or male.

All of these assumptions are now problematic, in part because of the changes in the social and intellectual world since the late nineteenth century that I discussed earlier. The equation of science and progress is questionable, to say the least, in the wake of two world wars and the possibilities of ecological and nuclear catastrophes. Europe and the US are not always benign models for the rest of the world, as their global domination is often based on economic and cultural imperialism. Race and gender mark social and personal identities in complex ways. Private and public identities are tied to cultural and linguistic processes, as well as economic ones.

I explore the classical sociological theorists through the lens of these contemporary issues and theoretical concerns. I focus on four areas: democracy and the public sphere; the paradox of rationality and the disciplinary society; colonialism; and issues of individual and cultural identity. I think these are the most pressing issues of our time. We live in a multicultural world where we have to develop new understandings of dialogue, democracy, and power, in order to live together in an egalitarian manner. Though I am critical of the classical social theorists, these thinkers can also contribute to a better understanding of these contemporary issues.

Marx, Weber, and Durkheim were complex thinkers, and I do not wish to force their thought into a straitjacket that distorts their work. I summarize each theorist's major arguments about social change and the dynamics of modernity. This synopsis includes Marx on capitalism and alienation, Durkheim on social solidarity and the sacred, and Weber on rationalization, bureaucracy, and the tensions inherent in modernity. Issues of class were of central importance to them. I also explore the philosophical influences on each theorist's perspective, from the Enlightenment through romanticism to Nietzsche's critique of philosophy, for they were interested in understanding such basic philosophical questions as the nature of freedom and the conditions for a good, just society. This philosophical dimension of their thought, combined with their attempts to understand and change society, gave their ideas a passion often lacking in contemporary social science. But in order to adequately grasp these various dimensions of classical theory's context and legacy, we need to add new thinkers from Freud to Du Bois to the classical theory mix, in order to appreciate its richness and possibilities for comprehending contemporary issues.

It is not that the public sphere, cultural identity, and the like were non-existent in the nineteenth century, but rather that they are on the fore-front of the public agenda now and reconfigured in different ways than in the nineteenth century. I argue that Marx, Weber, and Durkheim, Freud, Simmel, Mead, Du Bois, and Perkins Gilman have much of interest to say about these issues, though their arguments concerning them are some-times indirect, and their perspectives also demonstrate their theoretical limitations. Let's explore these issues in more depth.

Democracy and the Public Sphere

In the wake of the fall of communism in Europe and the rise of the new social movements, the requirements for the maintenance of a vigorous democracy have become a popular topic of discussion in the West. In the US as throughout Western Europe, many commentators contend that a crisis of democracy is at hand, demonstrated in a range of factors from tumbling voting rates in elections to the seeming incivility of public life.

This social context has prompted many contemporary sociological theo-rists, such as Jürgen Habermas, Anthony Giddens, and Alain Touraine, to formulate new approaches to the problems of contemporary democracy. While differing in many ways, they concur that the study and practice of democracy must move beyond representative parliamentary and legisla-tive institutions. A public sphere, where people can freely meet and dis-cuss issues of common concern outside of formal state institutions, is a necessary prerequisite for the exercise of a vibrant democracy. Democracy requires a culture fostering rational dialogue, openness, and tolerance. They are fearful that consumerism and an overemphasis on expertise can undermine democratic interaction. For example, Touraine and Habermas view the entertainment-driven mass media as an anti-democratic force, which encourages people to see themselves as passive consumers of pre-fabricated political images, rather than active citizens engaged in debate about the collective future of their society.[4] Touraine and Giddens also raise the problem of cultural fundamentalism, the defense of traditional beliefs without recourse to rational debate, as a threat to democracy. The twenty-first century has seen the rise of fundamentalist beliefs in religion and culture throughout the world.

The classical sociological theorists were not strangers to such concerns.

They too saw democracy endangered by capitalism, which encouraged bureaucracies and an instrumental reason that reduced concern for the public good. They advocated freedom of thought and research, contending that clericalism, state censorship, and nationalistic fervor could undermine these values. Such fundamentalist beliefs were impervious to argument. These theorists recognized that democracy was fragile, threatened by economic interests and fundamentalist beliefs, and had to be grounded in the actual collective experience of people if it was to be successful. They wished to expand the public sphere beyond voting, contending that public debate was crucial in the formation of citizenship, and were interested in political and economic rights for the working class.

The classical theorists wrote in a context different from that of the West today, which now includes a much more inclusive public life than that of their time. Since the nineteenth century, voting and civil rights have been extended to women and various minority groups. The state provides social and economic benefits, from public education to unemployment insurance, which existed only in rudimentary form, if at all, in the nineteenth century. Though Marx, Weber, and Durkheim did not question their gender and racial privileges to the extent that critics now do, they focused directly on social and political exclusion related to class. The male working class was the dominant group struggling for citizenship rights and economic benefits in the public sphere. This class attracted much of their concern and research interests, rather than the struggles of women and minorities.

For the classical theorists, democracy meant more than voting, more than the institutional guarantees for the exercise of political rights, such as freedom of speech. In different ways, Marx, Weber, and Durkheim, but also Mead and Du Bois, saw that political issues were always tied to economic power. Each theorist contended that democracy was threatened by divisions of wealth which concentrated power in the hands of the few, and that capitalism tended to promote a private, egoistic approach to social life which hampered democratic practice. An effective democracy demanded active participation in public life, and a culture of citizenship that would provide the impetus for this participation. The theorists drew on democratic republicanism, a tradition arising from the thought of Aristotle, Machiavelli, Rousseau, and Kant, which advocated active, participatory democracy as the key to a good society. The institutional dimension of democracy was always embedded in a larger cultural, social, and economic framework which dramatically influenced its functioning. Political rights and constitutions were dependent on a cultural and social infrastructure which was the true basis of democratic life. In different ways, these theorists recognized that modernity meant more plurality and diversity, and democracy had to respond to these new issues.

In sum, these theorists developed a rich notion of the public sphere. Du

Bois advocated the creation of a black public sphere outside of the state, where a new African-American culture could be cultivated. Mead recognized the necessity of free, open public spaces for social interaction and democracy to emerge. For Marx, unions and political parties could be spaces where workers could develop a sense of their distinctive heritage and values. Durkheim was interested in the public sphere as well, as an arena where moral individualism could be practiced and nurtured. Weber too, despite his criticisms of democracy, believed that the practice of democratic ideals by citizens was central to its success.

Rationality, Science, and Power

The argument that democracy is grounded in social conditions that must encourage autonomy and rational debate leads to questions of culture and power. The relationship of culture and rationality to power has been of central significance for many contemporary theorists. Cultural understandings have enormous consequences for the configuration of social power in a given society. Habermas focuses on how an instrumental reason oriented toward the control and prediction of social life validates the rule of technical expertise as the best way to solve social problems, inhibiting people's capacities to collectively create a meaningful existence. Thinkers who adopt some of Michel Foucault's tenets explore the ways in which dominant knowledges marginalize other cultural beliefs. These thinkers recognize the difficulties, if not the desirability, of achieving a just social consensus in the context of cultural differences and subtle forms of cultural power.

These ideas have been most powerfully presented in postmodern thinkers such as Foucault.[5] Foucault argues that rationality is tied to power rather than freedom. Beginning in the seventeenth century, European elites used state-supported science to control their populations, demonstrated in the rise of institutions such as prisons and asylums that established the rule of experts and doctors over a subject population. As modern governments gained power, they became interested in issues such as population and military capacity, developing techniques to better gain a handle on their subjects so that people could become docile and predictable.[6] What Foucault calls surveillance was at the heart of modernity, creating the preconditions for the rise of the "disciplinary society." Knowledge was intimately tied to power, as experts, from psychiatrists to Md.'s, defined normal and abnormal behavior, often using science to distinguish, classify, and institutionalize people who did not fit the norm, whether defined in terms of sexuality, madness, or criminality. Experts used science to justify a single morality as the only one possible for everyone.

Foucault saw the classical sociological theorists as part of a social scientific approach which created the knowledge base for the rise of the disciplinary society. He is right to some degree, for classical social theory was tied to this legacy. Marx, Weber, and Durkheim did not always adequately reflect on the ways that rationality can exclude and define others as irrational, and therefore inferior. For the most part, they did not view their theories as moral tales, stories or narratives that were not indicative of larger truths.

Yet to reduce the work of these theorists to this one perspective on disciplinary society is to misread them. The classical theorists understood reason and social science in a complicated manner. Though they tended to celebrate science and rationality, they were aware of some of their limits and pitfalls. They developed their scientific ideas in the wake of the romantic movement's criticisms of science and reason, and validation of sentiment and emotion. Their complex understanding of the potential and limits of science separated them from their more narrow-minded scientistic colleagues, as well as their Enlightenment ancestors. Their broad-ranging interests also differed from the specialized, expert-based scientists that often dominate our era.

Weber sees rationality and science as paradoxical, as creating the conditions for freedom while also promoting a nightmarish bureaucratic iron cage for modern peoples. Durkheim argues that reason was embedded in particular cultural traditions, and could take different forms in different societies. Marx contends that rationality and social experience were bound together, and that different classes would develop varying social knowledges. Rationality must be part of people's democratic experience rather than imposed on them if it is to be effective and lead to freedom.

These theorists recognized that people are reflexive agents who can change the social world that they live in, and are not just pawns of larger rationalization processes. To adequately study rationalization and the rise of disciplinary trends within society, they must be placed in their concrete historical context. The classical theorists at their best engaged in such a study.

Freud, Du Bois, Simmel, and Mead are also important figures who can contribute to an understanding of the relationship between rationality and culture not found in Marx, Weber, and Durkheim. They emphasize the emotional and artistic dimensions of experience, the importance of music and play, that are an integral part of social life. Much social interaction is fluid, always changing, and its coherence resembles a dance or a work of art more than a mathematical pattern. This aesthetic orientation gives these thinkers different and varied perspectives on science, the self, and democracy, than that found in Marx, Weber, and Durkheim. Du Bois and Perkins Gilman were interested in how the particular experience of African-Americans and women gave them different, critical viewpoints.

Freud argued that rationality had irrational bases in the unconscious. But for all these thinkers, these themes were often conflated with a celebration of modernity. Except for Du Bois, these problems become apparent in the theorists' relative inattention to colonialism.

Colonialism

The classical social theorists saw modernity as a world historical experience, transforming the lives of people throughout the globe. The sense of the modern as different from the traditional arose from the experience of the massive changes that capitalism and industrialism meant for everyday life, as traditions began to disintegrate and "all that is solid turns into air."[7] Despite some ambivalence about modernity, the classical theorists saw it primarily as a favorable process. Yet modernity's promise of freedom has a troubling relationship with its history of colonialism.[8] Colonialism did not just involve material control of non-Western resources, but also had cultural and philosophical dimensions. For example, much of the thought of Durkheim, Marx, and Weber defined modernity in terms of Western cultural and moral models, as images of "savage/civilized" helped contribute to the traditional/modern distinction which runs through classical sociological theory.

Many of these criticisms of social theory's interpretation of modernity were developed in Edward Said's influential 1978 book, *Orientalism*. Said argues that the self-comprehension of Europe was based on colonialism. Europe labeled itself as a place of order, reason, and power, in contrast to the irrational colonies which it strived to master. The notion of the Orient is a Western invention, and was imagined as an exotic place of passion and danger. Western scholars of the Orient synthesized these assumptions under the guise of the humanities and social sciences, as they "scientifically" demonstrated that the Orient was a primitive land whose values were divergent from, and inferior to, Western rationality, progress, and logic. Academic disciplines focusing on the Orient justified the West's incorporation and description of the inferiority of non-Western peoples. Orientalism is essentially an imperialist view of the world.[9]

Said's analysis of Orientalism can be applied to the role that men have played in labeling women, or the ways that whites define people of color. Such identities and power inequalities are not objective, natural categories. Knowledge cannot be separated from the operation of power; dominant identities are created by subjugating and negating the humanness of others, designating them as irrational.

Classical sociological theorists, like many Europeans, did not escape Orientalism. Irrationality was not just a philosophical problem; it became symbolized and carried by certain groups of people, from women to the colonized, who seemed to stand outside the assumptions of progress, reason, and morality that were so important to the European Enlightenment tradition. For many educated European men, the poor, women, and colonized were identified with unbridled passions. They were defined as wild, irrational, unable to control their impulses, and naturally prone to emotion. The very notion of reason developed in the context of these social definitions of irrationality and colonialism. Marx, Weber, and Durkheim participated in this discourse of colonialism and irrationality, as they defined non-modern peoples as less rational and less developed than modern Europeans. Women, too, were often labeled as representing the irrational. They rarely questioned the superiority of modernity, and often assumed it was inevitable.[10]

But these theorists were not consistent in their writings, as they sometimes critiqued colonialism and racism. Their historical approach prevented them from joining in the chorus that saw non-modern societies as simply "primitive," as many of their colleagues argued. They were influenced by evolutionism and Darwin's theory of natural selection, but often reinterpreted these ideas so that they were sensitive to locale and context. My point here is that these theorists were not entirely uniform on these points, and can be read in various ways. This is part of their attraction and frustration: they cannot be reduced to simple formulas.

This confrontation with other cultures also brought out some of the most interesting insights of Marx, Weber, and Durkheim. Their embrace of modernity and progress was tempered by their emphasis on historical and empirical study, for they struggled to make sense of the complex world around them. Their concrete investigations of cultures made it clear to them that human nature is not static, that it changes over time, and that laws and mores differ from culture to culture. Their wide-ranging comparative historical studies of different societies is almost completely absent from social theory today. They sometimes recognized that this complexity of human societies meant that other cultures could give the West insight into ways of living that could problematize some of its assumptions about superiority. This recognition allowed Marx, Weber, and Durkheim to identify and critique some of the distinctive characteristics of Western modernity. But on the whole, these thinkers were not sufficiently sensitive to the costs and complexity of imperialism. Their lack of reflexivity about these issues permitted them to see themselves as representatives of a better social order, with non-Western cultures as a prelude to a more rational modernity, for the most part. Of the thinkers we examine, only Du Bois consistently challenges this viewpoint. His analysis of the "internal colonization" of African-Americans complements his sense that African and Asian peoples have been casualties of European colonialism.

Individual and Cultural Identity

In today's world, many of our most vociferous and painful debates concern race, gender, and sexual orientation. We also live in a world where the established routes to selfhood, from marriage to careers, are in a state of change and flux. Many of us adorn our bodies in different ways, and we are very conscious about the "look" we are portraying to others. While Marx, Weber, and Durkheim sometimes recognized the complexity of what I call individual and cultural identity, they did not examine these issues with sophistication. Their explanations of race and gender were sketchy and underdeveloped at best, if not misguided. Thinkers such as Freud, Simmel, Mead, Du Bois, and Perkins Gilman addressed these topics in different and often more profound ways than did Marx, Weber, and Durkheim.

I want to explore individual and cultural identity in a bit more detail. Identity involves how we understand our experiences, and how we create a narrative or story about who we are. In the contemporary world, our sense of identity seems less sure, less rooted than in the past, as the traditional narratives about careers, marriage, sexual identity, and gender are breaking down. Many sociologists such as Alberto Melucci argue that we develop a "playing" self in such a context, more open to change and new experiences than in the past. Identity also concerns the relationship between the individual and group, for our sense of who we are is invariably tied up with how others see us. Frequently people today look to race, gender, sexual orientation, and/or the nation for definitions of self and community. Like colonialism, the issue of identity in the West thus involves questions of power, who has the power to construct identities. As the sociologist Robert Dunn puts it, the topic concerns "whether identities are self-constructed or externally imposed, an issue that in turn poses fundamental questions about the social and cultural relations of power."[11]

Marx, Weber, and Durkheim had a sense of some of these issues, though they did not phrase their analyses in this sort of language. Marx develops a complex theory about the creation of class identity, stressing the historically changing, conflicted relationship between classes. The capacity of workers to develop their own sense of cultural distinctiveness is almost non-existent under capitalism, as they have to struggle to develop a sense of identity in the context of capitalist domination. Durkheim's ideal educational system stresses cultural diversity and the learning of different cultural traditions. Individuals have to learn to understand and appreciate many different histories and cultures. In a highly complex modern world, the individual has to be flexible and adaptable to new conditions, and tolerant of other ways of life. Weber's study of the Protestant ethic showed the formation of a repressive individuality necessary for the rise of capitalism. He also sees cultural identity as always contested in a modern world where different religious and other ultimate values compete for allegiance. Individuality is complicated by conflicts between religious, artistic, and secular ways of defining identity. Power is at play in all constructions of identity.

But Marx's, Durkheim's, and Weber's understanding of individual and cultural identity was too rigid. In contrast to Marx, Weber, and Durkheim, the fluidity of identity, and how selfhood arises in a new, changing world is explored by Du Bois, Freud, Simmel, and Mead. I examine their complex understandings of cultural and personal identity, which challenge the assumptions of psychic and cultural coherence that so often characterize the thought of Marx, Weber, and Durkheim. These theorists recognize that people's sense of self is often not based on rationality and predictability; as people fashion their lives almost as a work of art, issues of bodily appearance, sexuality, and the like become increasingly important. Questions of aesthetic and emotional experience call for a rethinking of the rational assumptions of social theory.

I also examine the roles of race and gender in understanding society and identity. Most of the classical theorists started from a fundamentally different place in their understandings of society than, say, Du Bois. Du Bois begins his 1903 work, *The Souls of Black Folk*, with the question: how does it feel to be a problem? For Du Bois, African-Americans were conceived to be a problem in the context of the dominant US culture. Whites never had to confront this issue. I discuss Du Bois's analysis of how whiteness as an unexamined assumption informs much of European social science and culture. I also investigate Perkins Gilman's argument that gender relations are invisible in most social scientific perspectives. Issues of race and gender raise new questions about cultural power and its relationship to the formation of individual identity.

These classical thinkers, from Marx to Simmel, often believed that they were describing a new social reality. But their words helped create this very reality. Each author exemplifies Foucault's notion of an "initiator of discourse," a thinker whose work is so rich that it becomes a subject of ever-renewed interpretation by later commentators.[12] The shape of our lives owes much to these thinkers. That is why it is so important to return to them with new questions, to see what was theoretically lost, and what must be rethought.

Overview

Chapter 1 outlines the social world of the classical sociological theorists. I explore issues of industrialization, democracy, colonialism, and gender in the nineteenth- and early twentieth-century social worlds. In chapter 2 I examine the philosophical background of the classical social theorists, beginning with the Enlightenment. The complex legacy of the Enlightenment involved the critical use of reason against superstition and monarchy, and also promoted the initial philosophical foundations for the rise of the disciplinary society. I discuss Immanuel Kant, the key figure of the post-Enlightenment, who synthesized scientific and democratic themes into a coherent system. Many important philosophical strands emerged from various critiques and revisions of Kant. Republicanism, exemplified in the work of Tocqueville, helped inform the rise of the public sphere. Romanticism emphasized the authentic and natural individual and the diversity of cultures as counterpoints to Kant's rationalism. Hegel synthesizes many of these themes into his complex philosophical system. Pragmatist philosophers such as William James and the German philosopher Friedrich Nietzsche critiqued the Enlightenment's assumptions about morality, reason, freedom, and power, and argued for a more fluid conception of the self and identity.

In part two of the book, I move to a discussion of Marx, Weber, and Durkheim. I explore their thought in the context of the themes of the public sphere and democracy, the disciplinary society, colonialism, and individual and cultural identity. Their work was influenced by many philosophical figures and traditions discussed in chapter 2, including the Enlightenment, romanticism, republicanism, Hegelian philosophy, and often implicitly by Nietzsche's critique of science and morality. In chapter 3, I first discuss two early versions of social science: the thought of Saint-Simon and Comte. I then explore Marx's analysis of capitalism and alienation. Chapter 4 examines Durkheim's theories of the division of labor, suicide, education, and religion. Chapter 5 explores Weber's analysis of rationalization, religion, class, status, and bureaucracy. Part three analyses dimensions of cultural and individual identity neglected by Marx, Durkheim, and Weber. In chapter 6 I take up issues of self and cultural identity in the work of Freud, Simmel, and Mead, and the implications of their thought for conceptions of individuality, science, and democracy. Chapter 7 discusses the influence of race and gender on cultural identity, through examining the thought of Du Bois and Perkins Gilman. The theorists discussed in part three open up the classical sociological canon to new modes of conceiving of individual and cultural identity. They emphasize themes such as multiculturalism, the fluidity of self-formation, the place of emotions in individual and social life, the limits of science in understanding the self and culture, and the contributions that an aesthetic approach to analyzing society can make to social science.

Notes

1 Randall Collins and Michael Makowsky, *The Discovery of Society* (New York, 1998); Kenneth H. Tucker, Jr., *Anthony Giddens and Modern Social Theory* (Thousand Oaks, CA, 1998), pp. 14–15.
2 Anthony Giddens, *The Consequences of Modernity* (Stanford, CA, 1990).
3 R. W. Connell, "Why is Classical Theory Classical?" *American Journal of Sociology* 102 (May 1997), p. 1515.
4 Jürgen Habermas, *Between Facts and Norms: Contributions to a Discourse Theory of Law and Democracy* (Cambridge, MA, 1996); Anthony Giddens, *Beyond Left and Right: The Future of Radical Politics* (Stanford, CA, 1994); Alain Touraine, *Critique of Modernity* (Cambridge, MA, 1995).
5 Michel Foucault, *Discipline and Punish: The Birth of the Prison* (New York, 1977). Postmodernism is a difficult term to clearly define, having taken on a variety of meanings depending on who is using the concept. For my purposes, I distinguish modernism from postmodernism as follows: (1) The modern search for a stable community has been replaced by the postmodern attention to social differences. (2) The Enlightenment contention that rationality leads to a discovery of a timeless, placeless truth is criticized by postmodernists, who celebrate a diversity of truths. (3) Modernists argue that the social and natural worlds can be clearly represented by language. Postmodernists contend that language is always metaphorical; it structures our very sense of "reality," and language itself is always changing. (4) Modernists argue for a coherent, stable self. Postmodernists deconstruct this notion of the individual. They contend that individuality is shaped by class, gender, and racial factors, which are continually in flux. See Tucker, *Anthony Giddens and Modern Social Theory*, p. 133.
6 Zygmut Bauman, *Legislators and Interpreters: On Modernity, Postmodernity, and Intellectuals* (Ithaca, NY, 1987), p. 76.
7 Karl Marx and Friedrich Engels, "Manifesto of the Communist Party," in *The Marx–Engels Reader*, ed. Robert Tucker (New York, 1978), p. 476.
8 Ali Mirsepassi, *Intellectual Discourse and the Politics of Modernization: Negotiating Modernity in Iran* (New York, 1999), pp. 1–2; Tucker, *Anthony Giddens and Modern Social Theory*, pp. 54–5.
9 Edward Said, *Orientalism* (New York, 1978).
10 Bauman, *Legislators and Interpreters*, p. 115.
11 Robert Dunn, *Identity Crises: A Social Critique of Postmodernity* (Minneapolis, 1998), p. 3. See also Alberto Melucci, *The Playing Self: Person and Meaning in the Planetary Society* (New York, 1996).
12 Michel Foucault, "What is an Author," in *Language, Counter-Memory, Practice: Selected Essays and Interviews*, ed. Donald Bouchard (Ithaca, NY, 1977), pp. 113–38.

PART I

The Social and Intellectual Context of Classical Social Theory

CHAPTER ONE

The World of Classical Social Theory

The work of the classical sociological theorists developed during "the long European nineteenth century," dating from the French Revolution of 1789 to the Russian Revolution of 1917 and the end of World War I in 1918. Marx, Weber, Durkheim, and the other theorists we will consider were contributing to a shared intellectual project: the discovery of society. The "great transformation" of the nineteenth century, marked by industrialization and capitalism, the rise of the nation-state and democracy, and European colonialism, transformed the countenance of Europe and the world.[1]

Cultural changes were also important. The rise of the nation-state, the emergence of capitalism, and colonialism involved new conceptions of individualism and self-identity. In the wake of the European Renaissance, a new sense of the individual emerged in the West. Rigid inherited social roles broke down, urbanism gradually appeared, and social mobility slowly became possible for non-aristocratic people. These changes were tied to a new comprehension of individual agency, i.e. that one's actions could influence one's fate. The idea of the self became less constrained by social ties, more fluid and open to new experiences.

This new sense of self-autonomy depended on important institutional changes in the West. As democracy arose as a political system, public life became defined as an arena where decisions of common public concern could be discussed and debated by citizens, which Habermas labels the public sphere. Alongside this public realm a new private sphere developed, centered in the family. In the private sphere, one could be an authentic, passionate, and sincere individual, in contrast to the artificial, role-playing figure that essentially characterized the public self. Yet the public/private split also promoted a more complicated notion of the individual self whose make-up was inseparable from the social interactions that it encountered. This new sense of self was tied to the rise of the market as well as to democracy, for people increasingly worked outside of the household in occupations no longer linked to agriculture. These occupational changes encouraged the perception one engages in different behaviors and roles outside of the home than inside of it.[2]

This new configuration of public and private life created novel problems of political rule and self-development in democratic societies. The public and private spheres coexisted uneasily, as these domains seemed on the verge of collapse into one another. Never before had so many people been given the opportunity to govern themselves while having the possibility of changing their economic position; and this new political order, based on equality, emerged simultaneously with the inequalities generated by a capitalist economy and the production of unprecedented wealth in the nineteenth century.

I concentrate on the crucial transformations that I view as responsible for these changes, and that influenced the ambience of classical sociological theory: (1) the industrial revolution, consisting of the growth of technology, the market, and cities; (2) the French Revolution and the social and political changes it entailed, including the rise of the nation-state, nationalism, and democracy; and (3) colonialism, as history becomes world history as societies become interconnected. I end with a discussion of changing gender roles.

Industrialization and Urbanization

For almost all of history, the vast majority of people lived a rural existence, congregating on isolated, self-subsistent farms, in nomadic tribes, or in small villages. Under European feudalism (approximately 700–1500), before the rise of capitalism, the economy was submerged in customary social relationships. Tradition guided economic transactions. For example, feudal lords and peasants shared a system of mutual rights and obligations. Peasants gave a portion of what they produced to the lord, who in turn provided military protection (though this did not always work out in practice). Money and markets were an accessory to self-sufficient households, which produced chiefly for their own use, rather than for trade.

Feudal land and labor were ensconced in a traditional social organization, as money and trade were not major elements of the economy. Ownership of landed property supported the power dynamics of the feudal system. Land was the basis of military, judicial, and administrative systems, its functioning determined by legal and customary rules. As Polanyi states, "Whether it [land] was transferable or not, and if so, to whom and under what restrictions; what the rights or property entailed; to what uses some types of land might be put – all these questions were removed from the organization of buying and selling, and subjected to an entirely different set of institutional regulations."[3] Custom governed the relationship of master and craftsman, while worker guilds were subject to town and monarchical regulations.

Feudalism gradually transformed as markets became more important in economic development. Feudalism had no rational, regularized system of profit-making. Large profits were gained through war and plunder rather than economic activity. Beginning in the sixteenth century, social relations and institutions, from families to governments, were increasingly influenced by the market, rather than by tradition. For example, labor was separated from its traditional protective contexts. Workers, exposed to the vagaries of the market, often lived in poor conditions and worked in unsanitary factories in the early years of the industrial revolution. Machines, cities, and factories were equated with progress by many commentators, but feared by some such as the Scottish historian Thomas Carlyle (1795–1881), who saw them as harbingers of new forms of alienation and isolation. Workshops and factories demanded that more workers congregate in urban areas. Land and labor became commodities – land became private property that could be sold to another, not simply inherited, and workers labored for wages rather than in guilds guided by customary relationships.

Rural conditions predominated until the late nineteenth century. At the outset of the industrial revolution, around 1800, only a handful of people in Europe and the US lived in towns with more than 20,000 people. Over 90 percent of the people lived in the countryside. In the absence of highly developed agricultural technology, extensive roads, and sophisticated transportation, most people worked on farms to produce enough food to feed themselves and the few people who lived in towns. Even by 1848 the population was overwhelmingly rural. In Britain, the most industrialized nation, urban dwellers did not outnumber those living in rural areas until 1851, and then only 51 percent of Britons lived in cities. Only in France, the US and parts of Germany did more than 10 percent of the population live in cities of 10,000 or more people. Illiteracy was widespread; in 1860 75 percent of Spanish men and 89 percent of Spanish women were illiterate; in France in 1876 80 percent of rural men and 67 percent of rural women could not read or write.[4]

By 1900, social conditions had changed dramatically. Capitalism became dominant in the nineteenth century. People moved off the land into cities. In England, the US, and Germany especially, they moved into urban areas, so that more and more lived in towns that had at least 2,500 people by 1900. This trend in urbanization was due to a decrease in mortality, primarily infant mortality, as better sanitation and public health combined with more stable food supplies to increase population. The population of the world doubled in the period from the 1780s to the 1880s.[5] Industrialization created employment in factories near cities, and encouraged, indeed demanded, migration from the countryside to fill these jobs. These social changes were experienced by many people as the rise of a strange, new world. The dizzying pace of a new culture based on individualism, competitive struggles for wealth, and a secular worldview gave people a strong sense that they were living in a new era of constant change. The eternal truths related to tradition and religion became problematic, and people had more choices about everything from lifestyles to ethics than ever before. Marx and Engels's words in *The Communist Manifesto* exemplify this new sensibility: "All fixed, fast-frozen relations, with their train of ancient and venerable prejudices and opinions, are swept away, all new-formed ones become antiquated before they can ossify. All that is solid melts into air, all that is holy is profaned."[6] This experience contributed to the belief that a "modern" world was distinctively different from the "traditional" societies that preceded it, an insight formalized in social scientific ideas about traditional and modern societies. From the spectacular increases in technological growth, to the emergence of a consumer culture symbolized by the new "department store" such as the Bon Marché in France, a new world was at hand.

A scientific sensibility characterized late nineteenth-century European culture and left its marks on the emerging discipline of sociology. The advances of knowledge in the nineteenth century, such as Charles Darwin's (1809–82) biological theories of natural selection, and the exceptional improvements in technology symbolized by the railroad, encouraged a scientific ferment which influenced the quest for a science of society. This theoretical pursuit was evident in theories as diverse as Durkheimian sociology and the British sociologist Herbert Spencer's (1820–1903) emphasis on heredity and environment as explanations of human behavior.

Yet the late nineteenth century saw a reaction to the hegemony of science. Religious revivals swept through parts of Europe, coupled with a surge of interest in the psychological phenomena of suggestibility, hypnotism, and dream states. Writers such as Feodor Dostoevsky (1821–81) accented the irrational or non-rational sources of human behavior, located in the unconscious. In France, the philosopher Henri Bergson (1859–1941) and the novelist Marcel Proust (1871–1922) underscored the uniqueness of the individual, as her inner life escaped rational classifications. They contended that the subjective sense of time and experience differed radically from the mechanical time associated with the clock. Aesthetic modernism, especially the Cubism of Pablo Picasso (1881–1973), viewed the human world as fragmented, not obedient to uniform, predictable laws.

Methodologically, this attention to the singularity of the human spirit led the philosophers Wilhelm Dilthey (1833–1911) and Benedetto Croce

(1866–1952) to sharply differentiate between the "human" and natural sciences. They argued that the human sciences were invariably historical, as they studied an ever-changing social reality which demanded sympathetic understanding of the past and other cultures. The uniqueness of human life could only be fathomed by a sensitive interpretation of historical and individual context, for the spirit of an age or an individual could not be comprehended through trans-historical laws.[7]

These cultural changes were part of a new global culture and economy. In this period, the world became interconnected. Global agriculture faced pressure to develop new technologies, as demand for food increased and market competition became part of farmers' lives. By the 1880s almost all of the world had been mapped. The railway became the symbol of industrial might which forged an increasingly united globe. Between 1848 and 1854 the number of railway passengers in Britain almost doubled, from 58 million to 108 million, and companies' income from freight traffic increased two and a half times.[8] The railway and the steamship made international travel a matter of weeks rather than months, except in central Africa, continental Asia, and the interior of South America. The electric telegraph allowed communication across the globe in a couple of hours. Thus, more people traveled and communicated over long distances than ever before.[9]

Mass production through better machinery began to take hold. Mass education and higher learning became more important in the rise of powerful nations in Europe. While Britain industrialized first in the early nineteenth century, the 1860s saw the rise of new industrial powers in Germany, France, and the US, to be joined a little later by Japan. Industrialization became the main determinant of global power, for a nation could not impose its will in the international arena without a strong industrial base. The emergence of the US and Japan, combined with the colonizing adventures of many European businessmen, created the conditions for the possibility of worldwide conflict. The gap in wealth between the West and the rest of the world increased dramatically in the last part of the nineteenth century.[10]

Many cities grew exponentially: Vienna increased from 400,000 residents in 1846 to 700,000 in 1880; Berlin from 378,000 in 1849 to almost a million in 1875; Paris from 1 million to 1.9 million and London from 2.5 million to 3.9 million from 1851 to 1881. Newer cities such as Chicago and Melbourne increased their populations at an even faster rate. These cities tended to be centers of commerce, trade, transport, administration, and services rather than industry.[11]

The typical industrial town of this period was a medium-sized city. In the late nineteenth century, though heavy industry was increasing, industrial development was still often concentrated in factories employing

100–200 people, not the behemoths that would develop in the following fifty years. Capitalism was based on family ownership, on one-man rule. Most businesses in the first half of the nineteenth century were financed privately by family assets and reinvestment, rather than through borrowing from banks. Only with the rise of large industry did large investment banks and stock exchanges become important.[12]

Small firms often meant unstable working conditions. Insecurity dominated the lives of nineteenth-century workers, as they could be dismissed from their work at any time, and firms emerged and declined in an intensely competitive market. With the industrial revolution the working class became a subject of moral and analytical concern. Workers began developing a sense of working-class culture, of their distinctiveness from other classes such as capitalists, as they shared a common fate of wage-earning and manual labor, and increasingly congregated together in working-class communities.[13]

Many laborers saw that their economic and social interests conflicted with those who owned the establishments in which they worked. They began forming organizations and labor unions with a socialist orientation, as they believed that they were exploited, and did not receive the just rewards for their work. Labor movements developed differently in different countries. For example, France and Britain developed relatively popular socialist or labor-oriented political parties, and the US did not. However, working-class resistance to capitalism was remarkably similar in all three countries. Workers drew on their culture, such as traditions of workplace autonomy, to oppose capitalism. Labor organizations in the three countries defended their control of the labor process, often combining their craft traditions with a strongly democratic orientation. Workers were seen to be the carriers of the best parts of the democratic tradition of republicanism, or an active, participatory democracy. The British Chartists, and later the Guild Socialists, the French Confédération Générale du Travail, founded in 1898, and the American Knights of Labor drew on their respective republican heritages.[14] In each country, labor republicans critiqued the "egoism" that they saw corrupting society. They stressed the necessity of worker participation in state and economic institutions, tying worker control to labor emancipation. Each group also attempted to build distinctive working-class organizations that embodied the principles of democracy and free labor; fearful of the anti-democratic effects of bureaucracy and centralization, they looked to decentralized worker organizations as the path to working-class solidarity. They viewed the public gathering as the major forum for the forging of solidarity, rather than the back-room meetings of elites that concealed power and corrupted the democratic process.[15]

The emerging power of the working class, and its capacity to introduce a new vision of public life, was dramatically demonstrated in the Paris Commune of 1871. As France fell to German forces in the Franco-Prussian War of 1870–1, Paris was taken over by groups of radical workers, shopkeepers, and other militants. The Commune emphasized hostility toward the rich and equality over liberty. It practiced direct democracy, as people actively participated in its institutions. However, the Commune was crushed by the French military after less than a year of existence, and 12,000 militants and workers were executed.[16]

Though the Commune was an example of a kind of decentralized worker republicanism, socialism was not all of a piece, and other orientations arose which challenged the labor republicans. Marxism in particular became increasingly powerful as capitalism developed throughout the late nineteenth century. Though when we examine Marx we will see that his thought was quite complex, most Marxist parties adopted a simple version of his theory, stressing that the capitalist economy followed inevitable laws guaranteeing its destruction, and advocating a disciplined political party that could conquer state power. This version of Marxism, which ignored issues of culture and democracy, was demonstrated by the success of the Social Democratic Party in pre-World War I Germany, which had over a million members, the largest political party of any kind in the world. Though nominally Marxist and revolutionary, this party in reality was quite like any other large bureaucracy, its leaders interested in increasing the power of the organization within the existing status quo. Thus, it was not surprising that the SPD did little to protest German entry into World War I, and many workers flocked to the front to fight for the nation.

These massive social changes occurred for a number of reasons: from the rise of the bourgeoisie to a position as the ruling class, as Marx argues, to the emergence of the Protestant ethic, as Weber contends. I will not go into these reasons here, for the transition from feudalism to capitalism is a crucial dimension of Marx's, Weber's, and Durkheim's respective theories of social change, and will be discussed in future chapters. But it is clear that capitalism only reached its zenith when it combined with industrialism. Capitalism provided the inner dynamic of industrial expansion. Industrialism also transformed nature through urban expansion. The urban-created environment, the massive growth of cities, was the territory in which capitalism, industrialism, and the nation-state took hold.

The Nation-state

Marx's famous phrase, "Workers of all nations unite. You have nothing to lose but your chains!" is an interesting statement, and not only because of its passion. It demonstrates his vision of an international socialist community, which animated many other socialists besides Marx. But the reality of the nation-state is also apparent in this quotation. Nationalism proved to be a more powerful social force than Marxism or socialism in giving peoples, whether workers or not, a strong sense of cultural and social identity. The nation-state arose with the expansion of capitalism, as the state replaced the city as the major center of power and commerce shaping society. The expansion of capitalism was dependent on the centralization of violence in the modern state, as the police controlled populations internally while governments provided the military support for capitalist expansion abroad.

Capitalism could only gain world power in the context of a new state system which provided a structure of law and the fiscal guarantees of a peaceful social environment. The nation-state advanced this internal pacification process to a much higher degree than did feudalism. The internal control of the population involved the state ridding society of oppositional sources of rule, and centralizing the control of violence in the police and military. While this was to some extent a violent process, it depended more and more on subtle forms of social control, such as the expulsion of violence from labor relations. Economic compulsion and workplace surveillance replaced direct coercion as the primary practices of controlling labor. This new type of internal pacification that did not depend expressly on coercion was signified by the withdrawal of the military in internal affairs and the decline of violent forms of punishment and torture.[17]

As war became more technologically advanced, it accelerated state centralization and capitalist expansion. Armies became more professional, with an overriding organizational logic and routinized chains of command, exhibiting the discipline that Foucault sees as a central aspect of modernity. States became larger and more powerful. They created stable monetary systems which promoted the buying and selling of land and the establishment of wage labor. The administrative centralization of the state in the nineteenth century was tied to more efficient forms of communication and transportation, from the telegraph to the railroad. These changes demanded more uniform times and schedules, for mass transportation requires regularly timed and spaced movements. States needed information about its citizens, and developed new techniques to gather it. The government's surveillance capacities grew as it expanded more complex and formally centralized taxation and census systems.[18] Social science contributed much to these new systems of surveillance, systematically and scientifically gathering information about various social groups. The nation-state had other ties to the creation of a capitalist world economy. As the nation-state became the accepted political form in the sixteenth century, it enforced a statutory monopoly over a delimited territory and rule sanctioned by law. Diplomacy was a creation of a world system dominated by competing nation-states, with ostensibly "natural" frontiers and an internally coherent administrative government. The rise of the market demanded these stable institutions of rule and law, so that the entrepreneurship and long-term investment vital for capitalism could take place.[19]

The French Revolution

While the nation-state facilitated the expansion of industrial capitalism, it was also the place where democratic sovereignty took hold. The emergence of the nation-state and the political revolutions of the eighteenth and nineteenth centuries, especially the French Revolution, had important political and democratic repercussions. The French Revolution of 1789 was the most dramatic political event of this era, until World War I and the Russian Revolution of 1917. With the French Revolution, and to a lesser extent the American Revolution some thirteen years earlier, the idea became prominent that the old social order could be swept away in a revolutionary act, and society could be remade according to the dictates of reason. The Revolution affected the entire social structure of France, abolishing customary relations between the classes. The French Revolution invented the idea of political rather than religious revolution as the vehicle for fundamental social change, indeed a way to achieve salvation in this world. It accelerated the centralization of the government, while promoting the notion that the people had the right to participate in their own society and government.[20]

France, along with Britain, was the most powerful country in the world at the end of the eighteenth century. But it was a rural nation governed by a monarch, based on traditional relationships, which were reflected in the estate system, a remnant of feudalism. In France, the king ruled over three estates. The first estate consisted of the clergy, the second estate the nobility, and the third estate everyone else. Though the first and second estates only composed 1–2 percent of the population, they received the vast bulk of political and economic privileges. For example, they were not taxed, and all revenue came from taxes on the third estate. Estates were inherited or granted by the monarchy, though increasingly throughout the eighteenth century some noble positions could be bought.

The estate system became increasingly precarious as social change and conflict convulsed France in the eighteenth century. The French state had been engaged in fighting wars over territory with Britain since 1689, and needed increasing amounts of money to finance its military adventures. The monarchy centralized political and military power, taking away the local autonomy of many nobles. The king and his associates also needed money to finance their lavish lifestyle, and they raised taxes and increasingly sold noble titles for money, fostering corruption.

While the nobility had political and social privileges, merchants with incomes tied to trade were becoming economically powerful, as world trade grew with the colonization of the Americas. Peasants, too, became more prosperous in this economy. Trade and production for the market gradually replaced customary lord–peasant relations as the means to secure an income. As peasants and merchants became richer, they resented the taxes that they had to pay and their lack of a voice in governing the nation.

These conflicts were given philosophical articulation by the *philosophes* of the Enlightenment – men such as Denis Diderot (1713–84) and Adam Smith (1723–90). They argued that society should be based on rationality and the natural rights of man rather than on tradition and privilege. They believed that the progress of humanity was tied to the growth of reason, and saw the French monarchy and social structure inhibiting such progress. This was expressed economically by Smith in his influential book *The Wealth of Nations*, which contended that market forces, based on individual rational calculation, rather than tradition should control the economy. Allowing rationality free expression guaranteed wealth and happiness.

These tensions came together on the eve of the French Revolution. The French third estate refused to pay more taxes, the government had difficulty securing loans, and the monarchy started to collapse. The history of the French Revolution is tied to the increasingly radical demands of the third estate, as it moved from demanding a constitutional monarchy to the radical emphasis on political equality and a democratic republic, associated with the revolutionary Jacobin Robespierre (1758–94), to an early version of socialism, as workers and small artisans known as the *sans-culottes* called for a more equal distribution of wealth and goods. As the Revolution radicalized and new factions gained power, the guillotine was used to enforce government edicts, so that political opponents were often eliminated. This use of the guillotine and political purges became known as the Terror, and provided an example of revolutionary violence run amok for later generations.

Though the French Revolution ultimately failed, giving way to the dictatorship of Napoleon Bonaparte (1769–1821) in 1799, it had tremendous social, economic, and political consequences. The French Revolution instituted the rule of the people, if only for a short time. It freed property from public control, and abolished all estates existing between the government and individuals. The French Revolution inspired other democratic uprisings in much of Europe throughout the nineteenth century, and made issues of democracy central components in political discussions. It helped make the nation-state the primary focus of economic and social activity, and demonstrated the possibility of a successful insurrectionary movement led by committed revolutionaries, becoming an important symbol for later Marxists.

The French Revolution also gave a strong impetus to nationalism, as the French people were supposed to participate in the governing of the nation. Their main identity was to be as citizens of France. In the wake of the French Revolution, nation-building became extremely important. Waves of nationalist and democratic sentiment spread throughout Europe in the years 1848–70, as nations struggled to develop a common sense of history out of the many languages and ethnicities which composed them.[21] Nationalism was a new type of large-scale worldview over and above one's local village or region, which involved a common language and shared beliefs and symbols. As a political phenomenon, nationalism helped establish the notion that a people shared a collective history, expressed in elites' creation of common narratives that formulated the idea of a distinctive national past.[22]

The Public Sphere and Citizenship

The identity of the nation was not immutably given by nationality or culture, but was socially constructed through debate and discussion. This sense of national identity always involved culture and choice, and was crucially dependent on the existence of a public sphere.[23] In a public sphere, people come together in a realm that is outside of official state institutions to discuss problems of mutual concern. A public sphere is a prerequisite for an autonomous nation-state, whether the latter is based on civic unity in a territorial polity or on the merging of different cultures. Citizenship rights became an important arena of political struggle in the nineteenth century, as groups from workers to women who were excluded from the public sphere demanded a more wide-ranging definition of the citizen.

The public sphere "represents the potential for the people organized in civil society to alter their own conditions of existence by means of rational–critical discourse."[24] It gives rise to notions of citizenship and public opinion, the bases of popular sovereignty. Public discussion in an egalitarian public sphere is the necessary component of a functioning democracy. The public sphere was crucial for the democratization of Western society, inseparable from the rise of the modern nation-state and capitalist economy.[25]

The public sphere emerged as capitalism developed. Property owners attempted to secure the requisite information regarding commodity exchange in the market, demanding more information from the press.[26] Through newspapers a large-scale, critical public arose which contributed to the formation of public opinion. Individuals in the public sphere debated law, government, and the like, encouraging a more professional criticism based on principled argument.[27]

Public opinion and rational democratic debate provided new principles of political and social power. By bringing the control of the state under the guidelines of the franchise and an opinion guaranteed by public discussion, any rule of law had to answer to the sovereignty of the people. Parliament or some other form of legislative rule became the central institution of government. In addition to voting rights for males, a civil society composed of political clubs, a competitive press, and economic organizations provided citizens with the resources for popular government. A democratic public sphere also involved the triumph of liberal values, such as individualism, expertise, self-discipline, and achievement, which were widespread in Europe by the 1880s.[28]

This was not the only vision of public life, however. There were incipient public spheres based on groups excluded from participation in the public arena, from ethnic and racial minorities to women. But it was the working class which developed the major alternative public sphere in the nineteenth and early twentieth centuries. This proletarian public sphere differed from the dominant version. The proletarian alternative, arising as an independent public sphere after 1848, initially drew on a medieval, plebeian popular culture cultivated in carnivals, fairs, and independent spaces among peasants and craftsmen.[29] As workers congregated in cities, the unrestrained and boisterous atmosphere of the tavern and union hall provided them with a public space that contrasted markedly with the more orderly dialogue of the liberal public sphere's parliament. The expression of workers' own experience was the goal of the proletarian public sphere.[30] It valued the "producer," often the skilled union worker, as the principal actor of social life, rather than the citizen. The primacy of work blurred public and private spheres; militants argued that "moral collectivism" should inform all aspects of life, in opposition to bourgeois individualism. The proletarian public sphere emphasized community, cooperation, and production.[31] Workers often turned to collective action such as the strike rather than the ballot box to express their grievances.[32]

Both the liberal–bourgeois and proletarian public spheres were susceptible to demagogues who drew on nationalist rhetoric. Such leaders manipulated symbols and ideological appeals, contributing to an aggressive nationalism, in contrast to a more egalitarian nationalism associated with cultural diversity.[33] Nationalism often took on right-wing, xenophobic forms, in the face of massive inter-European migration and a new international economy. For example, France and Germany experienced a strong surge of conservative nationalism in the years preceding World War I. Germany, France, and Britain competed over colonial spoils that indicated new problems associated with the internationalization of the European economies. As new technologies of transportation and communication proliferated, business dealings and the circulation of information took on an international dimension. In this context, European governments could no longer assume that they had complete sovereignty over their internal affairs. Further, an increasingly interdependent planet required that old concepts of politics, government, and labor relations be rethought.[34]

Yet in *fin-de-siècle* Europe this new world order only existed in outline, and the emerging internationalist context only exacerbated a more rabid nationalism. A new type of militant nationalism arose that foreshadowed fascism and Nazism in many countries. Leaders promulgated the necessity and naturalness of a nationalistic, disciplined social order, and readiness for battle with one another.[35] War came in 1914, a horrible conflagration that would claim twenty million lives and usher in the era of worldwide conflict.

The Rise of the Disciplinary Society

This emphasis on military preparedness in the first decade of the twentieth century cast a bureaucratic shadow over European society, as countries prepared for war. Further, the social changes associated with industrialization, capitalism, the nation-state, and the public sphere contributed to the enthronement of bureaucracy, science, and rationality to positions of cultural power. They increased the rule of experts and educators. New institutions like schools, hospitals, factories, and the like promoted the surveillance of subject populations, whether students, patients, or workers. The rule of the knowledgeable was one important outcome of the rise of the public sphere. Bodies, emotions, and speech became more restrained and rationalized. Sexuality, death, and other behaviors central to human existence became private matters, to be disciplined and controlled by the individual with the help of social science.[36]

It is interesting to contrast these new forms of discipline with behaviors under feudalism. Before the rise of the nation-state there was no social center which could dictate conduct. Under feudalism, the notion that people lived in different God-given realities in a divine natural order meant that the lower classes did not try to emulate the upper classes. The powerful did not try to change the way of life of those less powerful. The medieval lord did not require that social inferiors act in a particular way as he mingled with them. The contrast between the noble's demeanor and that of peasants only heightened the noble's pleasure, confirming his superiority over the peasant.[37]

The noble's sense of mastery and contempt for social inferiors was strong in medieval times, in large part because nobles were not over-dependent on peasants to maintain their lifestyle. The social world centered around the noble knight. The sociologist Norbert Elias's vivid description of medieval life captures this world: "Hungry dogs, begging women, rotting horses, servants crouching against the ramparts, villages in flames, peasants being plundered and killed – all this was as much a part of the landscape of these people as are tournaments and hunts. So God made the world: some are rulers, others are bondsmen."[38] In medieval society there were few restraints on emotions, due in part to the lack of internalized social conventions. There was little embarrassment regarding public behavior, just as there was little need to control emotions.[39]

A kind of chaotic diversity existed in non-modern civilizations before the rise of capitalism. In the absence of a large, powerful state, rulers rarely directly commanded leaders of local villages, and peasants had much autonomy in governing their lives. The stability of the nation did not depend on ideological consensus; elites tended to be satisfied if their subjects paid their taxes and did not cause them trouble.[40]

This diversity could be seen in medieval France. At this time, people lived in close spaces, often in the same buildings, "masters and servants, children and adults, open at all hours to the indiscretions of callers."[41] Different social classes interacted with one another on a daily basis. Children and adults slept in the same bed, often bathed together, engaged in the same types of sex play, and wore similar types of clothes. Privacy, as we understand it now, did not exist. Until the sixteenth century in Britain, homes had no hallways, so to pass from one room to another, people had to walk through rooms where others slept. Individualism in its contemporary sense did not exist, as surnames were not commonly used until the seventeenth century. Before that time, all people from the same village or area shared the same last name.[42]

This cultural diversity was certainly made more uniform by the rise of a new capitalist and industrial society. Yet medieval Europe also lacked conceptions of universal human rights and democracy. Elites arbitrarily enforced laws, were intolerant of different religious beliefs, especially Judaism, and engaged in widespread violence and torture. Just visit the London Dungeon to see some of the more gruesome (and imaginative) tortures that were devised in the Middle Ages. Thus, the transition to a modern society was liberating in many senses – but we should be wary of embracing progress, just as we should not romanticize the past. The modern world instituted new, often subtle forms of power, from increased surveillance of people by the state to the creation of asylums, prisons, and the like, which institutionally segregated those who deviated from what was considered normal. Sexuality and death became sequestered outside the fabric of everyday life. These changes gave rise to social movements and philosophical perspectives that critiqued the costs of this new modernity, such as romanticism and Nietzschean philosophy, which I will address in the next chapter. One should not talk of progress in any simple sense, but examine closely the complexity of these social changes, placing them in their concrete historical context, a practice of the classical social theorists at their finest.

The feudal way of life declined with the rise of the nation-state, which consolidated power in a social center and promoted uniform standards of conduct, and a new, emerging capitalist economy. Capitalism and the nation-state often engaged in a war against forms of life that did not conform to their needs. This was particularly evident in colonialism.

Colonialism

Aggressive forms of nationalism helped give rise to European state rivalries which were played out overseas. The story of Europe and classical social theory is inextricably tied to colonialism. Europe has been intertwined with its neighbors throughout its history, but it was only in the nineteenth century that a clear-cut distinction between Europeans and others appeared. The notion of what an "advanced" nation should look like developed in the nineteenth century, in contrast not only to European feudalism, but also in opposition to non-European territories and empires. The ideal of the advanced nation involved a homogeneous territorial state that controlled economic development based on industrialization, governed by a set of broadly representative institutions based on the rule of law, and composed of literate citizens who shared basic political and legal rights.[43] Other territories that did not have these characteristics were seen as inferior and less developed, and helped justify colonialism.

Colonialism was not a smooth process, however. Overseas expansion increasingly gave Europe a sense of shared identity, but this was a haphazard, chaotic process. Until the eighteenth century, Europeans fought one another more than they fought the people they were colonizing, often entering into alliances with natives to oppose their European rivals.

After about 1815, Europeans did not fight among themselves for colonies so much as collectively turn on the natives. Still, by the middle of the nineteenth century virtually all of Asia and Africa, most of Latin America, and large parts of Europe existed outside of the compass of the railroad and telegraph, and had locally based economies. In the third quarter of the nineteenth century only India, Indonesia, and parts of North Africa were formal European colonies. But the non-European world was always threatened by the military capacity of the West and the inroads of capitalism. The social bases of the great non-Western empires or independent Asian and Islamic kingdoms, including the Ottoman Empire, Persia, China, Morocco, Burma, Siam, and Vietnam, were undermined by capitalist expansion. Morocco, Vietnam, and Burma were eventually occupied. European colonialism resulted in the conquest of Egypt in the late nineteenth century, and the beginning of the dissolution of the Chinese Empire, which grew increasingly dependent on the West in the wake of the Opium Wars of 1839–42 and the Taiping Rebellion of 1850–66. European colonization expanded after 1876. Between 1876 and 1915 a quarter of the world's land was distributed between a small number of European states, including Britain, Germany, France, Belgium, and Italy. Germany carved out bases in north Africa, the British enlarged Hong Kong and detached Tibet from China, and the French exerted stronger influence in their Indochinese empire. Mining was a major industry promoting colonialism, while the growth of mass consumption increasingly opened up and demanded new markets. Imperialism became a part of the political vocabulary of the 1890s.[44]

Despite nationalist rivalries, European colonists began to believe that they had more in common with one another than with the natives. They shared the same skin color, they had similar levels of technology, they shared common economic interests, and they faced the same problems of extracting resources from and governing the colonies. Telegraphs and steamships kept them in touch with Europe. Telegraphs and other forms of technological communication also heightened contrasts between those with these technologies and those people who lacked them. By 1900, European nations were combining in some imperialist ventures, as when they put down the Boxer Rebellion in China.[45]

In all regions of the non-Western world natives had to figure out how to deal with their white occupiers – whether they should copy them, resist them, or employ some combination of the two. Many of the colonized resisted the Europeans. Western forces were constantly troubled by guerrilla warfare in the colonies. Native Americans often fought the expansion of US settlers through much of the nineteenth century. Algerians rose against the French in 1871. In India in 1857–8 a large-scale revolt against the British occurred. The British sought to westernize India to better administer the colony, and rationalize economic control. The Indian revolt started as an uprising in the Bengal army, spreading to become a popular insurrection in the north under the leadership of traditional nobles and princes who wished to restore the Mughal Empire. These men rose against what they perceived to be the ruthless attempt by the British to eradicate their culture. Though the revolt failed, its aftermath saw the creation of the Indian National Congress in the 1880s, which would be the main instrument of Indian nationalism in the twentieth century. Britain later faced colonial revolts in Egypt and Ireland. The response of Europeans was often brutal, even if the natives were not actively resisting them. The Belgian King Leopold II (1835–1909) oversaw the deaths of millions of natives in the Congo in the nineteenth century.[46]

European expansion meant more cosmopolitan and multicultural European states, as different nationalities moved into them. During the nineteenth century there were enormous migrations, though these were primarily within Europe or from Europe to the US. By 1875 immigrants formed the majority population in New York, Chicago, Stockholm, Budapest, Berlin, and Rome. In some of the colonized areas large cities for capitalist markets emerged; Buenos Aires and Calcutta had over 500,000 residents in the 1880s. But most of the colonized world was rural at this time, with poor farming methods compared to the first world.[47]

As Europe experienced these great changes, European intellectuals began reflecting on its institutions. Colonialism and Empire were central ingredients of these considerations. Many saw similarities between eighteenth- and nineteenth-century Europe and ancient Rome, as Europeans viewed themselves as a warlike people who had a right to dominate others. Europeans defined themselves as more virile than other nations, bringing civilization to the "barbarians," as did the Romans. The idea of Empire also provided a common link for European workers and ruling classes, helping them share a national and European identity in opposition to the colonized. Moreover, as evidence of colonial atrocities mounted, most Europeans saw them as the result of the actions of a few bad men, rather than due to the systematic practices of colonialism.[48]

Colonialism was buttressed by much social science. European physical anthropologists became increasingly concerned with issues of race. Racism pervades this historical era in Europe and the US. Europeans had always had a healthy dose of racism, but this was sometimes mitigated by beliefs that other civilizations had qualities that could demonstrate the deficiencies of the West, as the eighteenth-century writer Montesquieu (1689–1755) argued in his work, *The Persian Letters.* Jean-Jacques Rousseau (1712–78) viewed Native Americans as "noble savages," whose "innocence" illustrated the corruption of European society by money and envy. The nineteenth-century innovation in viewing other cultures was to see non-European societies as subjects for conquest, "inferior, undesirable, feeble, and backward."[49] Many anthropologists and other social scientists developed an evolutionary model of social development, where races were seen as inferior because they represented earlier stages of biological or sociocultural evolution. This reflected the misguided social interpretation of Darwinism. Though many social scientists such as Marx, Durkheim, and Mead developed complex views of evolutionism, other less sophisticated social critics adopted Darwin's notion of the survival of the fittest in nature and applied it to society, often interpreting it in racist and nationalist terms (it must be emphasized that these were not Darwin's beliefs). Their technological, military, and economic success seemed proof for many Europeans of their superiority. Evolutionary change was equated with moral progress. Biology was often used to "explain" the supposed inferiority of people of color to whites, or of the working classes to the ruling classes.

Gender

Biology was also invoked to defend differences in rights and duties between men and women, and especially the dependence of women on men. While men participated in the public sphere, whether liberal or proletarian, women's domain was the private realm, the home. Not only were women subservient to their husbands and fathers, but when they did leave the household they were confined to poor jobs. Throughout the nineteenth century most working women labored in the agricultural sector and the home, supplementing the family's income by piecework in factories or in the household. Urban European women worked in domestic service or factories until married, and then in poorly paid manual labor. Working women saw little change in their lives at this time, except that they started to have fewer children. The sharp fall in mortality rates of infants under one year of age encouraged a lower birth rate. But life was difficult for most women. Widows and their children made up most of the paupers of Europe.[50]

Women's poor economic condition was matched by a lack of political and social rights. In most European countries women could not vote before 1918, in France not until the end of World War II. As the vote was extended to men after 1870, women were systematically excluded. In parts of central Europe until World War I, women could not belong to political parties or form political associations. Politics was a man's affair. In many countries women were barred from professions and from universities. Women's rights to sign contracts on their own, or to act independently of their fathers or husbands in legal matters, were severely constrained. Divorce was much easier for a man to procure than for a woman.

A double standard of morality was also apparent, reinforced by the cult of domesticity that was prevalent in the middle classes in the nineteenth century. For example, in middle-class, mid-nineteenth century Victorian Britain, there was a strong separation of public and private spheres. This split not only divided men and women into different social worlds, but also presupposed distinctive cultures and biologies divided by gender. A virile, active man participated in public life, while passive, emotional women controlled the household. Men focused on careers and public acclaim, and the destiny of women was marriage and motherhood. These differences were believed to be God-given, as men and women differed as radically in mind as they did in bodies. Cults of masculinity and domesticity presupposed one another, and reinforced the lack of rights and social power for women.[51] Many men argued that women would become too much like men if they engaged in public life, and neglect their most important duty, that of motherhood. The mother should represent purity and virtue, teaching children these values in the home.

But greater rights for women were implicit in the democratic ideals sweeping through Europe and the US. Especially among middle-class women, new aspirations developed in the decades before 1914. Schools of secondary education for women grew from zero in 1880 to 138 by 1913 in France, for example.[52] The ideal of the vigorous outdoors-woman competed with that of the delicate, shrinking female. The notion of competence for women beyond the kitchen grew. For example, women started playing tennis singles in Wimbledon and the US Open in the 1880s. It would have been inconceivable for women to appear in public without men and/or their families some twenty years earlier.[53] Increasingly, women were seen as individuals, who even had erotic tendencies of their own.

Still, because women were excluded from much of public and political life, feminist movements developed throughout much of Europe and the US. The first wave of European feminism was connected to nationalism, often concerning the role of women in transmitting the new cultural heritage associated with the nation to the next generation. By 1900 feminist movements were often controlled by professional, middle-class women, who advocated opening up the professions and extending the vote to women.

This, then, was the world of classical sociological theory. Marx, Weber, Durkheim, and the other theorists we will consider were attempting to understand the dynamics of industry, capitalism, and democracy. Marx, Weber, and Durkheim, like almost all educated Europeans in the nineteenth century, believed in progress, and took for granted many of the prejudices that accompanied this belief. Most social scientists did not reflect on the importance of gender and colonialism for the theoretical perspectives they were confronting. Du Bois and Perkins Gilman were exceptions to this rule, as Du Bois examined the role of race and colonialism in the

European and American consciousness, and Perkins Gilman critiqued the social sciences' neglect of gender. A more complicated understanding of individual and cultural identity arose in the nineteenth century, finding expression in the work of Freud, Simmel, and Mead, whose complex interpretation of the psyche and small-group behavior radically changed visions of society as well.

Notes

1 Karl Polanyi, *The Great Transformation* (Boston, 1957).
2 See Richard Sennett, *The Fall of Public Man: On the Social Psychology of Capitalism* (New York, 1978), and Jürgen Habermas, *The Structural Transformation of the Public Sphere: An Inquiry into a Category of Bourgeois Society* (Cambridge, MA, 1989). See also Kenneth H. Tucker, Jr., *Anthony Giddens and Modern Social Theory* (Thousand Oaks, CA, 1998), pp. 155–6.
3 Polanyi, *The Great Transformation*, p. 70.
4 E. J. Hobsbawm, *The Age of Capital, 1848–1875* (New York, 1975), pp. 173–92.
5 E. J. Hobsbawm, *The Age of Empire, 1875–1914* (New York, 1987), p. 14.
6 Karl Marx and Friedrich Engels, "Manifesto of the Communist Party," in *The Marx–Engels Reader*, ed. Robert Tucker (New York, 1978), p. 476.
7 See H. Stuart Hughes, *Consciousness and Society* (New York, 1958); Tucker, *Anthony Giddens and Modern Social Theory*, pp. 36–7.
8 Hobsbawm, *The Age of Capital*, p. 209.
9 Hobsbawm, *The Age of Empire*, pp. 13–14.
10 Ibid, p. 15; *The Age of Capital*, p. 80.
11 Ibid, p. 211.
12 Ibid, pp. 213–15.
13 Ibid., pp. 219–23.
14 For Britain, see Gareth Stedman Jones, *Languages of Class* (New York, 1983); Patrick Joyce, *Visions of the People: Industrial England and the Question of Class, 1840–1914* (New York, 1991). For the US, see Sean Wilentz, *Chants Democratic: New York City and the Rise of the American Working Class* (New York, 1984); and Leon Fink, *In Search of the Working Class: Essays on American Labor History and Political Culture* (Urbana, IL, 1994). For France, see Claude Nicolet, *L'Idée républicaine en France: essaie d'histoire critique* (Paris, 1982); and Kenneth H. Tucker, Jr., *French Revolutionary Syndicalism and the Public Sphere* (New York, 1996), pp. 6–7.
15 For France, see Alain Cottereau, "The Distinctiveness of Working Class Cultures in France, 1848–1900," in Ira Katznelson and Aistide Zolberg, eds, *Working-Class Formation: Nineteenth-Century Patterns in Western Europe and the United States* (New York, 1986). For England, see Paul Pickering, "Class Without Words: Symbolic Communication in the Chartist Movement," *Past and Present* 112 (August 1986), pp. 144–62; and Robert Gray, "The Deconstructing of the English Working Class," *Social History* 11, no. 3 (1986), pp. 363–73. For the US, see Leon Fink, *Workingmen's Democracy: The Knights*

of Labor and American Politics (Urbana, IL, 1983); Mary Ryan, "Gender and Public Access: Women's Politics in Ninteenth-Century America," in *Habermas and the Public Sphere*, ed. Craig Calhoun (Cambridge, MA, 1992), pp. 259–88; and Victoria C. Hattam, *Labor Visions and State Power: The Origins of Business Unionism in the United States* (Princeton, NJ, 1993).

16   Ronald Aminzade, *Ballots and Barricades: Class Formation and Republican Politics in France, 1830–1871* (Princeton, NJ, 1993), pp. 249–51.

17   Tucker, *Anthony Giddens and Modern Social Theory*, pp. 119–20; Anthony Giddens, *A Contemporary Critique of Historical Materialism, Vol. 2: The Nation-State and Violence* (Berkeley, CA, 1985), pp. 190–2, 288–9.

18   Ibid, pp. 102, 114–15, 148–57, 172–80.

19   Ibid, pp. 80, 85, 90.

20   On the French Revolution, see Simon Schama, *Citizens: A Chronicle of the French Revolution* (New York, 1989); and Francois Furet, *Penser la révolution française* (Paris, 1978).

21   Hobsbawm, *The Age of Capital*, pp. 82–3.

22   Tucker, *Anthony Giddens and Modern Social Theory*, pp. 120–1; Anthony Giddens, *A Contemporary Critique of Historical Materialism, Vol. 1: Power, Property, and the State* (Berkeley, CA, 1981), pp. 13, 191.

23   Craig Calhoun, *Critical Social Theory: Culture, History, and the Challenge of Difference* (Cambridge, MA, 1995), p. 248.

24   Ibid.

25   Jürgen Habermas, *The Structural Transformation of the Public Sphere*, pp. 15–18.

26   Ibid, p. 54.

27   Ibid.

28   Tucker, *French Revolutionary Syndicalism and the Public Sphere*, p. 75–6.

29   On the development of popular culture among the "plebeian" classes, see Mikhail Bahktin, *Rabelais and His World* (Bloomington, IN, 1984); and Peter Burke, *Popular Culture in Early Modern Europe* (New York, 1978).

30   See Peter Uwe Hohendal, "Critical Theory, Public Sphere and Culture: Jürgen Habermas and His Critics," *New German Critique* 16 (winter 1979), pp. 105–7.

31   Oskar Negt and Alexander Kluge, *Proletarian Public Sphere and Experience: Toward an Analysis of the Bourgeois and Proletarian Public Sphere* (Minneapolis, MN, 1993), pp. 83–4.

32   On the development of the proletarian public sphere in France, see Tucker, *French Revolutionary Syndicalism and the Public Sphere*; Alain Dalotel, Alain Faure, and Jean-Claude Freiermuth, *Aux origines de la commune: le mouvement des réunions publiques à Paris, 1868–1870* (Paris, 1980); for the United States, see Ryan, "Gender and Public Access," in Calhoun, ed., *Habermas and the Public Sphere*, pp. 259–88; for England, Jones, *Languages of Class*; for Germany, Mary Nolan, "Economic Crisis, State Policy, and Working-Class Formation in Germany, 1870–1900," pp. 352–93; and Jürgen Kocka, "Problems of Working-Class Formation in Germany: The Early Years," pp. 279–351 in Katznelson and Zolberg, ed., *Working-Class Formation*.

33   Giddens, *The Nation-State and Violence*, pp. 217–20.

34   See Stephen Kern, *The Culture of Time and Space, 1890–1918* (Cambridge, MA, 1983); and David Harvey, *The Condition of Postmodernity: An Enquiry into the Origins of Cultural Change* (Cambridge, MA, 1989), pp. 264–5.

35   See Tucker, *French Revolutionary Syndicalism and the Public Sphere*, pp. 162–5.

36   See Michel Foucault, *Discipline and Punish: The Birth of the Prison* (New York, 1977); and Zygmut Bauman, *Legislators and Interpreters: On Modernity, Postmodernity, and Intellectuals* (Ithaca, NY, 1987).

37   Norbert Elias, *The History of Manners: The Civilizing Process, Vol. 1* (New York, 1978), pp. 106, 117, 210.

38   Ibid, p. 212.

39   Ibid, p. 214; see also Stephen Mennell, *Norbert Elias: An Introduction* (Cambridge, MA, 1992), pp. 57–8, and Tucker, *Anthony Giddens and Modern Social Theory*, pp. 73–4.

40   Giddens, *The Nation-State and Violence*, pp. 59, 76.

41   Philippe Aries, *Centuries of Childhood: A Social History of Family Life* (New York, 1962), p. 405.

42   Ibid. See also Andrew Cherlin, "I'm Okay, You're Selfish," *New York Times Magazine*, Oct. 17, 1999, p. 44.

43   Hobsbawm, *The Age of Empire*, p. 24.

44   Ibid, pp. 59–63, 281; *The Age of Capital*, pp. 60–8, 127–31.

45   V. G. Kiernan, *Imperialism and Its Contradictions* (New York, 1995), p. 157.

46   Hobsbawm, *The Age of Capital*, pp. 117–18, 122–5.

47   Hobsbawm, *The Age of Empire*, p. 20.

48   Kiernan, *Imperialism and Its Contradictions*, pp. 159–64.

49   Hobsbawm, *The Age of Empire*, p. 79.

50   Ibid, pp. 193–4.

51   Peter Gay, *The Cultivation of Hatred: The Bourgeois Experience Victoria to Freud* (New York, 1993), pp. 289–97; Tucker, *Anthony Giddens and Modern Social Theory*, p. 185.

52   Hobsbawm, *The Age of Empire*, pp. 202–3.

53   Ibid, pp. 206–7.

CHAPTER TWO

From the Enlightenment to Nietzsche: Science, Republicanism, and Identity

In this chapter I trace some of the philosophical ideas of the eighteenth and nineteenth centuries that influenced the rise of classical sociological theory. As I have already presented the historical background in the previous chapter, much of this discussion will be an internal philosophical affair. Theoretical perspectives are not determined only from the outside, as social changes occur; they also respond to internal, immanent philosophical questions and problems. I think that the classical social theorists attempt to answer some basic philosophical questions, including: What is freedom? How is freedom tied to reason, moral conduct, individuality, and democratic community? What inhibits freedom and morality? Who can exercise freedom? The classical social theorists' answers to these questions are not simple. They require an investigation of the various philosophical currents from the eighteenth-century Enlightenment to late nineteenth-century pragmatism to adequately understand the philosophical background of thinkers such as Marx, Weber, Durkheim, Freud, Simmel, Mead, Du Bois, and Perkins Gilman.

I underline the tensions in rationality, democracy, republicanism, and individualism that characterize this era, and how they influenced the rise of the public sphere, the disciplinary society, and a new sense of cultural identity. We will cover a lot of thinkers quickly in this chapter, so it might seem a bit like going through the Louvre on skates. But remember, I examine this wide range of thinkers to provide a sense of the rich framework for the classical social theorists. These various philosophies and critiques set the intellectual stage for thinkers from Marx to Perkins Gilman.

I begin with the Enlightenment emphasis on critical rationality and its theories of science and progress, which set the philosophical agenda for the modern epoch. The Enlightenment left a rich legacy for subsequent social thought, from a stress on human rights to a critical attitude toward tradition. Yet it also contributed to the rise of a disciplinary society, for Enlightenment *philosophes* were often insensitive to cultural differences, emphasizing one way of life as right for all people. The philosopher Immanuel Kant was a central figure in synthesizing and rethinking many Enlightenment themes about science and morality. Kant's approach cemented a split between idealism, a philosophy emphasizing the free human spirit, and naturalism, which stresses the world of nature which follows deterministic laws. I explore three important developments in the wake of Kant's philosophy. First, I examine the vicissitudes of republicanism, especially the French social thinker Tocqueville, which influences the rise of the public sphere, developing democratic ideas in a more historically and culturally sensitive manner than does Kant. Second, I investigate the romantic movement's emphasis on feeling and art in opposition to Kant's abstract rationality. I analyze the philosophy of Hegel, who develops themes of rationality, republicanism, and romanticism into an overarching philosophical system. Third, I explore the new sense of cultural and personal identity associated with pragmatic philosophy and the philosopher Friedrich Nietzsche. I discuss their criticisms of Kant's view of the individual as a coherent, rational being.

The Enlightenment

The eighteenth-century European Enlightenment provided a philosophical and cultural basis for the industrial and political revolutions that ushered in the modern era. The Enlightenment is often seen as a march of progress, as the rise of reason and science overcoming the superstitions of the Middle Ages. Such an optimistic viewpoint is now questioned. Some contemporary authors argue that it promoted a single way of life and worldview at the expense of local traditions and beliefs.[1]

The Enlightenment advanced the belief that society was best understood through reason rather than tradition. The Enlightenment emerged in the wake of the scientific revolutions of the sixteenth and seventeenth centuries, which challenged the dominant philosophical and religious visions of the universe. Before these revolutions, spirits and essences were believed to govern the natural world. For example, the Greek philosopher Aristotle (384–322 BC) contended that objects gained speed as they approached the ground because they became more joyful when they came closer to their natural resting place, the earth. Society, too, seemed to exist on a natural basis. Every person had his or her rightful place in a great chain of being, with the monarch, whose rule was guaranteed by the divine right of kings, at the top of the chain, and peasants at the bottom.[2] In the wake of the scientific thought of Copernicus (1473–1543), Bacon (1561–1626), Galileo (1564–1642), and Newton (1642–1727), there arose a new perception of an orderly universe, which was governed by natural laws of motion and gravity rather than spirits. Science could grasp these laws in mathematical form. There was no need for a divine purpose to explain the workings of nature. The natural world became subject to humankind's prediction and will.

Many Enlightenment *philosophes*, such as Adam Smith, Denis Diderot, and the Marquis de Condorcet (1743–94), viewed themselves as scientists fighting intolerant and irrational traditions, associated with the rule of the monarchy and the church, which inhibited the growth of science and reason. In their writings they look to the natural sciences as a model for social science. Yet they were also motivated by profound moral concerns. They thought that the possession of reason defines humanity, and grants humans a special dignity. The goals of reason and science should be to reduce human suffering and increase human happiness.

Most *philosophes* tended to be utilitarians, in that they thought that everyone had natural desires to maximize pleasure and minimize pain. The feudal idea that social life was structured according to a providential plan seemed ridiculous to these thinkers. Moral ideas of good and bad could not be drawn from a natural order, but only from the calculation of the consequences, the costs and benefits, of individual actions. Reason can help people in this calculus, by determining whether actions are likely to result in pleasure or pain.

The *philosophes* understood people as natural beings whose desires should not be judged as sinful or wicked. These egoistic desires were part of the human condition, and should be evaluated positively. Indeed, the public good arose from the confluence of different actions among citizens "looking out for number one," looking after their own self-interest. One important argument, advanced by British utilitarians and economists such as Smith, David Ricardo (1772–1823), and Jeremy Bentham (1748–1832), was that monarchies and traditions prevent individuals from understanding their best interest, and acting rationally upon it. They advocated the elimination of government and customary regulation of the economy, allowing the free market, through the "invisible hand," to maximize everyone's self-interest and the good of society as a whole. Capitalism, based on the rule of the market and the private pursuit of profit, was the best economic system to promote such a society. However, the *philosophes* had no analysis of society as a social system, and focused instead on the self-interested individual bound by few social constraints. They concentrated on the importance of personal rights, such as freedom of speech, assembly, and the like.

Thus, the Enlightenment view of science was motivated in large part by a strong moral vision which still has appeal today. The use of reason and science to alleviate suffering continues to be a major goal of our civilization. The belief that all people are rational beings with inherent rights is a powerful and important antidote to repressive regimes throughout the world. Enlightenment ideals promoted values of open and public inquiry, the free flow of information, and the importance of rational education for all people. Enlightenment ideas are also influential in some versions of contemporary social science and social policy. Some scholars and public policy experts believe that the self-interested individual should be the basis of public policy decisions. They contend that the extension of market principles to all aspects of society, from schools to government, will solve social problems, and that the public good will arise from self-interested economic transactions.

I think that such arguments about contemporary public policy are naive, and they demonstrate the problems of the Enlightenment perspective. These perspectives do not analyze culture, institutions, and other sociological factors which profoundly influence the market. Self-interest cannot guarantee social stability. A market system can promote unbridled egoistic individualism and undermine any shared sense of the public good, advancing a competitive economic system with no moral or institutional restraints. For example, many countries throughout the world, as in contemporary Eastern Europe, have difficulty developing stable capitalist economies because they lack the requisite institutional infrastructure and moral and legal frameworks to keep unbridled individualism in check. As the sociologist Michael Burawoy states, capitalism "requires a stable institutional environment – contract enforcement, rule of law, stable rates of taxation, and so on – to promote risk taking and long-term investment."[3] This institutional environment does not automatically develop from a market economy of self-interested individuals. The classical social theorists recognized these problems, and argued that capitalism needed strong moral and institutional frameworks in order to develop.

The beginnings of a disciplinary society can also be seen in the Enlightenment. For the *philosophes*, nature is a neutral domain which people had to master. Conceptions of ecological destruction are foreign to them. They had little sensitivity to cultures other then their own. These orientations provided legitimacy for states and social systems which were insensitive to the destruction of different, seemingly "irrational" ways of life which did not conform to the Enlightenment model, whether feudal or non-European. The *philosophes* define human happiness primarily in terms of instrumental efficiency and calculation.

The *philosophes* were more effective as critics than as governors of society. They did not adequately reflect on their ideas of progress, science, and the like, celebrating them as antidotes to a reactionary, suspicion-dominated society. It is no accident that the popular term for the medieval period came to be the "Dark Ages." However, in the wake of the Enlightenment, science and reason took on different meanings beyond instrumental calculation as philosophers began reflecting on its principles. The philosopher Kant was an important figure in this rethinking of the Enlightenment, as he defended – yet also fundamentally revised – many of its basic tenets.

Immanuel Kant

Kant (1724–1804) was a philosophical revolutionary who challenged the dominant views of science and morality in his time. For all his philosophical adventurism Kant, a German professor, never left his native city of Königsberg. He led a very orderly life: his neighbors set their clocks by the precise time of his afternoon walks.[4] Kant only missed his daily walk once, when he became entranced while reading Rousseau's *Confessions*. His rule-governed behavior conformed to his philosophical beliefs. Kant states that people must follow an inner law, which is "the autonomous ethical law in its pure and unalterable validity."[5] Unlike the *philosophes*, Kant does not believe that right actions derive from a consideration of self-interest and/or the calculation of individual costs and benefits. The unity of individual desire and the common good through the use of reason is the centerpiece of Kant's moral philosophy.

Kant searches for answers to basic questions about knowledge and morality. He encapsulates his quest in a famous statement: "Two matters fill me with ever renewed wonder: the starred heaven above me and the moral law within me."[6] Kant's motto *Sape Aude*, "dare to know," captures the spirit of the Enlightenment. Systematic knowledge of the world is necessary if humankind is to rule and control it effectively. For Kant, as for the Enlightenment *philosophes*, to know something means to use one's reason. But Kant does more than just criticize superstitions and other obstacles to people's use of rationality. He sees reason as the basis of freedom, for to be rational means to be autonomous, to determine one's own beliefs and actions, and to obey only those laws which are informed by argument and evidence. He defends reason against its skeptics, while simultaneously demonstrating the limits of rationality. This emphasis can be seen in all of his work. Writing in 1784, Kant defines enlightenment as the public use of reason by citizens, which guarantees freedom of thought through criticism of received beliefs, from religion to science to government. Kant's equation of freedom and rationality are major themes in his discussions of knowledge, morality, and art. Reason can lead to the truth if publicly exercised by people of good will.

For Kant, our use of reason structures the world as we understand it. We cannot help but rationally order our experience, and approach nature like a judge "who compels the witnesses to answer the questions that he puts to them."[7] We have *a priori* (prior to experience) categories in our mind, such as time, space, causality, quantity, etc., which shape our experiences. The natural and physical world is captured by sciences such as physics, which mathematically plot its structure. These sciences give us valid *a priori* knowledge, for they are universal and necessary. They are the model for all knowledge, as they provide foundations for the progress of knowledge "throughout all time and in endless expansion."[8] Reason provides the principles which regulate and inform processes of understandings.[9]

Yet for Kant, paradoxically, reason is finite, for people can never understand all of complex reality. While reason provides the principles of knowledge, it cannot know anything outside of the categories of the mind. Like the inhabitants of Plato's cave who were unable to see beyond its confines, reason cannot know what is exterior to the categories of perception. Nevertheless, people have a tendency to search for a first principle or presupposition on which all knowledge rests, but such a voyage is doomed to fail. What Kant calls "noumena" or things in themselves, outside of the categories of the mind, are by definition unknowable. Philosophers have constantly searched for a rosetta stone of philosophy which will unlock the mysteries of God, history, nature, people, indeed all of life (and death). Such a search is futile, for philosophers must recognize that reason is limited to phenomena, what we can experience, and cannot look past its own categories of understanding.

Kant develops a different point of view when he examines society and morality rather than nature. When Kant turns to the human world, he views people as free beings who can determine their own actions. Of course, he realizes that people are often influenced by factors outside of their own will, from heredity to upbringing. But for Kant, this tension between our inclinations to act in predetermined ways, and our individual capacity to select the best and right course of action, provides the groundwork for freedom. If we lived in a world where our choices were determined beforehand by our environment or genetic make-up, we would have no freedom. We must be able to freely select the right thing to do; thus freedom is tied to morality.

Kant looks within the individual conscience to find the basis of freedom and morality. Morality cannot be imposed from outside the person, but is determined by the motives that inform her actions. It makes a huge difference to Kant whether or not the individual has good intentions for engaging in an act, regardless of the outcome. Moral acts are based on good intentions, immoral acts on bad intentions. But how do we arrive at good intentions? Kant does not locate moral freedom in sentiments or emotion; rather, he finds it in reason. For moral action to exist, motives must be dictated by the nature of reason. The moral person acts according to rational principles which can be generalized to all of humanity. She does not opportunistically calculate the advantages and disadvantages of a situation. If the individual behaves according to selfish desires, she is not acting in a principled way. For example, in Kant's view, a person should not break any promises she has made, even when keeping the promise might prove disadvantageous to her. Keeping a promise is a universal principle, applicable to everyone.

Kant calls this the "categorical imperative:" one should only follow those moral principles which one thinks everyone else should observe. Thus, we act virtuously because we can posit without contradiction that everyone else should also act virtuously. For example, we should love our neighbor as ourselves and act out of charity and compassion, even if this restricts our individual happiness and self-interest. We should do our rational duty no matter the cost. Reason unencumbered by self-interest can provide us with insight into the universal bases of our actions. Kant envisions "a society of rational beings each obeying a common law, but a law which he has imposed on himself, in accordance with the principle of autonomy."[10]

Reason gives us moral laws to follow regardless of circumstance, exemplified in principled acting. Kant is saying that we owe it to ourselves to live up to the demands of our reason, that it is our duty to do so.[11] Kant focuses on developing the capacity to act rationally, which he regards as a higher end than human happiness. The moral individual behaves according to universal principles, represented in ideals such as justice, and treats other human beings as ends, not as means to fulfill her instrumental desires. Law rather than force can compel peace among nations; following moral laws can ensure humankind's freedom; recognizing the laws of the mind and of nature can guarantee the progress of science and enlightenment; and the lawful harmony of aesthetics provides the key to art. People are able to follow laws when they are not influenced by their passions or self-interest.

Kant is a seminal thinker for social thought. He equates modernity with rationality and freedom. His idea of reason differs from that of the Enlightenment *philosophes*, for it is based on generalized principles that follow no calculus of pleasure or pain, but lead directly to universal aspirations such as justice. His arguments abut the connection of reason, freedom, and morality, the role of perception in structuring knowledge, and the potential limits of reason provide the backdrop for discussions of these issues by the classical social theorists. He separates the natural and social worlds from one another. This split between nature and morality inaugurates a split between materialism, which sees humans as determined natural beings, and idealism, which sees them as free spiritual beings. This split is a major philosophical divide throughout the nineteenth century. Kant is also a forerunner for the idea of the public sphere, for mutual discussion in a public realm can allow people to realize their common reason, and act on it.

Kant's idea of living according to freely chosen principles still has a powerful attraction. I just finished reading *Will*, the autobiography of G. Gordon Liddy. While I do not agree with his politics, there is something admirable about his complete commitment to his principles, even if he does take this commitment to the edge of lunacy. However, this example demonstrates some of Kant's problems. Liddy clearly believes that he has arrived at his conservative principles through rational thought. Yet most people are not as conservative as Liddy. Kant assumes that because all people possess reason, they will act rationally in more or less the same way. There are no different rules of rationality for different peoples, because everyone shares the same basic rational ways of thinking. This is a problematic assumption at best. Anthropologists have demonstrated that people in non-modern cultures can give persuasive reasons for their behavior and beliefs, and that rational action is culturally defined in specific social circumstances.

Further, Kant's philosophy can slide into ethnocentrism. In our multicultural world it is hard to believe that the same values can be applied to all cultures without revision. Indeed, a Kantian universal approach which is insensitive to cultural differences can promote a disciplinary society, where one way of acting is applicable to all, regardless of circumstances or cultural and personal background. Finally, Kant believes that there is no real joy in following principles and doing one's duty. He invites us to love our neighbor, but this not an emotional love that will give us happiness, but must be completely altruistic. Kant thinks we must repress our emotions and desires for happiness in order to act dutifully according to moral principles. This is a cheerless moral perspective that I do not find attractive.

We will explore many of these criticisms in this chapter. The romantics criticize Kant's rationalism, arguing that sentiment and imagination are more important faculties than reason for granting insight into reality and individuality. The romantic tradition attempts to overcome the dichotomies of society and nature, reason and feeling, posited by Kant. The romantics place the individual's search for happiness and a sense of authenticity over and above obediently doing one's duty.

Related to the romantic critique is the criticism that Kant does not take into account experience, instincts, and power relations in the shaping of the individual. Nietzsche argues that the self is marked by power, and it is not nearly as coherent as Kant makes it out to be. He criticizes Kant's idealistic view of perception and rationality, as if the mind had no body. For Nietzsche, instincts and power considerations invariably influence the use of reason. Individuals are shaped by psychological and social forces outside of their control, and even outside of their consciousness. The pragmatist philosophers James and Dewey join Nietzsche in contending that the individual's sense of self is more fluid and fragile than Kant realizes.

The ideas of Kant and criticisms of them inform the work of the classical social theorists in many ways. Freud, Simmel, Du Bois, and Mead argue that Kant has a too simplistic and rational view of self-development. Durkheim and Weber are attracted to Kant's idea of free moral action uninhibited by passions or interests. However, they join Marx, Simmel, and Mead in arguing that Kant does not take into account the historical and natural dimensions of morality and democracy. For these thinkers, morality and rationality must be studied empirically, in different eras and societies. Rationality and morality are not abstract, innate in the human mind, but intimately tied to particular societies. Weber, while influenced by Kant, believes that reason cannot determine which beliefs we should follow. He argues that different cultures develop different values, whose relative worth cannot be adjudicated by reason. Marx does not believe that reason can ever be pure, but is influenced by class interests.

In sum, for the classical social theorists, Kant does not sufficiently recognize that people are social and historical creatures, whose moral principles and understandings of rationality differ from one another. He remains trapped in the Enlightenment belief that reason can show us the one best way to act. This assumption affects his idea of democracy, for Kant does not consider how different people with different ideas might democratically interact with one another. While Kant drew on the republican ideal that people must create the laws which govern them, his view of democracy and the public sphere does not take into account the cultural and social conditions underlying citizenship and democracy. The quality of the community defines individual experience, for people are shaped by the society in which they live. The capacity to act according to the public good and the dictates of reason depends fundamentally on the customs and community in which people live and actively participate.

The classical social theorists drew on this republican tradition of democracy, which informed the rise of the public sphere and modern notions of citizenship. Unlike the *philosophes* and Kant, republicans were cautious about the inevitability of progress, sensitive to historical and social differences, and recognized the problems of a market-based society. The republican tradition's lineage runs from Aristotle to Machiavelli (1469–1527), to Rousseau, Kant, and Tocqueville. To get a more flexible and culturally sensitive view of democracy and the public sphere, we will now turn to republicanism.

Republicanism

In the US and elsewhere, we take for granted our democratic rights. Indeed, the US advocates democracy throughout the world. Yet people rarely reflect on what democracy means, besides voting and political rights. Democracy is often analyzed concurrently with capitalism, though the homology of democracy and capitalism is far from clear or accepted.[12] For instance, in the context of the post-communist regimes of Eastern Europe, critics of the idea that democracy and capitalism are automatically coupled point out that the formation of a market economy and a democratic government follow different logics. The republican tradition contends that capitalism and an unequal division of wealth are anathema to democracy, which requires an active citizenry concerned about the public good rather than the accumulation of money. For example, Thomas Jefferson (1743–1826) argues that unequal divisions of wealth, a concern with private over public pursuits, and a citizenry obsessed with money are problematic for democracy.

Jefferson wrote in the tradition of classical republicanism – different from the Republican Party in the US – which continues to be a vital theory of political and social life.[13] Variants of republicanism are important components of the thought of Marx, Durkheim, Weber, and Du Bois. The classical republican or civic humanist tradition is based on the "liberty of the ancients," of the ancient Greeks and Romans, who advocated the governing of a people through the public-spirited actions of a community of autonomous, equal citizens.[14] This tradition dates back to Aristotle, who argues that people are inherently social creatures, and that problems of human freedom are inseparable from the types of community and forms of government in which people live. Citizens need to develop their capacities of judgment to effectively participate in and maintain these communities. As this tradition was transformed through the Enlightenment, the quality and mutuality of the ties between rulers and ruled became its defining features. Political virtue, the capacity to act on and understand the public good rather than self-interest, supplied the principle that governed the individual's relationship to society.[15]

This tradition entered modern political and social theory through the writings of the sixteenth-century Italian thinker Machiavelli. Machiavelli is often interpreted as the prototype manipulator, who gave advice to leaders about how to gain and maintain power through deception and coercion. But he is more complex than this characterization. He is also interested in the cultural and social conditions necessary for a republic to survive.[16] According to him, a republic, based on the sovereignty of its people, can only endure if the populace are virtuous. For Machiavelli, a virtuous people cannot live in economic servitude, and must develop a martial spirit and a strong sense of their responsibilities to the public good which is immune from corruption by wealth.

This virtue–corruption dyad characterized the language of republicanism and became prominent in the French and American Revolutions of the late eighteenth century. Aristocrats were often accused of corruption, for they were seen to lead idle and dissolute lives, having power with no responsibility. The themes of the republican tradition include a suspicion of the potential corruption engendered by commerce and credit which encourages selfishness, and a fear that an abundance of wealth and luxury can endanger concern for the public good. Political and economic factions inhibit the development of public spiritedness, while the possession of land and/or weapons was considered central to economic independence.[17]

These republican themes and critique of Enlightenment science and culture were given dramatic expression by the great French social thinker Rousseau. Drawing on the ancient Greeks and Romans and his experience in the Republic of Geneva, Rousseau assigns citizenship its modern definition of the union of rulers and ruled, in which people democratically make the laws that they obey. Individuals in such a community create the rules that they follow; they are dependent on the quality of the community in which they live for their freedom. There is nothing inevitable about the relationship of community and freedom, however. In fact, most societies tend toward corruption, with power concentrated in an elite which rules a passive citizenry. Only in a participatory political community composed of activist, equal citizens can people develop the moral qualities of responsibility and autonomy necessary for a good republic. In a successful republic, virtue, the capacity to act ethically, is dependent on people pursuing the common good rather than private satisfactions.[18] If Rousseau's approach sounds like Kant, it is for good reasons. Rousseau is a major influence on Kant's understanding of morality.

Rousseau also developed some dangerous ideas. Although he argues that people need a political, democratic space, a public sphere, in which the general will can arise, he thinks that the good republican community emerges almost magically, for it expresses the undivided will of the people. There is little room for divergent opinions, the give and take of people with different beliefs, in such a community. Rousseau's ideal of republicanism looks suspiciously like cultural or religious fundamentalism. He had little concern for the rights of those who did not agree with the general will. He also did not think that women had the mental capacity to adequately participate in the formation of the general will.

Indeed, the type of republicanism associated with Rousseau and later the French Revolution was often very rigid and austere, personified in figures such as the radical leader Robespierre. Robespierre emphasized that citizens should act only for the public good. They should become patriots who live for the nation, and overcome all selfish and egoistic desires which might inhibit such patriotism. He thought that all citizens should share the same beliefs. Those who did not have the interests of the nation at heart he defined as traitors, and guillotined them, until he himself was eventually beheaded by his opponents. Republicanism was revised in a more balanced direction by Tocqueville, known for his criticisms of the power of public opinion and desire to protect the rights of minority points of view in a democracy.

Tocqueville

Tocqueville (1805–59), in his two-volume work *Democracy in America*, written in the 1830s, assimilates many of the lessons of the French Revolution, criticizing its excesses and looking to America for a republican alternative to France. Republicanism should not be an abstract puritanical model of society, but should be informed by a particular community's history and culture, its version of public virtue linked to "enlightened self-interest." Tocqueville sees the future of democracy and republicanism in the US, which has avoided the centralized government and strong ideological politics of European nations such as France. Yet Tocqueville also critiques the dangerous social and cultural factors that are bound up with the development of democracy in the US. He is among the first to analyze the desire for money and wealth and the mediocrity of the arts that a democracy produces, which weaken participation in public life while simultaneously encouraging a culture of individualism and privatism.

Tocqueville contends that nineteenth-century European and American societies were undergoing a great transformation, as an aristocratic social condition gave way to a democratic one. Tocqueville does not mean only that democratic political institutions were replacing monarchies. Rather, the change in social conditions involves a new culture and new ways of understanding the social world. Aristocracies based on feudal social relations, inherited privileges, and traditional justifications of social life, were gradually being replaced by an anti-traditional, materialistic, fluid democratic culture, whose essential values were equality and individualism. While generally favorable to this trend, Tocqueville does not believe that the rise of a democratic social condition necessarily results in more freedom.

Republican democracy requires a strong measure of public spiritedness on the part of its citizens if it is to flourish. Democracy demands that people be able to act together to make good laws and realize that their self-interest is intertwined with the communal interest. Such a concern for the common good has to be cultivated and regularly renewed in each generation, for democracy demands sacrifices on the part of the people.

A thriving democracy calls for political life to be infused into communal life, in order to make citizens "constantly feel their mutual interdependence."[19] Decentralized town governments, as in nineteenth-century New England, provided the best arenas for the realization of democracy. Participating in the public world of the township compels people to consider more than their own self-interest. In Tocqueville's words, "Local freedom . . . perpetually brings men together and forces them to help one another in spite of the propensities that sever them."[20] Participation in government gives people the crucial, irreplaceable experience of democratic life. In order to govern effectively, citizens must learn to work together. A populace educated in republican principles is required for a good democracy. Voluntary organizations, from churches to political parties, are also important vehicles for learning a republican way of life and the importance of the public good.

If people do not participate in their institutions, a type of democratic despotism can emerge which does not have to rely on direct coercion and terror, for it involves the silencing of minority viewpoints in the face of the overpowering might of popular opinion, what Tocqueville famously labels the tyranny of the majority. Further, democratic despotism, which concentrates power in the state, creates a depoliticized political culture. Governmental centralization of power will work to divest local communities of their rights and political efficacy, weakening citizen cooperation in the process.

When people are relatively equal yet have no communal ties to one another, and tradition loses its power as an overriding cultural belief system, the pursuit of money and riches becomes increasingly prominent. The US has always prided itself as the land of individualism, lacking a strong sense of national traditions. Yet individualism easily translates into the characteristic US incessant striving for wealth, for nothing else holds Americans together. Money is something that everyone in a democracy wants to have. It is a means of distinguishing people from one another, yet it is a very temporary one. This concern with money and social mobility gives Americans a particularly melancholy and impatient character. Tocqueville states, the American "clutches everything, he holds nothing fast, but soon loosens his grasp to pursue fresh gratifications."[21] Such a man in pursuit of wealth "is always in a hurry, for he has but a limited time at his disposal to reach, to grasp, and to enjoy it."[22] This sounds like the relentless "24/7" lifestyle of work that many Americans have adopted today.

This restless pursuit of money promotes a culture of egoism and individualism, rather than one of public participation. There is little concern for past or future generations. Democracies reinforce egoism, "a passionate and exaggerated love of self, which leads a man to connect everything with himself and to prefer himself to everything in the world."[23] Yet more insidious than egoism for a democracy is individualism. While egoism "originates in blind instinct," individualism "is a mature and calm feeling." Each person comes to suppose that friends and family are the most important parts of his or her life, and that the public realm is at most a hindrance to the happiness of his or her private world. Individualism saps the virtues essential for participation in public life, and threatens to decline into egoism. Individualism is the concomitant of equality, for it involves circumstances where people feel little attachment to one another and to their ancestors, but know very clearly their own self-interest.

The culture of equality and the market has other effects, especially on the arts. Democratic arts encourage a society of images, in that artisans attempt to give their products "attractive qualities which they do not in reality possess." This social mirage is a particular instance of an unstable democratic society obsessed with social mobility. As Tocqueville states, "In the confusion of all ranks everyone hopes to appear what he is not, and makes great exertions to succeed in this object."[24] Democratic arts favor shock, novelty, and sensationalism over substance and continuity. Does any of this sound familiar? I think so. Just turn on the "Jerry Springer" show and its many brethren.

Democracies tend to support inferior works of art and handicrafts. Tocqueville contrasts the position of the artist and artisan in an aristocracy and a democracy. In an aristocracy, the arts are a privileged sphere, where the artisan has a reputation to preserve. The guild ties of artisans ensure that he "is not exclusively swayed by his own interest or even by that of his customer, but by that of the body to which he belongs." The speed of production is subordinated to "the best possible workmanship."[25] In a democracy this social tie is dissolved, and for the artisan "the will of the customer is then his only limit."[26] But the customer also changes as well, as artisans and artists produce for an anonymous and expanded market rather than for a particular patron.

In effect, Tocqueville is stating that the market promotes mass production. As people desire more products and works of art, the artisan and artist attempt to supply them, which induces them "to produce with great rapidity many imperfect commodities, and the consumer to content himself with these commodities."[27] Such swiftly produced works of art and handicraft are often unchallenging and mediocre. When quality declines, people are more attracted to art and crafts for their novelty and shock value.

Tocqueville understands the costs and benefits of modern democracy. He recognizes that progress is problematic. He sees democracy as a fragile political and social system, requiring a high level of public participation. Unlike Kant, Tocqueville emphasizes the social, cultural, and institutional requirements of a good democracy, which must promote a reflexive, active citizenry.

Tocqueville recognized that republicanism could run amok. He was shocked by the excesses and horrors of the French Revolution, during which republicans beheaded one another while they tried to reform society according to an abstract ideal of virtue. They had no sense of its limitations, or its dependence on shared community and customs. For Tocqueville, republicanism must be tempered by experience and a strong sense of culture and history. The exercise of reason, and of good judgment generally, is dependent on cultural traditions. People must participate in voluntary associations and their institutions if democracy is to be effective. The quality of political and social institutions is inseparable from a good society, a point made by contemporary US political commentators from Robert Putnam to Robert Bellah, who bemoan the lack of participation in contemporary voluntary organizations and political groups. Democracy and a vibrant public sphere require institutions and a culture promoting political participation.

Romanticism

Romanticism reacted to austere republicanism, as well as to the overly rationalistic philosophy of Kant. While romantics, like republicans, distrusted the instrumental and monetary emphases of emerging capitalism, romantics did not reject sensuality, vividly demonstrated in the German poet Heinrich Heine's (1797–1856) criticism of republicanism: "You demand simple clothing, reserved manners, and unspiced delicacies; we on the other hand demand nectar and ambrosia, robes of royal purple, expensive perfumes, voluptuousness and luxury, nymphs dancing and laughing, music and comedies – do not be annoyed by this, you virtuous republicans."[28] Another important dimension of romanticism, the centrality of feelings over reason, derives from Rousseau. This is a theme which resonates in contemporary Western culture. (Think of the first Star Wars movie, which combines romantic themes with advanced technology. Obe Wan Kenobe tells Luke Skywalker to "trust the force," in other words to follow his feelings, restrict his reason. That is the way to find and experience that primordial life-force that will guide the chosen few, the

Jedi Knights, to wisdom and power.) Let's investigate Rousseau's ideas in greater depth.

Rousseau and the Romantic Impulse

We have already encountered Rousseau as a proponent of republicanism. He was also deeply interested in the rise of an authentic individuality that he saw threatened by the competitive European society of his time. Rousseau began as a friend of the *philosophes*. He shared their opposition to monarchy and their desire to rid society of superstition. However, he soon became their major critic. For Rousseau, the *philosophes* elevated egoism and the pursuit of wealth as the highest human goals. In actuality, he thought that such aims increased human corruption and depravity. The *philosophes* had a simple and rational notion of the individual, whom they saw as motivated by pleasure and pain. In Rousseau's view, the depths of our desires and emotions are mysterious. People are not solely rational creatures, but complex emotional ones, who must look within themselves to find their authentic self.

Rousseau is famous for his idea of the "noble savage," a kind of dignified figure who existed before the dawn of European civilization. The noble savage exemplified Rousseau's contention that people are naturally good, or noble, in a state of nature, for they do not desire to dominate or control others. As the state of nature disappears with the development of civilization, people become increasingly corrupt and depraved. They are concerned with what others think of them, they desire wealth and fame, they become envious and competitive. In sum, they become distasteful creatures. People no longer act authentically, in harmony with their inner voice and feelings, but according to the conformity demanded by society. For Rousseau, people naturally have a sympathetic attitude toward others, and are moved to help them when they see human pain or suffering. Our conscience, a remnant of the goodness of the state of nature, is where this sympathy is located. However, modern civilization emphasizes self-love and competition between individuals for money and power. It inhibits the exercise and cultivation of conscience, and promotes a lack of sympathy for others and a deficiency of personal authenticity.

Rousseau is not nostalgic for a return to the state of nature, however. Once people left the state of nature, they could never return. A new, virtuous community lacking dependence and egoism has to be created. His republicanism is important here, for it supplies the means to achieve this community. Individual wills and desires have to be transformed from selfishness to a concern with the public good if a good, virtuous society is to be achieved.

For Rousseau, education was central to this process. Society could not become better without people changing their individual character, undergoing a psychological transformation. Rousseau believed that children should be educated to become authentic, autonomous individuals who could develop their own strong sense of identity. Children should be taught increasingly complex moral challenges, so that they learn to think independently and act rightly, and find their own unique inner voice.

Rousseau recognizes the costs of Enlightenment progress to individual authenticity and communal solidarity. He helps inaugurate the romantic reaction to Enlightenment rationalism. A new vision of individuality, based on feelings and intuition, can provide more profound insight into experience than a cold, calculating reason.

Later poets and artists such as William Wordsworth (1770–1850) who adopted many of romanticism's tenets searched for the natural and authentic core to humanity and nature. A desiccated, objective reason that is indifferent to human feelings and nature has created the impersonal world of capitalism and instrumental bureaucracy. For romantics, nature is not a realm to be dominated by technology, but should be celebrated, as the best life is one rich in ex-perience and sensuality. Romantics extol nature as a mysterious life-force which can give humanity a new vitality. For many romantics, humankind must be reconciled with nature, and reason informed by emotions.

Romantics desire an authentic existence, not an artificial life separated from nature and feeling. Authenticity requires each individual to discover her inner voice and/or path. Finding this inner sense is not a rational process, however. Reason can make us lose contact with authenticity, and we must unlearn our rational assumptions, as Luke Skywalker had to do in order to merge with the force. People have to open themselves up to their feelings and their experiences. For romantics, people's duty is not to live up to the demands of reason, as it is for Kant. If we have a duty, it is to express the unique inner voice that is within each of us. This demonstrates a new kind of individualism, where each person is obliged to follow her distinctive life-calling. This is not a calling in a traditional or religious sense, for there are not necessarily any models that individuals can follow. They must create their lifestyles themselves.

Art becomes increasingly important in this context. It is the expressive and creative medium *par excellence*. Music and laughter, emotion and art, go together. Romantic art opposed the classical style of the time, calling for more experimentation in artistic forms. Romantic art is not an imitation of the natural world or an expression of dramatized religious or civic themes, as was most of the art which preceded it, but a manifestation of a unique inner self. Many painters, writers, and musicians believe that art exemplifies the creative imagination, providing more insight into truth than rationality or science. For example, Beethoven's (1770–1827) emotional and romantic symphonies contrast with the more measured and precise music of Mozart (1756–91). Many romantics embrace a kind of mysticism and celebration of nature, in opposition to the crass commercialism they saw arising around them. Art becomes a realm of beauty in and of itself, and the artist should live for her art. We still have the idea that some artists "sell out" when they change their artistic style to make it more popular and commercial. It seems that many popular musical genres, from rock and roll to rap, begin as expressions of alienation and difference from mainstream society and commercialism, only to become taken over and produced by large corporations, losing their critical edge.

Romanticism had cultural and social implications beyond the individual and artistic levels. The philosopher Johann Herder (1744–1803) uses romantic ideas to develop the notion of unique national cultures. In an early version of multiculturalism, Herder states that every nation has a distinctive culture which should be recognized and respected. Paradoxically, while extolling individual experience, strands of romanticism also value tradition as more powerful than reason. As the philosopher Hans-George Gadamer states, "We owe to romanticism this correction of the Enlightenment, that tradition has a justification that is outside the arguments of reason and in a large measure determines our institutions and our attitudes."[29]

These romantic views of history, art, and the self are important in the development of classical social theory. Though Marx, Weber, and Durkheim adopt rationality, it is not that of the Enlightenment. Each of these thinkers has a view of rationality that cannot be severed from the complexities of human experience, which gives them a rich sense of reason. Weber, Durkheim, Freud, and Simmel in particular have a strong awareness of the irrational forces that influence human behavior. Marx's theory of labor has a powerful romantic dimension. Each theorist is also sensitive to the conflicts and drama of history that problematize the linear Enlightenment theory of progress.

Yet the ideas of the classical social theorists were also profoundly influenced by the philosopher Hegel. The romantics' critical perspective on progress, which celebrates tradition, experience, and the individual, is connected to rationality by Hegel. While Hegel sees the social world becoming more rational over time, as do the Enlightenment *philosophes*, his view is different than theirs. History is more like a spiral than a linear progression, moving from a simple beginning through various conflicts to a higher realm of freedom. Unlike Enlightenment progress, this historical perspective emphasizes crisis and drama, alienation and reconciliation. It grants a central place to the complex development of self-discovery in the historical process, without which progress is impossible.[30]

Hegel

People often speak of the "spirit" of an age. For example, we frequently label the 1970s in the US the "me decade," or the 1980s the "decade of greed." We also think that certain people embody the spirit of the times. Thus, Martin Luther King, Jr. is said to personify the spirit of the 1960s, Ronald Reagan the spirit of the 1980s. Who exemplified the spirit of the 1990s? Bill Gates? Hillary Clinton? Kurt Cobain? Tony Blair? In any case, these notions imply that ideas and great individuals dramatically influence, if not rule, historical eras. A particular epoch can be understood as a unity, as a totality, held together by a particular "spirit."

These ideas can be traced in large part to the influence of the great German philosopher G. W. F. Hegel (1770–1831). Hegel's philosophy is based on idealism, the theory that mind and ideas govern the material world. The evolution of ideas provides the key to history. The true history of humankind is the history of what Hegel variously terms consciousness, spirit, or philosophy. Hegel is a great synthesizer of various philosophical strands. He develops many romantic themes discussed above, such as the notion that each historical era is distinctive and that self-understanding is a complex process, but ties them to rationality. His view of reason is enriched by a sense of its cultural and historical dimensions. He draws on republicanism as well as romanticism. People make their history in part through the institutions, such as the government, that they create. Society and the individual cannot be separated from one another. The nature of public life, the community in which one lives, profoundly influences the individual.

Hegel views history as a progressive, rational process. Humankind will eventually reach a level of complete self-awareness, where people fully understand who they are and the reasons underlying their actions. To reach this goal entails reconstructing the history of philosophy, which represents the history of rational understanding. Hegel claimed that previous philosophical systems had been partial and incomplete; only his philosophy could explain the social and natural worlds in their totality.

Hegel arrives at his philosophical conceptions largely through criticizing Kant. Like Kant, he argues that human thought, exemplified in science, philosophy, and theology, unlocks the key to understanding history and human nature. However, Hegel thinks that Kant's philosophy is ahistorical, that Kantian categories of cognition and morality are not timeless universals, but develop and change over time. They arise through complex and contradictory historical processes. Overcoming conflicts allows humankind to reach a higher stage of understanding. Change is the only constant in existence. Philosophical, social, and individual change and development emerge from struggle. Further, morality is tied to the community in which people live. It is not an abstract, universal form of obligation, as it is for Kant. Different moralities are appropriate for different historical eras.

Hegel recognizes that much of human existence is not pleasant. Knowledge is the source of great unhappiness, for we recognize that we are mortal beings. Further, people are dependent creatures, subject to the vagaries of nature. The institutions and ways of thinking that they create can come to dominate and regulate them. For example, many people today believe that the government and/or economy control them, rather than providing a space where they can fulfill their desires. This can also occur in the realm of thought and culture, where stereotypes, say of women or people of color, can feel oppressive to these groups. For Hegel, when people think that the institutions and culture that they create do not express their desires and goals, they are alienated. But only through knowledge can people escape this dependency.

One might say that Hegel extols the power of negative thinking. For Hegel, we only understand things through their opposites, through what they exclude. To know freedom, I must know the lack of freedom; to know love, I must know the lack of love. We also can learn the nature of freedom when we experience oppression, or understand love through encountering hate. Knowledge arises through this process of negation and contradiction. It progresses through the playing out of these contradictory qualities. Knowledge is a kind of unstable unity, for it is always changing, never static. Individual development too emerges through this process, as the self struggles to comprehend its history, throwing off its dependence on others until it can determine its own existence and achieve a higher level of understanding. If one experiences love and hate simultaneously, overcoming this conflict can be the source of great insight. Hegel's famous triad of thesis, antithesis, and synthesis is applicable here. Love's antithesis is hate, and their struggle results in a synthesis, a new mature affection based on commitment, perhaps. For example, children often adopt the values of their parents in their early years, rebel against them in their adolescent years, and develop a mature synthesis as adults which allows them to evaluate the strengths and limitations of their parents' beliefs. But this process always takes place in a social context, in a community which supplies the values and ideals which inform people's identities.

Reason develops as people attempt to comprehend and change the world around them. History represents the attempt to make the world adapt to the growing potentialities of humankind. Hegel calls this the dialectical process. Through thought, humankind transforms the world, which in turn transforms humankind, which transforms the world, etc., in a continual progression toward a more rational existence. This dialectic informs his study of philosophy. Every philosophical system encounters its opposite, its negation, and the ensuing conflict produces a higher synthesis, which eventually results in a philosophy better able to reflect on and comprehend existence.

Each historical era represents a stage in the development of reason. Every historical epoch is a self-contained whole, represented by the prevailing ways of thinking and living, the political and social institutions, and the science and philosophy of the time. This is the spirit of the age. The ultimate goal of history is the merging of reason and reality, where ideals can be realized in practice. In Hegel's ideal community the requirements of duty and the desire for individual happiness can be reconciled. Hegel thinks that when he was writing history had reached a stage where such goals were realizable; universal desires for freedom could be realized in how people actually lived and thought. He contends that the German government of his time, which gave people limited political and civil rights, actually accomplished this unity of the individual and society.

In sum, history is a process whose meaning reveals itself by stages. Each succeeding historical era represents humankind's growing awareness of its role in creating the social world. Hegel's philosophical system gives an account of all preceding philosophies, as the stages of philosophy culminate in his system. Hegel argues that reason has a history which he has comprehended. People must reach a stage of self-consciousness and awareness for freedom to become real. But this process is fraught with conflict and contradictions, which are the motors of progress.

Hegel's philosophy has had a profound influence on subsequent social thought. The classical social theorists, especially Marx and Du Bois, build on his ideas that the individual, society, and history are bound together in a complex and contradictory process. Though progress toward a better world occurs, it does so through conflicts and struggle, on both the individual and social levels. Hegel advances the republican theme that people's experience is shaped by the communities in which they live and the cultural traditions and ideals that inform their experience. The best society fulfills the individual's desires and aims. When public ideas conflict with people's private beliefs and goals, alienation exists. Hegel also problematically argues that his philosophy represented absolute knowledge, that all of reality could be understood rationally. This is a dangerous notion, for it implies that conflicts and different points of view will end in modern history.

Such ideas were influential in the work of Marx, Durkheim, Mead, and Du Bois. Marx views history progressing through stages, as does Hegel, with conflict as its motor. People are historical creatures, who create themselves through their institutions. He equates Hegel's dubious notion of absolute knowledge with the communist revolution. Durkheim also adopts a theory of history, and sees people as social creatures, influenced by the beliefs of the societies in which they live. Mead and Du Bois see the development of the individual as a complex, conflictual process, culminating in a condition of increased self-awareness.

Cultural Identity and the Self

Alongside the rise of rationality, the public sphere, a romantic appreciation of nature, and a new sense of history, modernity involved a new concern with the self and its capacity for creating its own story, its own life-history. Many philosophers developed a complex notion of the self that emphasized the difficulty of forming a coherent sense of identity. While Hegel touches on this idea of the self, it was developed in much more depth by the pragmatist philosophers John Dewey and William James, and the German philosopher Friedrich Nietzsche.

These thinkers recognize that the self could be multiple and creative, and that art can provide the best means to understand this playful, fluid self. This sense of creativity, art, and playfulness has a kind of subterranean influence on classical social theory. Foucault sees the French poet Charles Baudelaire (1821–67) as personifying this sensibility. Baudelaire constructs his individuality as a work of art, almost like a character in a text. While this emphasis on the self might sound like romanticism, there are important differences. This self for Baudelaire is consciously constructed by the individual. It is an artificial, artistic creation, not a return to nature as found in the romantics. The nineteenth-century dandy, obsessed with appearances and style, exemplifies this notion of the self. There is no search for an authentic, deep self that strives to express its innermost being, but an individuality emerges whose openness to experience means that it is always in transformation, and not necessarily coherent. This ideal posits a fluid, constantly changing, dramatic sense of self. Experience is multidimensional. These latter ideas were expressed in the philosophy of pragmatism.

Pragmatism

Toward the end of the nineteenth century a group of American philosophers, led by James (1842–1910) and Dewey (1859–1952), developed a philosophical approach labeled pragmatism. They wanted to move beyond the Kantian split between nature and spirit, natural and human science, idealism and materialism, by returning to experience, which they saw as open-ended, always changing, and uncertain. They viewed individuality as fluid, much like experience itself. James focused on the sense of self and knowledge arising from pragmatism, while Dewey explored art and politics. For James, we experience an ever-changing stream of consciousness. Experience is the source and test of our ideas, which are not timeless truths. Knowledge is experimental, always growing and expanding. Beliefs are not necessarily true or false, but are habits that can be changed and corrected so that people can achieve their goals. Abstractions that are not tied to experience drain life of its fullness, its richness. Morality does not refer to timeless truth, but ethical values that change over time.

Dewey's understanding of political life is based on this notion of experience. Politics is experimental problem-solving that varies according to time period and social context. People accumulate cultural experience over time, which helps them choose among different political options, but such decisions are never certain. People also possess many different values, which have to be adjudicated and harmonized for citizens to live together. This is why democracy is the best system of government and has to be extended into all areas of life. Because people live such uncertain, contingent existences, they must be free to try out new ideas and ways of living together, to be decided upon by equal citizens. Only the expansion of social justice and freedom could guarantee this capacity of groups to live together in a tolerant way, with different ways of life existing side-by-side.[31] This view of experience and democracy has affinities with republicanism, for they require the active participation of people.

Dewey sees people as rationally choosing among different courses of action in determining their conduct. But Dewey also understands society and experience from an artistic perspective. The flux of experience, or stream of consciousness, has emotionally charged, dramatic qualities that escape rational categories. Art provides a form for this rhythmic quality of life. Aesthetic experience is an interplay between harmony and tension. The anthropologist Victor Turner summarizes Dewey's view well:

> Because the actual world, that in which we live, is a combination of movement and culmination, of breaks and reunions, the experience of a living creature is capable of aesthetic quality. The live being recurrently loses and reestablishes equilibrium with his surroundings. The moment of passage from disturbance to harmony is that of intensest life.[32]

People learn to integrate these different qualities into their experience, which gives it a creative and dramatic quality.

Thus, for Dewey, people must solve problems that constantly arise for them. This is not only a scientific process, but has an aesthetic dimension. Because people's experience is shaped and shared communally, aesthetic sensibility develops through social interaction. This process requires sensitivity and empathy as well as instrumental rationality. Thought invariably calls forth imagination and feeling because it is an active encounter with the social and natural worlds.

This theory of society and human experience is pluralist, requiring a sensitivity to different beliefs and values. This new sense of self demands an empathic understanding of divergent values and is alert to the possible repression of those who hold different beliefs from the mainstream. It is open to new experiences, and recognizes that there are no absolute truths. The individual is shaped by and shaper of experience, ideas which influenced the perspectives of Mead and Du Bois. These themes are also taken up by the philosopher Friedrich Nietzsche, though he takes them in some different directions. He too emphasizes the limits of science and the uncertainty of knowledge, the self as a work of art, and the importance of experience in the shaping of the self. But he is no democrat; further, he sees instincts shaping many people's ideas, and contends that the very notion of the individual owes much to power dynamics.

Nietzsche

To get a sense of what Nietzsche (1844–1900) thought of himself, consider his last work, an unusual intellectual biography entitled *Ecce Homo.* First of all, the title: "Here is the Man." In John's Gospel, Pontius Pilate uses these words to indicate the flogged and humiliated Christ. In *Ecce Homo* Nietzsche explicitly compares himself to Christ. Next consider the various chapter titles: "Why I am so Wise;" "Why I am so Clever;" "Why I Write such Good Books;" and "Why I am a Destiny." Nietzsche begins the latter section with a self-appraisal. He writes: "I know of my fate. One day my name will be associated with the memory of something tremendous – a crisis without equal on earth, the most profound collision of conscience, a decision that was conjured up *against* everything that had been believed, demanded, hallowed, so far. I am no man, I am dynamite."[33] Are these words the ravings of a megalomaniac madman? Many think so, as Nietzsche was frustrated at his lack of fame during his lifetime, and he did go insane shortly after penning these lines. But Nietzsche has been in a sense "born posthumously," as he thought he would be. His philosophy has echoed through modern history. He has been incarnated at different historical junctures as a critic of bourgeois morality and Christianity, a Nazi, and most recently a postmodern hero. For our purposes, he has had a central influence in classical sociological theory.

Nietzsche states that he likes to philosophize with a hammer, to destroy old idols and Gods. He sees himself as a prophet who captures the coming crisis of Western civilization. This crisis will involve the overthrowing of old gods, especially Christianity, and a fight between those who develop a capacity for an active life and a reactive, repressive resentment against such strong-willed individuals. Nietzsche, like Kant, views the enthronement of reason as a major result of the European Enlightenment. But he is even more critical than Kant in exploring the limits of rationality. Unlike Kant, Nietzsche argues that reason is a tool for increasing power rather than finding objective truth. He sees people ruled by bodily desires and instincts, contending that philosophy has long ignored this reality in its love affair with reason. Our belief that reason sets us free only reinforces the illusion that we can act autonomously. Most people are not masters of their own destiny; this is reserved to the few, strong "overmen," whom Nietzsche sees as the future of the human race.

Themes of wandering, loneliness, homelessness, illness, and health pervade Nietzsche's work. This is not surprising given his own constant poor health. Illness prompted him to resign from a professorship at the University of Leipzig in 1879. As his health deteriorated, he moved constantly, searching for a suitable climate in which to live and write. When he went insane in 1889 he was just beginning to achieve fame. He lived a nomadic, solitary lifestyle.

Nietzsche's work was taken up by the Nazis as a precursor to their philosophy of the master race when they came to power. This fascist interpretation was encouraged by his sister, Elisabeth Förster-Nietzsche, an anti-Semite with strong German nationalist sympathies. She edited the 1901 volume *The Will to Power*, published the year after Nietzsche's death and eleven years after his insanity, in which she gave his writings an anti-Semitic and nationalist twist. Nietzsche's reputation was rescued by the American philosopher Walter Kaufmann, who translated many of Nietzsche's works into English in the 1950s. Kaufmann emphasizes the tender Nietzsche, the master of language and metaphor who is not anti-Semitic, who opposes German nationalism, who speaks of the war of ideas rather than armies, and who tolerates a great variety of perspectives.[34]

I think Kaufmann's interpretation is the right one, though there are undoubtedly some troubling aspects of Nietzsche's work, from his sexist view of women to his unsettling comments about a "blond beast" master race. Yet Nietzsche is averse to politics and causes of all types, whether liberal or reactionary. He sees politics inhibiting the critical capacities of the "free spirits" he thinks can save the modern world. In his view, any society needs artists who continually test the community's limits, more than it needs petty politicians. Nietzsche views himself as an artist, and he identifies strongly with the Greek god Dionysus, the God of wine. In his earliest work, *The Birth of Tragedy*, Dionysus represents the dissolution of the individual into ecstatic, intense, and intoxicating feeling. Nietzsche contrasts Dionysus with Apollo, the god of sunlight, music, and poetry. Apollo represents form and balance, the capacity to dream. Art is an integration of Dionysus and Apollo, a higher form of reality, where the mundane world is left behind in intoxication or in aesthetic form and balance. Nietzsche hoped that a rebirth of art could occur through the German composer Richard Wagner's (1813–83) music, whose operas returned to the irrational, intense world of tragedy. Nietzsche thinks that Greek culture can provide a source of inspiration for the alienated, shallow, and materialistic modern West.[35] One of Nietzsche's enduring themes is that art provided better interpretations of reality than the positivist science of the nineteenth century. The world operates like a text, open to endless interpretations and creative possibilities, rather than following natural laws that determine existence.

Nietzsche eventually became disillusioned with Wagner, and identified with Dionysus almost completely, dropping any reference to Apollo. Dionysus represents the irrational reality beneath the surface of life. Later, Nietzsche redefines Dionysus as the Antichrist. Nietzsche opposes Christianity's interest in the afterlife, and its virtues of renunciation and humility. The greatest humans are the most deviant, living beyond good and evil, rich in will and desire, master of their own virtues, and living life to the fullest.

Nietzsche thinks that people are motivated by a will to power. This will is not an urge to physically dominate others; rather, it refers to the capacity to shape the world according to one's imagination. The best examples of the will to power are in the realm of values. For example, philosophical and historical perspectives do not arise out of a devotion to truth, but from a will to power, exemplified in the passion and fanaticism of scholars, who wield reason as a tool to defend their convictions. Philosophies and histories are infused with the personal viewpoints of those propounding them, and reflect the scholar's desires and wishes in some way. Figures such as Jesus and Socrates typify the will to power. Their will was so great that they managed to mold the world based on their beliefs. Their interpretations were so powerful that it was forgotten that they were just versions of the world, and people elevated them into the absolute beliefs of Christianity and philosophy.

Behind seemingly true and objective systems of thought, from Christianity to science, stands the will to power. Nietzsche advocates a transformed, "gay" science, where serious thinking need not be dull, but can sizzle and sing. Though he has great respect for science, he contends that science as practiced in the nineteenth century cannot adequately portray a chaotic world that is more complex than people's capacity to understand it. Knowledge does not reflect reality, but is rather a projection of will, desires and values, onto the external world. Because there is no absolute truth, different truths coexist side-by-side, depending on the way of life of the observer. Knowledge and power are intimately linked to one another; people often follow particular doctrines because they are imposed on them, not because they are true.[36]

This critique of knowledge extends to science. Science contributes to the removal of the divine from the understanding of nature, but it must avoid becoming a new religion itself. The universe has no inherent meaning, it is not rational. There is no law in nature, for no one commands and no one obeys. Modern peoples need to complete the "de-deification of nature," which means that all beliefs in absolute truth, whether religious or scientific, must be abandoned.[37] For Nietzsche, science cannot dictate values. When it becomes the overriding value system of society, it often justifies the domination of others.[38]

Pain and cruelty lie at the bottom of all things we value as good. Lasting ideas of justice, beauty, etc. only come about through repressing our instincts. A big hurt survives in our memory – people only remember those things which wounded them in some profound way, though they repress and reinterpret this memory.[39] The self-torture that results from such internalization of pain is most obvious in religious ascetics, who deny the world of the flesh and are consumed with guilt. Such figures like to make others suffer, like the Protestant reformer John Calvin, who we will encounter again in our discussion of Max Weber.

Nietzsche devotes much criticism to Judaism and Christianity. He is adamant that people are inherently different from one another, so that there is no one right way to live for everyone. Individuals have a tendency to concoct various moral tales which they assert as universally true for everyone. Theologians are particularly apt to engage in such conceptual imperialism. Nietzsche admires the ancient Greek nobility, who did not try to transform the lives of those under their control. Christianity in particular not only creates guilt and self-punishment, but also a fear and denial of sensuality, a repudiation of what is human.[40]

Judaism and Christianity are based on the inability of people to achieve their desires. Religious leaders react to this impotence by making those in power feel ashamed of their behavior, or immoral. This resentment infects modern cultures, influencing doctrines from democracy to socialism. Powerless people, whether the proletariat or average citizens, often feel resentful, and attempt to make people ashamed of their distinctiveness, to make anyone who is outstanding or achieves great acts feel guilty for doing so. Nietzsche calls this the morality of the "herd," for it reverses the values of ancient nobility, which are based on strength and distinction, because not everyone can achieve these characteristics.

Weak people wish to alleviate suffering, because they cannot realize their desires. There is no supernatural reason for suffering, but many people wish to find an interpretation that explains and justifies it. This is the origin of religion, which tries to explain the significance of suffering. Often, it makes people who do not suffer feel guilty, commanding them to adopt the values of the herd. Much of contemporary individualism arises from guilt and resentment, tied to notions of morality and responsibility. Once the concept of an individual who is responsible for her deeds exists, this individual can be made accountable, she can be blamed and punished for her actions.

For Nietzsche, suffering is not good or bad in itself, but depends on what is made of it. This view of suffering informs his understanding of the self. What is significant for each person differs from individual to individual. People's very sense of self can be changed by a new way of life, a new way of thinking. They always have the possibility of changing the stories by which they interpret themselves, because life is fluid and ever changing. We must incorporate good and bad into our sense of self, so that we do not repress "evil." The self is something to be achieved, not a given in our experience.[41] People should not just contemplate life, but actively transform it. The will to power means channeling desires in a creative direction rather than repressing them (what Freud would later call sublimation). People have to actively shape their lives, rather than react to what others think of them. They must "live dangerously," accepting that there are no absolute truths. Rather than following an absolute morality, we should strive to be "the poets of our life," and lead a life rich in meaning and experience, though without any guaranteed truths to guide us.[42]

Nietzsche is in many ways the "bad conscience" of the modern world. He punctures cherished beliefs about reason, morality, truth, progress, and science, demonstrating that power and desire inform many of our most altruistic sentiments. After Nietzsche's devastating critique of morality, scholars would have to confront a world where absolute truth and morality are chimeras. In Nietzsche's powerful language, "God is Dead. ... And we have killed him," in that science and reason have made the idea of God more unbelievable in the modern world.[43] There are now no sure foundations for our existence, no basis on which we can hold firm, whether it be religion, morality, science, or the self. We have trouble accepting this fate, as in Nietzsche's poetic phrasing, "Woe, when you fell homesick for the land as if it had offered more *freedom* – and there is no longer any 'land'."[44]

This search for land, for the foundations of truth, for a sure footing for our beliefs, will be a temptation for many of the theorists that we discuss, though Nietzsche thinks such sure foundations for our beliefs are impossible in the wake of the "death of God." Nietzsche's contention that there is no absolute morality, and that we need new ways of life in this new context threatens to shatter the most confident statements of the classical social theorists, and always lurks in the background of their thought.

Nietzsche is most directly influential in the thought of Weber, Freud, and Simmel. Weber shares Nietzsche's contention that religion originates in the attempt to understand suffering. The world is chaotic, and we impose our particular perspectives on it. For both thinkers, particular interests often masquerade as truth or morality, and ideas often rationalize interests. Power and struggle exist in all societies. Like Nietzsche, Weber sees rationalization as depersonalization, as the loss of meaning in modernity. Weber also adopts Nietzsche's will to not deceive and be deceived.[45]

Freud shares Nietzsche's idea that the body and consciousness, knowledge and instincts, cannot be separated. Guilt is based on the repression of instincts and desires. Rational thinking is often based on illusions and wishes. Indeed, humankind will rationalize a lot of behavior in order to hide the desire for power, and the quest to hurt and control others. Beliefs and morality have a hold over us not because of their truth, but because they help us get what we want, or hide what we truly desire. Only a transformation of instincts in a self-conscious direction, what Freud calls sublimation, can allow people any sort of autonomy from their instinctual life.

Simmel, Du Bois, and Mead, like Nietzsche, sense that contemporary experience is fragmented and ever-changing. A new protean, fluid self, flexible and playful, arises in this context. Simmel and Mead define much of social life as playful, and argue that science cannot grasp this dimension of social experience. Simmel shares Nietzsche's emphasis that much of society can be understood in aesthetic terms, like a text. Like Nietzsche, he does not necessarily see the social fragmentation of modernity as an alienated condition to be bemoaned, but delights in its possibilities for social creativity.

Nietzsche contributed to a critique of the emerging disciplinary society that he saw around him. He is suspicious of claims to disinterested truth, which camouflage the will to power motivating them. Power and knowledge are intimately tied to one another; most philosophers, from the Enlightenment through Kant, view their beliefs as universal, true for everyone regardless of time or place, ignoring other ways of life and forms of knowledge. Nietzsche thinks such universal theories should be rejected. He states: "I mistrust all systematizers and I avoid them. The will to a system is a lack of integrity."[46] Nietzsche also criticizes modern notions of individuality and responsibility, arguing for a more fluid sense of individuality "beyond good and evil."

For Nietzsche, the idea of a moral individual is not a timeless universal figure, but a historical creation. The modern idea of the individual arises in a historical context which cannot be severed from considerations of power and control. Once the concept of an individual who is responsible for her deeds exists, this individual can be made accountable, she can be blamed and punished for her actions. The origins of rational law are not found in the pursuit of moral freedom, but in the punishment of accountable individuals. The sovereign, responsible individual can be made into a biographical case by authorities from schools to the penal system, so she can be controlled and judged.[47] Many of us internalize these ideas, and accept the definitions of our identities given to us by powerful institutions. I once taught a student who came to my office hours after she received a B+ on her midterm examination, complaining that she was not a B+ person. She had equated a grade with her very sense of self.

According to Nietzsche, the moral self is linked to the rise of a powerful state and centralized institutions, which can define and punish individuals. Like Foucault, who admired him, Nietzsche argues that the idea of the individual originates in power. It contributes to the rise of the disciplinary society. People are controlled, watched, and measured by a host of new social institutions, when they are not confined in asylums, factories, or schools.[48] For Nietzsche, this is the ultimate result of the Enlightenment. Its version of reason informs institutions which marginalize and control anyone who wishes to think or act differently.

But the Enlightenment heritage is much more complex than simply being a precursor of the disciplinary society. In the wake of the Enlightenment, cultural identity and the self become issues to be reflexively analyzed and understood in new ways. Individuality is more than just an effect of disciplinary power. Ironically, Nietzsche, like the romantics he detested, helped promote a notion of a fluid, creative individuality that also challenged the hegemony of the instrumental rationality of a disciplinary society. It is instructive to compare Nietzsche and the pragmatists here, for they had two different visions of how new cultural identities arose in the modern era. Both Nietzsche and the pragmatists believed that knowledge was not an end in itself. Rather, the formation of knowledge contributes to people getting what they desire, and can promote a capacity for a richer and fuller experience. For Nietzsche and the pragmatists, the self is fluid and changing, open to a diversity of new experiences, often more like a work of art in progress than a predetermined, fixed narrative. But for the pragmatists these ideas led to an emphasis on egalitarian democracy, tolerance, and a proliferation of new beliefs. Nietzsche, on the other hand, emphasized great individuals, the overmen, who would transform the social world, whose will to power was so great that society became a canvas for their artwork.

This aesthetic and fluid view of the individual influenced Simmel, Mead, and Du Bois, opening up the possibilities for new, complex understandings of self-identity that exploded the boundaries of the disciplinary society. People can be active agents in creating society and resisting power. They are not just pawns of a disciplinary authority.

The rise of the public sphere and republicanism is also a strong counterpoint to disciplinary trends. Republicanism emphasizes democratic participation in social institutions and is suspicious of experts who centralize power apart from the people. Republicanism remained powerful throughout the nineteenth century. The issue of forming a "political culture of citizenship" became paramount at this time. This tradition supplied a vision of active citizenship, stressing political or social activity as the core of life, a strong responsibility to govern, and a full commitment to the public world. Throughout the nineteenth century these values often conflicted with more limited versions of democracy, based on voting and representative institutions, and contrasted with the belief that government's responsibilities consisted of protecting the sanctity of legal rights and private life. The republican concern with rights was based not so much on legal and institutional guarantees, but on the moral and communal foundations of such rights. Ruling must be a partnership where independent individuals exercise their capacity for self-government. Moral autonomy could only be secured by political and economic equality, which allowed a proper regard for the public good.

This participatory orientation led to a critique of state and economic centralization, in which power was concentrated in the hands of the few. The problem of sustaining virtue, a recurring problem in republican theory, was echoed in later debates about creating public spiritedness; or, in Durkheimian terms, social solidarity, a participatory socialist society for Marx, a legitimate government for Weber, and a democratic society for Mead and Du Bois.[49] Marx, Weber, Durkheim, Mead, and Du Bois argue that democracy requires active participation and a moral capacity for judgment and to work for the common good, which must be learned by participation in democratic practices.

Republicanism certainly has limitations. Any single notion of virtue can define specific groups as non-virtuous, or incapable of concern for the common good. This particularistic vision of virtue and community may contribute to the disciplinary society, because it may prohibit competing definitions of the public good, and forbid the participation of those defined outside of its parameters. For example, the exclusivist dimensions of Rousseau's version of republicanism result in a gendered public sphere, with women relegated to domesticity in the private realm, for they were viewed as incapable of working for the public good.[50] Those outside of Europe, the colonized, also were often defined as incapable of virtue, outside of the boundaries of republicanism. In my view, however, republicanism in classical social theory most often served as an important democratic counterpoint to disciplinary trends.

This chapter has explored the Enlightenment and its legacy. It has examined various responses to some fundamental philosophical problems which I mentioned at the beginning: What is freedom? How is freedom tied to reason, moral conduct, individuality, and democratic community? What inhibits freedom and morality? Who can exercise freedom? The answers to these questions provide the intellectual background for the social theorists I will discuss in the remaining chapters. The *philosophes* of the Enlightenment criticized the monarchies of their time on the basis of reason, and inaugurated a new, rational approach to understanding society. They advocated the rule of science rather than custom, and some form of popular rule instead of the divine right of kings. The equation of rationality, freedom, and progress became a major issue for all subsequent social thought. Enlightenment rationality was not just benign, however. It also promoted a new type of modern disciplinary society through criticizing all forms of social life that did not meet the standards of its version of rationality.

I will trace this paradoxical relationship of rationality to freedom *and* power throughout the work of the authors in this text. Classical social theorists did not just blithely recreate the tensions of Enlightenment thought, however. As I have shown in this chapter, many philosophical movements and traditions intervene between the Enlightenment and thinkers like Marx, Weber, and Durkheim. The link of rationality to freedom is rethought by Kant, and criticized by thinkers from Rousseau to the romantics to Nietzsche. Kant places the dignity and uniqueness of the individual at the centerpiece of his philosophy, but for him the individual is a rational rather than an emotional being. Kant rethinks the Enlightenment argument that rationality is instrumental, oriented toward the pursuit of liberty and the maximizing of pleasure and the avoidance of pain. For Kant, rationality and universality belong together. General principles and ideals such as justice rather than individual desire should guide human morality and conduct. While Kant's vision of human freedom promotes a kind of cosmopolitanism, a sense of being a citizen of the world with concern for all its inhabitants, it can also contribute to the notion that one way of acting, one morality, is true for all cultures, for men and women, for blacks and whites.

This Kantian search for the general principles underlying human behavior was taken up in different guises by Hegel. Hegel *contra* Kant contends that reason has a history, and societies progress through stages toward a more rational, sovereign existence. Hegel revises the Enlightenment idea of progress, emphasizing the dramatic conflicts and contradictions that inhere in historical progression.

Theorists from Marx to Mead are concerned about the meaning and substance of rationality and progress. Like Hegel, they reject Kant's abstract and eternal notion of reason, adopting some type of a theory of history. The relationship between the individual, reason, and a rich, authentic experience also becomes a major theme for classical social theory. These themes of cultural identity and the self are raised by Rousseau, who helped to initiate the romantic movement's emphasis on inner experience rather than rationality as the pathway to a rich human existence. Romantic themes appear as a critical perspective on modern society in Marx, Durkheim, and Du Bois. I sketched individuality's conflict with scientific reason through the romantic movement and the philosophies of pragmatism and Nietzsche. Nietzsche points out that modern individuality may be linked to scientific rationality and disciplinary power by making the individual into a guilt-ridden moral being who is accountable for his actions, who can be punished and controlled by authorities. However, I think that the fluid and artistic notions of individuality tied to romanticism and especially pragmatism provide a counterpoint to the rigid, disciplining rationality of the Enlightenment. For the pragmatists, art becomes increasingly important as a way to understand society and experience the self, a theme taken up by Simmel and Mead, among others.

Republicans also criticize the Enlightenment's impoverished notion of democracy, drawing on Aristotle and Machiavelli for a stronger sense of community based on popular sovereignty and the connection of ruler and ruled. Rousseau ties republicanism to the public sphere, the space where public opinion is formed. Kant, too, discusses the democratic public sphere as a realm where individuals can freely engage in rational discourse on issues of general concern to society. Tocqueville criticizes this abstract view of democracy. For him, democracy is tied to moral experience; both are inseparable from the community in which one lives. He explores democracy and republicanism in a richer cultural and social context than do Rousseau and Kant, arguing that democracy requires moral action based on concern for the public good. Such moral and democratic conduct does not arise automatically, but must be grounded in the institutions, customs, life-experience, and history of a culture if it is to be successful. Historically, republicanism was sometimes used by elites to limit the participation of workers, women, and ethnic and racial minorities in the public sphere, for they were judged to lack the requisite intellectual and moral qualities for democratic action. Yet I think this theory of participatory republican democracy problematizes the idea of a modern disciplinary society, for it is based on the principles of active democratic participation in social institutions. Citizens must govern themselves through participation in an egalitarian public sphere, or a plurality of public spheres. These institutions do not simply shape people, but are fashioned by them.

Marx, Weber, Durkheim, Mead, and Du Bois discuss the cultural and social prerequisites of democracy and the public sphere, often drawing on republicanism in doing so.

This brief summary demonstrates the complex factors that influenced classical sociological theory. Thinkers from Marx to Freud inherited the distinctive dilemmas and tensions arising from the Enlightenment and its aftermath, and developed them in different ways. We will now turn to these theorists, summarizing their major arguments and placing them in the context of democracy and republicanism, the rise of the disciplinary society, colonialism, and issues of cultural identity.

Notes

1 See Zygmut Bauman, *Legislators and Interpreters: On Modernity, Postmodernity, and Intellectuals* (Ithaca, NY, 1987); Steven Seidman, *Contested Knowledge: Social Theory in the Postmodern Era* (Cambridge, MA, 1994).

2 Ibid, p. 20.

3 Michael Burawoy, "Review Essay: The Soviet Descent into Capitalism," *American Journal of Sociology* 102 (March 1997), p. 1,436.

4 Carl J. Friedrich, Introduction, *The Philosophy of Kant: Immanuel Kant's Moral and Political Writings* (New York, 1949), p. xviii.

5 Ibid, p. xxiii.

6 Quoted in ibid, p. xiv.

7 Ibid, p. xxvii.

8 Immanuel Kant, *Critique of Pure Reason* (New York, 1965), p. 19.

9 John Kemp, *The Philosophy of Kant* (New York, 1968), p. 39.

10 Ibid, p. 73.

11 Charles Taylor, *Sources of Self: The Making of the Modern Identity* (Cambridge, MA, 1989), p. 364.

12 See, for example, the classic work of C. B. Macpherson, *The Political Theory of Possessive Individualism: Hobbes to Locke* (New York, 1962).

13 See Steven Seidman, *Liberalism and the Origins of European Social Theory* (Berkeley, CA, 1983), pp. 152–60; Anthony Giddens, "Classical Social Theory and the Origins of Modern Sociology," *American Journal of Sociology* 81 (1976), pp. 703–29.

14 Keith Baker, "Defining the Public Sphere in Eighteenth Century France: Variations on a Theme by Habermas," in *Habermas and the Public Sphere*, ed. Craig Calhoun (Cambridge, MA, 1992), p. 202. On the republican tradition, see the classic work by J. G. A. Pocock, *The Machiavellian Moment: Florentine Political Thought and the Atlantic Republican Tradition* (Princeton, NJ, 1975).

15 Charles Maier, *In Search of Stability: Explorations in Historical Political Economy* (New York, 1987), p. 235. See also Adrian Oldfield, *Citizenship and Community: Civic Republicanism and the Modern World* (New York, 1990).

16 Alan Ryan, "Property," in *Political Innovation and Conceptual Change*, ed. Terence Ball, James Farr, and Russell L. Hanson (New York, 1989), p. 317. See Pocock, *The Machiavellian Moment*; also Quentin Skinner, *The Foundations of*

Modern Political Thought (New York, 1981).

17 Ryan, "Property," pp. 317–25; Kenneth H. Tucker, Jr., *French Revolutionary Syndicalism and the Public Sphere* (New York, 1996), pp. 80–1.

18 Jean-Jacques Rousseau, *The Social Contract* (Baltimore, MD, 1968). Of the many books on Rousseau, see Judith Shklar, *Men and Citizens: A Study of Rousseau's Social Theory* (New York, 1969); Jean Starobinski, *Jean-Jacques Rousseau: La Transparence et l'obstacle* (Paris, 1971); and Alessandro Ferrara, *Modernity and Authenticity: A Study of the Social and Ethical Thought of Jean-Jacques Rousseau* (Albany, NY, 1993).

19 Kenneth H. Tucker, Jr., *Anthony Giddens and Modern Social Theory* (Thousand Oaks, CA, 1998), pp. 157–9; Alexis de Tocqueville, *Democracy in America*, Vol. 1 (New York, 1990), p.103.

20 Ibid, p. 111.

21 Alexis de Tocqueville, *Democracy in America*, Vol. 2 (New York, 1990), p.136.

22 Ibid, p. 137.

23 Ibid, p. 104.

24 Ibid, p. 51.

25 Ibid, p. 50

26 Ibid, p. 51.

27 Ibid, p. 52.

28 Heinrich Heine, *Samtliche Schriften*, ed. K. Brieglub (Munich, 1968), Vol. 3, p. 670, quoted in Jürgen Habermas, *The New Convervatism: Cultural Criticism and the Historians Debate* (Cambridge, MA, 1990), p. 84.

29 Hans-Georg Gadamer, quoted in Richard Wolin, "Untruth and Method," *The New Republic* 452 (May 15, 2000), p. 39.

30 Taylor, *Sources of the Self*, pp. 370–89.

31 James Kloppenberg, *Uncertain Victory: Social Democracy and Progressivism in European and American Thought, 1870–1920* (New York, 1986), pp. 26–45, 59–75, 123–40.

32 Victor Turner, "Dewey, Dilthey, and Drama: An Essay in the Anthropology of Experience," in *The Anthropology of Experience*, ed. Victor Turner and E. Bruner (Urbana, IL, 1986), p. 38.

33 Friedrich Nietzsche, *Ecce Homo*, in *The Basic Writings of Nietzsche*, ed. Walter Kaufmann (New York, 1992), p. 782.

34 For a biographical discussion of Nietzsche, see Walter Kaufmann, *Nietzsche: Philosopher, Psychologist, Antichrist* (Princeton, NJ, 1974), pp. 23–71.

35 Friedrich Nietzsche, *The Birth of Tragedy*, in *The Basic Writings of Nietzsche*, ed. Walter Kaufmann (New York, 1992).

36 Friedrich Nietzsche, *The Gay Science* (New York, 1974).

37 Ibid, pp. 167–8.

38 Robert J. Antonio, "Nietzsche's Antisociology: Subjectified Culture and the End of History," *American Journal of Sociology* 101 (July 1995), p. 11.

39 Friedrich Nietzsche, *On the Geneaology of Morals*, in *The Basic Writings of Nietzsche*, ed. Walter Kaufmann (New York, 1992), pp. 497–8.

40 Ibid, pp. 464–9.

41 Alexander Nehamas, *Nietzsche: Life as Literature* (Cambridge, MA, 1985), p. 182.

42 Nietzsche, *The Gay Science*, pp. 228, 239–40.

43 Ibid, p. 181.

44 Ibid, pp. 180–1.

45 On Weber and Nietzsche, see William Hennis, *Max Weber: Essays in Reconstruction* (London, 1988), pp. 147–61.

46 Friedrich Nietzsche, *Twilight of the Idols* (New York, 1998), p. 8.

47 Judith Butler, *Excitable Speech: A Politics of the Performative* (New York, 1997), p. 45.

48 See Pierre Rosanvallon, *La Crise de l'état providence* (Paris, 1985); François Ewald, *L'État providence* (Paris, 1986); and Giovanna Procacci, *Gouverner la misère. La question sociale en France 1789–1848* (Paris, 1993).

49 Michael Walzer, "Citizenship," in *Political Innovation and Conceptual Change*, ed. Terence Ball, James Farr, and Russell L. Hanson (New York, 1989), p. 216; Tucker, *French Revolutionary Syndicalism and the Public Sphere*, pp. 82–3.

50 Joan Landes, *Women and the Public Sphere in the Age of the French Revolution* (Ithaca, NY, 1988).

PART II

Social Science and the Canon: Marx, Durkheim, and Weber

CHAPTER THREE

Marx: Modernity and Capitalism

The Rise of Social Science: Saint-Simon and Comte

The emerging social sciences in the late eighteenth and early nineteenth centuries, associated with the thought of Henri Saint-Simon (1760–1825) and Auguste Comte (1798–1857), draw upon many of the philosophical ideas discussed in chapter 2. Like Kant, Saint-Simon and Comte are interested in the relationship of rationality and science, but they argue that empirical study rather than *a priori* reasoning can demonstrate the laws underlying the human community. They contend that social science, conceived along the lines of natural science, can uncover the principles of morality and social development.

Saint-Simon and Comte reject much of the romantic tradition's emphasis on individual authenticity and return to a version of Enlightenment scientific naturalism. They contend that history progresses through stages and that individual life is greatly influenced by society, which has its own laws and dynamics separate from the individual. These authors embrace industrialization, seeing it as the latest stage in the progress of humanity. They argue that social scientists are the experts best fit to rule the new economy and the state. Saint-Simon and Comte differ from republicanism in these respects. Industrialization and a linear theory of progress were anathema to classical republicanism, as was the social scientists' denial of popular participation in governing.

These earliest social scientific thinkers utilize biological imagery to analyze society, as they believe that society is similar to the human organism. Evolutionism is an important component of their thought, for they argue that societies progress to superior forms, with industrial society as the highest point of social development. They move from philosophically speculating about society to attempting to understand its actual dynamics.

Saint-Simon, Comte's teacher and mentor, wrote in the wake of the

French Revolution and was impressed by the emerging industrial society. He argues that new classes with potentially divergent interests characterize industrial society. Social knowledge can help to unify these opposing classes. Science should replace religion as the key principle uniting people; it is to be a new religion of humankind, based on reason and empirical study, that will be open to all.

Liberty is founded on positive scientific principles which guarantee progress and the responsibility of an enlightened elite to lead and construct a social order. Saint-Simon turns from the political to the social realm as the true arena of human solidarity. He advocates social science as the foundation of a new solidarity, for the administration of society should be in the hands of its most competent members. Saint-Simon values the producer, elevating industrial production as the major organizing principle of modern society.

In his view industrialism succeeded feudalism. He is one of the first thinkers to argue that modernity was distinctive, compared to the society which preceded it. Industry is the key feature of modern society. As feudalism collapsed, conflicts became prominent between "idlers" such as aristocrats and the priesthood (the remnants of the first and second estates before the French Revolution) and "producers" (the third estate, from merchants to workers). All those involved in industry shared similar interests and would unite to overthrow the rule of the idlers.

Within the broad category of producers conflicts might result because the wealthy can become narrowly egoistic and not develop any solidarity with the impoverished. Social scientists can rescue society from conflict through rational knowledge and administration. Centralized planning and the efficient distribution of resources can unite all industrial producers. A strong moral education inculcating citizens with scientific values will help maintain social order.

In sum, modern societies are industrial societies. Saint-Simon recognizes that new classes, and possibly new types of class struggle, arise with industrialism. He posits a key role for the social scientist, who understands the laws underlying social life and unifies society. The selfish egoism of the wealthy must be corrected by an informed, empirical social science.

Comte was Saint-Simon's secretary and intellectual partner, despite being forty years his junior. The two men later argued and cut-off contact with one another. Comte developed many of Saint-Simon's ideas in a more systematic manner. He wrote in an era of upheaval after the French Revolution, as republicans struggled with those favoring monarchical rule for the control of society. Comte advocates a new social scientific perspective that would transcend these two conflicting orientations and provide social stability and prosperity. He coined the term "sociology," deriving it from the notion of social physics. A scientific approach to society could ensure its smooth functioning. A strong government, run by sociologists and industrialists, is a necessary component of the modern era.

Comte conflates the history of rational thinking and the history of society. He argues that all societies had traversed three stages, each informed by particular ways of viewing the world. In the first "theological" stage, associated with aristocracies, fantasies construct experience, as people believe that spirits and divine intervention rule the world. Reason is just a crude instrument that is often subservient to divine beliefs. In the second "metaphysical" stage, corresponding to the Enlightenment, reason assumes social power, but it is too abstract and formalistic, unable to fully grasp empirical reality. People construct unrealizable utopias based on rational principles that have little to do with reality. In the final "positive" stage, the era in which Comte lived, the intellect is able to rationally grasp the laws underlying social and natural development. Institutions are founded on scientific knowledge, which can integrate custom and cultural traditions into a mature understanding of society. The *philosophes* problematically believed they could change all of society overnight according to the dictates of reason. For Comte, people and societies could not be so easily shaped. The study of a particular nation's past, combined with scientific principles, offer the best means for social progress.[1]

Comte was impressed by the development of the natural sciences and mathematics, and he thought they had already achieved the positive stage of scientific development. Sociology is just reaching the positive stage, and it has to become as powerful and effective a science as its natural counterparts. For Comte, this new social science should attempt to gather objective data, avoid positing divine or natural essences that determine this data, and derive laws which can explain empirical findings. If sociology can follow these methodological principles, it can become the queen of the sciences. Its broad scope and late-blooming scientific maturity mean that it can comprehend the rise of knowledge in all scientific disciplines.

Sociologists should combine with industrialists to rule society. A new industrial order guided by sociological knowledge will overcome the warfare of the Europe of Comte's immediate past. Society will be based on secular moral principles of natural human sociability. But such moral beliefs can only become widespread through the medium of the family, which inculcates the necessary social values of cooperation and altruism. Comte views the family founded on a "natural" division of labor between intellectually inferior but emotionally sensitive women, who take care of their children and husbands, and rational men, who work outside of the home.

Saint-Simonian and later Comtean conceptions of positivism left an important legacy for social science. They recognized that society had its own laws of development, independent of the state. Society could be rid of chance and made more rational through scientifically grasping the laws underlying social life. Applications of science and technology guaranteed continual economic expansion, and the growth of science provided a model for future social progress.[2]

Comte's analysis clearly demonstrates some of the problems of this early form of sociological theory. He equates progress with a kind of imperialistic rationality that overtakes all previous forms of life, with Europe as the model society. He has no sensitivity to the possible relationship between reason and power. His work has a strong conservative element, emphasizing community, order, and authority. For instance, Comte's rigid view of gender, which is echoed in many of the other sociological theorists we will discuss, views hierarchical relations between men and women as natural. He also does not take democratic social processes seriously, for in his perspective a technocratic, scientific elite should govern society. Finally, Comte states that his moral vision is grounded in his scientific perspective, and he fails to grasp how his scientific corpus derives from his moral passion to overcome the social conflicts of his time.[3]

Comte and Saint-Simon incorporate evolution into their work, which became powerful ideas in much classical sociological theory. Evolutionism has complex roots. One of its earliest manifestations was Christianity's notion of the progress of linear time toward judgment day, which replaced ancient notions of time as cyclical. Various forms of biological evolutionism also inform classical sociological theory, as society is seen to follow organic processes like the body.

The importance of biological imagery was reinforced by the power of Darwinian evolutionary theory in the 1860s, as biology challenged physics as the predominant social science in Europe and the US. Darwin's ideas about natural selection posit a world which changes by accident, where pain and will play a great role. When applied to society, social Darwinism became a veil for imperialism and racism, arguing that racial or national bases of natural selection determine those groups who are fittest to survive. But Darwinism is a complex phenomenon, as were theories of evolutionism in general. Many nineteenth-century biologists argued that organisms and their habitats did not exist in harmony, as classical science assumed. Rather, organisms had to adapt to the foreign environment of their "milieu," which promoted the idea that the environment interacts with the organism in a complex way. The particular conditions of specific situations determined the relationship between the organism and its milieu, so that there was no simple linear progress.

While classical social theorists adopt the notion of evolution as moral and social progress, they also incorporate these complex understandings of evolutionism and Darwinism. For theorists such as Durkheim, society progresses through stages, with organic, necessary connections between each step of evolutionary growth. Though the organism has to adapt to the environment, this adaptation need not be in terms of a Darwinian survival of the fittest, but rather entails a symmetry both between the organism and the environment and within the organism itself. Durkheim adopts the metaphor of equilibrium to describe this process. A healthy society holds social forces in equilibrium, while a healthy individual balances desires with morality. Marx, too, draws on evolutionary theory, arguing that society advances through historical stages of development. Like Comte and Saint-Simon, Marx contends that a science of society must study the actual social forces influencing human conduct. Yet Marx is much more complex and sophisticated than these thinkers. Figures from the romantic philosophers to Hegel profoundly influenced Marx, and themes such as the scope of reason and the nature of freedom are always in the background of his thought. It is to Marx's work that we now turn.

Karl Marx

Whenever I am fortunate enough to visit London, I trek to Highgate cemetery to view Karl Marx's grave. The gravestone depicts one of Marx's most famous portraits. His leonine head, framed by long hair and a full beard, his fierce eyes, and his determined countenance convey the very essence of a revolutionary. Marx's passionate writing and stylistic verve complement this strong presence, as befits one who wants to change the world. His impatience with intellectual criticisms of society that do not lead to action is symbolized by the famous saying on the gravestone: "Philosophers have only interpreted the world, in various ways. The point, however, is to change it."[4] It is no wonder that Marx's favorite Greek mythological hero is Prometheus, the Titan who stole fire from the heavens to benefit humankind. Marx saw himself as unlocking the mysteries of human society and history, which will unleash the power of a rationality and technology forged by revolutionary action, to create a new egalitarian, communist society.

Yet Prometheus was punished by the gods for his theft, and Marx seems to also identify with this part of the Promethean myth. The socialist revolution that he hoped for never came to pass during his lifetime, and he saw radical worker movements crushed time and again in different countries. Rather than sharing in the fruits of socialist victories, militant workers throughout Europe shared "a solidarity of defeat."[5] Contemporary events appear to confirm this interpretation. Marx's hope that the working class would inaugurate revolution throughout Europe has not come to pass. The heyday of communist regimes is now over in the wake of the break-up of the Soviet Union, as few governments still exist that call themselves communist. Socialism and communism did not represent the progress of humanity toward freedom, as Marx believed, but seemed to be a retrograde step toward oppression. In actually existing communist countries, a party elite consolidated control in a centralized government, the working class had little actual power, and the people few human rights. It is an open question as to whether or not Marx would have approved of such regimes. In my opinion, he would have found contemporary communism to be a distortion of his theories, in much the same way that he judged the French Marxists of his time. After reading the French workers' party interpretation of his work, an exasperated Marx is reputed to have said: "I am not a Marxist."

Many of Marx's main arguments cannot be transferred to the 1990s from the nineteenth century without serious modification. Any analysis of stratification, particularly of class, is surely more complicated now than in the nineteenth century. Not only have new issues around race, gender, ethnicity, and sexual orientation come to define more of our experiences, but Marx also wrote in a time before the worldwide expansion of the mass media, and he could not have foreseen the ways in which the media shape our perceptions of ourselves and others. Throughout the Western world, too, the occupational structure has changed. Marx's view of the proletariat seemed to mean unskilled factory workers, yet manufacturing jobs as a percentage of the total workforce in the West have declined since 1970, with retail, service, and white-collar jobs expanding. The technological revolution associated with the widespread use of computers has only increased this trend away from factory work in the West.

Nevertheless, Marx's argument for the union of theory and practice, the link between understanding society and changing it, continues to resonate with many contemporary theorists, myself included. For example, Cornel West, the African-American philosopher and social critic, is attracted to Marx because he shares Marx's vision of justice, which involves criticizing and changing the economic inequalities created by capitalism.[6] Indeed, much of Marx's critique is living and relevant. It is undeniable that class divisions still exist, whether between the rich and poor within countries like the US, or between wealthier and poorer nations in the global economy. Capitalism has expanded throughout the world, as Marx foresaw, and multinational corporations dominate the globe. It is clear that capitalism creates many social problems, from the destruction of the environment to the experience of alienation in the workplace, as many people feel powerless in their jobs.

My task in this chapter is not to discuss whether or not Marx was right in his specific predictions about the demise of capitalism and the victory of communism, but rather to explore his ideas with some contemporary themes in mind. I examine the major Marxist theories of class struggle, historical materialism, social change, and the critique of capitalism. I want to move beyond these relatively familiar components of Marx's thought to some other issues. I explore Marx's work in the context of the major issues that I have raised earlier: individual and cultural identity, Empire, democracy and the public sphere, and the disciplinary society.

I argue that Marx had interesting things to say about the problems and possibilities created by European colonialism, and the strengths and limitations of contemporary democracy. I think that many of Marx's writings implicitly deal with the cultural identities of different groups, though he did not formulate his ideas in this way. Marx foresees aspects of a new disciplinary society in his analysis of the workplace. In sum, Marx demonstrates the richness and problems of the post-Enlightenment heritage. He embraces many Enlightenment ideals, such as rationality and progress, but this attraction is always qualified. He adopts and reinterprets Hegel's view of the contradictory process of history, which problematizes any simple notion of progress. His view of rationality is influenced by a romantic sense of the costs of progress, which inform his expressive notion of alienation. Marx also recognizes that knowledge, like cultures more generally, has to be understood in its particular historical context, though he was not always consistent on this issue.

In order to fully understand these issues, it is necessary to explore the intellectual circumstances of Marx's life. This provides an important and necessary context for thinking about the classical thinkers, Marx included. We have discussed the general economic and social circumstances of their work in previous chapters. Marx's thought was also shaped by philosophical traditions and the political battles of which he was a part. Marx cannot be understood as an intellectual giant who strode upon the world scene and suddenly reshaped the history of social thought. Rather, his strengths and limitations also represent the soundness and weaknesses of the traditions which influenced him. Marx incorporated many of the ideas of these traditions into his theory, and changed them accordingly. Comprehending Marx means understanding those ideas and debates which influenced him and which he utilized in some ways, and criticized in others. Resurrecting them can not only lead to a better comprehension of Marx's thought, but also shed light on the formation of sociological thought in general, and some of the ideals and beliefs it left behind in its ostensible progress.

Marx and His Time

Before moving on to Marx's intellectual context, I want to say a few words about his life. Marx, like many revolutionaries in nineteenth-century Europe, lived a nomadic existence. Born in 1818 in Germany, during his lifetime he was exiled from Germany, France, and Belgium, eventually settling in London in 1849, where he lived until his death in 1883. Marx was a well educated man. He studied philosophy, history, and law at the universities of Bonn and Berlin, receiving his doctorate in 1841 and eventually becoming fluent in eight languages. Marx was banished to Paris in 1843, which turned out to be a seminal experience in his life. He was introduced to French socialism and met many radical working-class leaders. In 1844 he also encountered Friedrich Engels (1820–95), who would be his lifelong colleague and benefactor. Marx lived a difficult life of intermittent employment, working as a journalist from 1851–62, but always looking to complete his theoretical work on the dynamics of capitalism.

Marx's life had its share of tragic defeats. He survived the death of four of his children. Marx had a great love for his family. In a touching remark after the death of his young son, Edgar, in 1855, he wrote to a friend, "the house seems empty and deserted since the boy died. He was its life and soul. It is impossible to describe how much we miss him all the time. I have suffered all sorts of misfortune, but now I know what real misfortune is."[7]

Marx was a complicated man. He was able to inspire fierce loyalty in many people, but regarded his opponents within the socialist movement with little charity, as rivals (especially the anarchists Jean-Pierre Proudhon (1809–65) and Mikhail Bakunin (1814–76) to be dispatched as quickly, and as sarcastically, as possible. He was abnormally vindictive, suspicious, and sure of the correctness of his views.

I do not want to spend a great deal of space on Marx's life, however, as there are many fine biographies of him. I rather wish to explore the intellectual influences on Marx's life, as Marx played a profound role in my intellectual development. As a college student in the 1970s I was intrigued by the young Marx's writings on alienation. For Marx, alienation refers to the process whereby people produce a kind of Frankenstein world, where their own creations dominate them without their realizing it. This concept resonated with me. I had always wondered why people often treated one another so callously, like commodities to be discarded. Marx provided me with an answer: capitalism created a society where people were defined and understood as commodities, something to be bought and sold. In such a context, it is not surprising that many people treat one another badly. As I became more familiar with Marx's writings I saw this theme of alienation connecting all of his many works. From his critique of religion to his criticisms of capitalism, Marx argues that people's creations come to define, and indeed, dominate them.

While I still find Marx's theory of alienation appealing, I think he also gives us some insights into contemporary issues of globalization and capitalism. There is now much talk about how globalization is changing the world, as the planet becomes increasingly interconnected. There is some truth to this argument, but Marx demonstrates that globalization and capitalism have always been intertwined. Globalization cannot be separated from the search for markets and profits, and its shape in different countries is based on a balance of power between capital and labor, which now heavily favors corporations. From a Marxist perspective it is not surprising that many people are organizing against the policies of the International Monetary Fund and the World Bank, which privilege capital over labor.

Marx did not formulate these ideas out of whole cloth. He develops them through a critique of Hegel and his own involvement in working-class politics. Marx represented but one current of thought among many others competing for dominance in nineteenth-century revolutionary circles. The anarchist movement in particular fought Marx for control of the revolutionary soul of the working class in the nineteenth century. In our times anarchism has experienced something of a small revival, as shown by the recent black-clad anarchist protesters at the International Monetary Fund and World Bank demonstrations. Yet for many people anarchism is almost a dirty word, as it connotes crazed bomb-throwing sociopaths who simply want to destroy society. This is a caricature of anarchism as an actually existing social movement. While there were some terrorists *avant la lettre* among anarchists in the nineteenth century, the movement was very complex, with many different strands. Most anarchists, like Marx, criticized capitalism and advocated the abolition of private property. They saw themselves as practical materialists and scientists who wished to change the world and inaugurate a new society, in opposition to the abstract reveries of idealist philosophies and theologies. They, too, saw class struggle as the major dynamic of modern societies. The anarchists' major differences from Marx included a stronger critique than Marx of the state, which they saw as an authoritarian institution. For anarchists, the state as well as capitalism was responsible for oppression. Anarchists also disputed Marx's exclusive focus on the working class as the agent of revolutionary change, for they believed that all of the oppressed, including the poor and peasants, were potentially revolutionary (not just the workers).

One of Marx's major opponents was Bakunin, who may have been even hairier than Marx. The son of a Russian aristocrat, Bakunin was charming and impressive in appearance. He was certainly as intimidating as Marx, if not more so, his bearded face encased in a muscular 6'4" frame. Bakunin became something of a legend among workers and peasants in Europe, as he fought in the revolutionary uprisings in 1848–9, was jailed in Russia from 1851–61, and managed to escape in 1861 and resume his revolutionary activities. Bakunin considered Marx to be authoritarian, and he worried that a Marxist revolution would simply result in increasing a centralized state power controlling all of society. He thought that non-industrial peasants could be as revolutionary as workers, for they lacked only leadership. He advocated direct action that sometimes resembled today's terrorism, believing that destroying capitalism by violence would help usher in a new egalitarian world.[8]

Bakunin's intimidating presence contrasted with the more diminutive Frenchman Proudhon, another of Marx's anarchist rivals. Proudhon famously wrote that "property is theft," a theme that united radical leftists in the nineteenth century. But Proudhon's anarchism was more sedate than Bakunin's, for he eschewed violence, even opposing strikes, and advocated workers banding together peacefully in associations to promote their interests. Marx vehemently criticized his anarchist opponents, in a sarcastic but sometimes witty way. For example, Marx wrote a book called *The Poverty of Philosophy*, which criticized Proudhon's major text, *The Philosophy of Poverty* (to continue this theme, in the 1960s the philosopher Karl Popper wrote a text critical of Marx entitled *The Poverty of Historicism*).

Marx, Bakunin, and other leftists tried to merge the various strands of radicalism into a cross-national organization, the International Working Men's Association. The first meeting of the International Working Men's Association took place in London in 1864, and was dominated by followers of Proudhon.[9] Proudhon's anti-revolutionary stance contrasted with Marx's position, while Bakunin wished to make the International into a training center for the "shock troops of the revolution."[10] As Marx and Bakunin came to dominate the International and Proudhon's influence faded, their mutual hostility grew. Marx thought that Bakunin was leading a vast conspiracy against him, while Bakunin believed that Marx wished to exercise authoritarian control over the entire working-class movement. Their confrontation came to a head in 1871, with Marx's support of a socialist working-class party whose aim should be to take over the state, and Bakunin's vehement opposition to this program. In the wake of these disagreements and the defeat of the Paris Commune of 1871, the International fell apart in 1872.[11]

Despite these battles, Marx and his anarchist opponents share several ideas beyond the critique of capitalism and private property. Notwithstanding many of Marx's comments to the contrary, and the highly centralized governments under communist regimes, Marx shares the anarchists' criticisms of the limitations of representative democracy, and the importance of decentralized, participatory democracy as an alternative to a centralized state. Anarchists, like Marx, believe that democracy and socialism can only succeed if the workers themselves create them and participate in the very institutions that they make. This is a learning process for workers, a way of combining the theory of socialism with its practice, that could not be short-circuited in any way. For Marx and the anarchists, the experience of participation in making social change is a central, identity-forming activity for workers. This is why they place so much emphasis on labor unions. Liberation cannot be granted to workers; it must be earned by the proletariat itself.

Marx argues that experience and identity cannot be separated, that the particular experiences of the proletariat are necessary to the success of the communist revolution. This relationship between experience and identity for Marx can be seen in his reinterpretation of Hegel and Feuerbach, particularly Hegel's ideas about the relationship of lordship and bondage.

Hegelianism and Feuerbach

Back in the early 1970s I remember reading some liner notes (which unfortunately have disappeared in the age of CDs) from a Rolling Stones album written by former Stones bassist Bill Wyman. He stated something to the effect that everyone's experience is different, just as everyone's identity is different. I thought, yes, that's right, no one is like me. But I also realized that identities do not exist in a vacuum; individuals only form them in association with others, who must recognize the distinctiveness of who they are. For example, I felt that my generation was locked in a struggle with an older generation for a definition of what could be done and said about a variety of issues in the US, from Vietnam to sexuality. The assertion of new identities, from women to African-Americans, to gays and lesbians, also came to public prominence during this era, and they invariably involved struggles over social and cultural power. The issues of recognition and identity are still prominent today. In contemporary language, being "disrespected" is seen as an almost physical injury by many individuals and groups.

As I investigated these issues I found that they had been taken up in Hegel's philosophy, in a very abstract way. These are difficult concepts which I will explain below, but keep in mind that they form the backdrop for Marx's understanding of the dynamics of class struggle, in particular the important distinction between the experience of the proletariat and the bourgeoisie. In Hegel's view, our identity (or consciousness, as Hegel puts it) is in large part based on the desire to have others recognize us as both unique and equal. This can take many forms. For example, it can mean recognizing someone's achievements, someone's special qualities, or the rights of someone to the ownership of private property. It also means being respected by another as an equal. We all know how important it is for our peers, our families, and authority figures to recognize who we are. But this recognition is shallow if it is forced. It must be freely given, and we must be respected as equals.

Hegel extends this analysis to entire groups of people, and examines how different types of group recognition have developed historically. The first historical instances of recognition were not egalitarian, but resulted in the egoistic control and mastery of others. This interaction originally took place as a violent struggle between peoples who could only assert their identity at the expense of others, through dominating them. This is how Hegel explains the origins of history: history begins with the clash of peoples and the victory of one over the other, which gives birth to the inequality and differential power relations that have existed in all societies. Hegel theorizes a distinction between lord, the ruling group, and the bondsman or slave, the subservient groups, to explain this history, which is really an analysis of the dynamics of servitude and mastery as they have developed throughout the past.

Hegel states that once the lord controls the bondsman, the lord's superior power is recognized by him, if only grudgingly. But the lord only gains recognition through domination, as his freedom comes at the expense of the bondsman. This is a superficial form of freedom and recognition, for the lord is not recognized by an equal partner, and consequently the lord remains individualistic and shallow. This is a simple, bare level of life for both the lord and the bondsman, for there is no mutual recognition between equals, between peers. In order for true human recognition to occur, the lord–bondsman dichotomy must be transcended.

The bondsman has the potentiality to overcome the conflicts between lord and bondsman, because of his unique social position and historical experiences. The bondsman only has control over the world of things, through his labor. But the bondsman can actually develop a more profound sense of identity because of this particular relationship to the world, and his experience of changing nature. Through labor, the bondsman transforms nature and makes himself as an authentic and independent being, shaping a social world, from buildings to institutions. This allows the natural and social worlds to reflect what the bondsman has made, and he sees the products of his labor as an extension of himself.

The bondsman's toil and suffering provide the basis for a more profound understanding of human consciousness. Unlike the lord, the bondsman achieves independence through transforming the conditions of his existence, and eventually becomes aware of his role in this active transformation. He becomes conscious of the possibility of freedom and autonomy as the result of his own efforts. He develops an idea of freedom to be realized through his own activity. Since the bondsman creates the world that the lord lives in, he deserves the recognition that the lord denies him. The lord enjoys what the bondsman makes, but he did not struggle to create it. Further, the lord is not independent, for he relies on the material products that the bondsman has produced. Because of his particular experience through labor, and his understanding of the links between his actions and the transformation of his experience, the bondsman has a richer identity than does the lord. Until the bondsman is respected, however, he will not be free. To attain this respect, he must abolish the relationship of servitude, and create a world of equality.[12]

This distinction between lord and bondsman provides an interesting way to understand Marx's distinction between classes and the various struggles between them. Hegel outlines this process in a very abstract manner, while Marx sees classes struggling in the material world. For Marx, the members of the working class, like Hegel's bondsmen, have a more profound understanding of themselves and the world because they actually create it. A large part of the struggle between classes concerns the powerful's lack of respect and recognition of the independence and dignity of the bondsman, as well as material inequality. The experience and identity of the working class are inseparable from the process of labor. Revolution involves an assertion of working-class identity, the desire of the proletariat to be fully recognized, as well as the redistribution of wealth. Equal recognition and respect are central aspects of identity.

Marx was also influenced by the German philosopher Ludwig Feuerbach (1804–72). In his book *The Essence of Christianity* (1842) Feuerbach criticizes idealist philosophies such as Hegel's, that equate the progress of humankind with the advance of spirit or abstract reason. Feuerbach argues that the starting point for the study of humanity must be real people living in the material world. People are natural beings; the real does not emanate from the divine, but from nature. In fact, people project their real powers onto the idea of a God, creating a fantasy religious world of harmony and beauty, while the real world is one of pain and misery. The idea of God only exists because humankind is alienated, divided against itself. The criticism of God can allow humankind to return these alienated powers to itself.

Marx adopts much of Feuerbach's materialism but contends that Feuerbach does not sufficiently comprehend that material circumstances can be altered through conscious social change. People are natural creatures, according to Marx, but they are also historical ones. Feuerbach's approach is ahistorical, for he posits an abstract human nature that exists outside of society and does not understand that people change as society changes. People can actively change the world, and it is this interaction between humankind and the material world developing through history that forms the basis of Marxism.

Marx's Critical Sociology

Armed with Marx's background in Hegel, Feuerbach, and anarchism, it is now possible to discuss his social theory. Marx, like Hegel, saw a progressive logic in history. Marx incorporates Hegel's notion that the oppressed have a distinctive experience of the world based on labor, which develops over time and ultimately provides them with a vantage point from which they can criticize their rulers. Marx was fond of saying that he turned Hegel right-side up, that Hegel's abstract philosophy captured the major contours of human history, but that it was not grounded in the real world or the struggle of classes. Marx's rich view of reason was also grounded in a romantic impulse, which sees capitalism destroying the possibility of authentic human experience.

Marx is a philosophical materialist. He contends that the material has primacy over the spiritual world, as matter conditions mind. Material factors, especially the production and reproduction of existence through labor, are the driving power in people's lives. The problems facing any society are inseparable from the organization of the labor process. Marx states: "Life is not determined by consciousness, but consciousness by life."[13] To understand any society it is necessary to grasp the labor process, the ways in which people transform nature through work. Labor fundamentally shapes people's identities, their sense of who they are.

Human history is the process of people producing their material lives. Labor produces a "definite mode of life," and human nature is dependent on the material conditions of production. The labor process is socially organized in distinct ways in different societies. The manner in which production is arranged forms the basis for the distribution, exchange, and consumption of goods, which varies from society to society. Every type of productive system presupposes a set of social relations as well as a particular approach to mastering nature. The reproduction of a people through labor is not accomplished by isolated individuals, but by members of a society.[14] For Marx, material inequality and the different experiences of classes are intertwined and cannot be separated.

As the arrangement of labor becomes more complex, a division of labor emerges. The division of labor distributes the conditions of labor (the tools and materials) into different, unequal groups. It promotes a more efficient economic system that allows a surplus to be created beyond that needed for subsistence. When a surplus develops, one group can live off the labor of another, akin to the master's dominion over the slave. Classes arise when the surplus of goods produced by the division of labor can be controlled by a minority of people. Class is defined by ownership or non-ownership of the means of production in a particular society. Any community in which an elite possesses the surplus is an unequal society. Further, the ways in which a ruling group extracts the surplus from another class provides insights into the type of inequality and exploitation generated in that society. In feudalism class domination occurs through coercion and traditional regulations, while under capitalism exploitation rests on seemingly impersonal mechanisms such as the labor contract and the market. Marx and Engels write that capitalism "has pitilessly torn asunder the motley feudal ties that bound man to his 'natural superiors,' and has left remaining no other nexus between man and man than naked self-interest, than callous 'cash payment.'"[15] In Marx's view, not only are classes different under capitalism, but modern peoples live in a different experiential world than in the past.

The Theory of Social Change

Classes develop divergent economic interests and conflict with one another, which is the engine of social change. Class conflict takes place within different modes of production, which are the totality of material and economic circumstances that "condition[s] the social, political, and intellectual life process in general."[16] Marx differentiates between Asiatic, ancient, feudal, and bourgeois modes of production "as progressive epochs in the economic formation of society."[17] Each succeeding mode of production displays progressive technological growth, organizational sophistication, and rational comprehension of the world. Marx distinguishes between the forces and the relations of production to explain these social changes. The forces of production are the technological and organizational capacities of a given society, while the relations of production refer to the type of ownership of the productive apparatus of a society (whether ownership is private or public, for example). The relationship between the forces and relations of production cannot be abstracted from the social and historical context in which they occur. Most significantly, the forces and relations of production are in constant conflict, and, in concert with class struggle, social change is impelled by their internal contradictions.

Marx is sometimes depicted as a technological determinist who believes that the expansion of technology within the forces of production determines the direction of social change. However, Marx argues that the relations of production are an equally important variable in social change, for in one historical era they can contribute to the increase of productive forces, while in another epoch they may inhibit them. The relations of production often seem to be the natural and inescapable features of social life during a particular historical period. For example, the lord–peasant relationship and its corresponding system of estates appeared to

be the eternal order of being under European feudalism, while the possession and control of private property by individuals and firms seems to be
the natural order in capitalism. Marx argues that this is not the case, and
that these relations of production become fetters on the further advancement of the productive forces, and have to be "torn asunder," in his
colorful language. Capitalism does not avoid contradictions, but creates
new ones, such as the opposition between the capitalist's private ownership of the means of production and the laborers' lack of ownership and
collective work to manufacture goods. Capitalism is steadily wracked by
crises which destroy productive forces, throw workers into unemployment, and create widespread hunger and misery. Socialism and later
communism will establish a more rational organization of the means of
production.

The Communist Manifesto

Marx concisely lays out many of these themes in the famous work, *The
Communist Manifesto*, co-authored with Engels in 1847. This pamphlet
was written when movements for democracy were threatening the rule of
monarchs. From Chartist demands for universal manhood suffrage in Britain
to demands for Polish national independence, the European continent
was in upheaval. Marx and Engels wrote for a small, obscure group known
as the Communist League.

Marx and Engels explore the logic whereby capitalism arises and will
destroy itself. The key to this process lies in class struggles between the
proletariat and the bourgeoisie, whose conflicts can only be resolved with
the victory of the working class and the establishment of socialism. They
begin the essay by stating that all history is the history of class struggle.
From the earliest forms of civilization, a ruling class has controlled production and politics, ensuring that it maintains economic control over an
oppressed stratum. As social conditions change, new classes come into
prominence. Marx and Engels briefly trace the history of capitalism, tying
it to the destruction of feudalism and the rise of the bourgeoisie. The
colonization of the Americas and other non-European lands is a key development for the rise of the bourgeoisie, who incessantly search for markets. In their words, "The East-Indian and Chinese markets, the colonization
of America, trade with the colonies, the increase in the means of exchange and in commodities generally, gave to commerce, to navigation,
to industry, an impulse never before known."[18]

Marx and Engels appear to praise the bourgeoisie. They write that "the
bourgeoisie, historically, has played a most revolutionary part."[19] The rise
of the bourgeoisie establishes a worldwide market system, encouraging

the development of industry, commerce, and communications. It creates massive industries and unprecedented wealth, subjecting nature to machinery and technology. The bourgeoisie demolishes the superstitions of feudalism, putting "an end to all feudal, patriarchal, idyllic relations."[20] It produces a more cosmopolitan and urban world, destroying, in one of Marx and Engels's most unforgettable phrases, "the idiocy of rural life."[21] With the rise of the bourgeoisie "national one-sidedness and narrow-mindedness become more and more impossible."[22]

But this progress comes at quite a cost. Bourgeois rule "has left remaining no other nexus between man and man than naked self-interest, than callous 'cash payment'".[23] All seemingly natural relations between ruler and ruled, all mutual rights and obligations, are severed by capitalism. The bourgeoisie upsets all social relations, throwing them into anarchy, as it scours the world for new markets, uproots communities by moving production to new, cheaper locations, and revolutionizing the workplace by introducing new technologies and laying off workers. Moreover, the rule of the bourgeoisie translates into the dominion of money over all of society. As Marx and Engels write, capitalism promotes the dizzying pace of modern life, and "all that is solid melts into air, all that is holy is profaned."[24] Not only do social conditions continually change, but everything has a price under capitalism. There is nothing outside of the market, nothing sacred or holy, that cannot be bought or sold.

Most property becomes private property under capitalism, owned by private individuals rather than by the state or the community. Ownership of industry replaces ownership of land as the major source of wealth. Capitalism is an internally contradictory economic system, in large part because private property ownership is not controlled by any larger public entity, and production and consumption are often not in equilibrium. This results in crises of production, when too many commodities are produced and cannot be consumed. The bourgeoisie either lays off workers when crises occur, looks for new markets to conquer, or tries to exploit existing markets more efficiently. Because capitalism is a worldwide system, crises quickly become international. All nations are drawn into the capitalist system and share in its problems.

The conflict between the bourgeoisie and the proletariat is the major contradiction of capitalism. Workers are brought together in factories and workshops to produce goods, yet the commodities they produce belong to the capitalist, a private individual. In their search for profits capitalists closely monitor and discipline workers. Marx and Engels use military metaphors such as describing workers as an "industrial army" to capture the experience of the workplace. Labor loses all joy, mass production reigns, and the worker "becomes an appendage of the machine, and it is only the most simple, most monotonous, and most easily acquired knack, that is required of him."[25] There is constant pressure on wages to decline, as the capitalist attempts to cut wages in order to increase profits.

Yet the proletariat is growing ever larger as capitalism develops. Workers under capitalism can more easily recognize their oppression, for they have few ties, outside of economic ones, to the ruling class. More and more people are forced to leave farms and enter wage labor, and mass production makes conditions of work increasingly similar. As the bourgeoisie extends throughout the world it creates its own gravediggers in the proletariat, for it needs new workers to exploit. The proletariat will become conscious of its differences from the bourgeoisie, as workers are forced into unions to represent and defend their interests. Laborers will demand that the state regulate the labor process, and class struggles will become politicized. The victory of the proletariat will be unique in history, for the proletariat represents the great masses of people. Marx and Engels write: "All previous historical movements were movements of minorities, or in the interests of minorities. The proletarian movement is the self-conscious, independent movement of the immense majority, in the interests of the immense majority."[26]

Such a struggle for power on the part of the proletariat will not be easy, however. This is in part because, in another famous phrase, "the ruling ideas of any age have ever been the ideas of its ruling class."[27] Marx designates such ruling ideas as ideologies, which are distorted, fragmentary representations of reality that justify the dominance of the ruling class. Ideologies idealize existing conditions, positing the existing society as the best of all possible worlds. Any ruling class which comes to power tries to show that its interests are the interests of all classes in society. Rulers appeal to universal ideals, whether they be religious, nationalistic, or political. The bourgeoisie inaugurates the ideal of the universal rights of man, such as freedom of speech, freedom of assembly, freedom of religion, etc. These are ideologies because they supposedly allow everyone equal freedom, when in reality freedom is dictated by economic power. Those who control the material means of production control intellectual production. The owner of a large newspaper has much more of an ability to practice freedom of speech, and get his ideas heard by millions, than the average worker. Those with wealth control schools, the media, and other sources of information. The economically powerless have difficulty publicizing their views. Thus, the dominant ideas of the age are the ideas of the ruling class.

Under capitalism the rule of the bourgeoisie is reinforced by the power of the state, which is "the executive committee of the bourgeoisie," in Marx's terms. The state, through police and the military, enforces existing property relations, and laws are set up to protect the wealthy. From Marx's perspective it would not be surprising that 95 percent of the people in US prisons are from poverty backgrounds. They have little access to political and legal power, and crimes against property are punished harshly.

Marx and Engels discuss how communism will change this situation. Communism will abolish the rule of private wealth over workers, so that workers do not produce more capital for capitalists but can enjoy the fruits of their labors. They argue that ridding society of capitalism and instituting socialism will change all social relations, such as gender relations, in a more egalitarian direction. Marx and Engels advocate several steps to realize their goals, from a progressive income tax to free education for children, many of which have been realized in contemporary Western nations.

The Theory of Capitalism

Marx contends that capitalism is an essentially exploitative system, which he explains in his labor theory of value. He states that a commodity's exchange value, or price, is directly measured by the amount of labor embodied in it. As it takes a greater amount of work and more sophisticated labor to make cars rather than pins, cars cost more than pins. Yet making pins and making cars involve very different types of labor. To compare them, the concrete differences between types of work must be erased and defined in regard to abstract labor, whose value can then be calculated in terms of wages. Abstract labor allows the computation of socially necessary labor time, i.e. the average amount of time required to produce a commodity in a given industry. Commodities exchange at their values, or the amount of socially necessary labor time that it takes to make them.

The exploitation of labor can be understood through the concept of socially necessary labor time. The worker is paid her full value as a commodity, for she receives a sufficient wage to reproduce herself as a laborer (the socially necessary labor time to recreate her existence). Yet the laborer produces more wealth than is necessary for the cost of subsistence, for only a proportion of the working day is necessary to reproduce the worker's life. The rest of the working day the proletarian produces profits for the capitalist. Exploitation occurs entirely within the sphere of production, as the worker creates revenue for the capitalist and does not receive her just share of resources.

Marx on Manufacture, Modern Industry, and Crisis

Marx traces the rise of capitalism through several stages. In medieval times, guild production predominated, when each worker produced

independently for trade in the home. What Marx labels simple cooperation arises with the beginnings of capitalism. Workers come together in a
single workplace and budding capitalists supply the capital (equipment
and raw materials) for production. Laborers increase their productivity in
this setting, for they can produce items more quickly than when working
completely independently of one another. At this stage, workers still perform their work at their own pace. The capitalist pays these artisans a
wage and markets their products for a profit.

The capitalist soon realizes that he can increase profits and efficiency by
extending the division of labor in the workplace. Marx names this phase
of capitalism manufacture. Workers lose control over production, as each
laborer specializes in a single, simple operation. The striving for capitalist
profits dominates the organization of the workplace. Under manufacture,
the capitalist becomes an essential part of the production process, for he
supplies the capital necessary for production, while workers supply the
labor.

This is not in any sense a "natural" process. In *Capital* Marx demonstrates that in early nineteenth-century Britain farmers were forced off
the land through various enclosure laws and poor people were compelled
to work or face jail time through the Poor Laws. The state, through its
coercive powers and legal and police forces, supported the rise of capitalism, not only in Britain but throughout the world. We can see the same
sorts of things happening now, as many governments in the Third World
aid corporate production efforts in their countries. The market disrupts
existing ways of life and forces production for the market upon the people.

The final stage of capitalism that Marx documents is modern industry.
Capitalists utilize machinery to increase profits through lowering costs,
increase the specialized division of labor in large factories, and deprive
workers of any control over the production process. Modern industry
exacerbates a major contradiction of capitalism, for production is planned
and socialized within the workplace, which is highly rationalized. Exchange, the consumption of products, is not planned, but dependent on
market forces. Thus, many firms fail when they cannot sell their products,
and recessions and sometimes depressions occur. Firms attempt to overcome these problems by becoming larger so they can control more of the
market and centralize production. But monopolies cannot stop the crises
of capitalism.

The accumulation of capital, the constant increase of capital, is a major
dynamic within capitalism. Capitalism is dependent on sustained economic growth, requiring continual reinvestment and the search for new
markets. Capitalists wish to increase profits, which means cutting costs,
especially labor. The wages of labor are kept low because of what Marx
labels "the reserve army of workers," the unemployed, who compete for

jobs. Capitalists also reduce costs by replacing workers with new technology, or attempting to increase the productivity of workers. This process is at the heart of the crisis-ridden nature of capitalism. As capitalists accumulate they require more labor, wages rise as unemployment drops, rising wages eat into profits, capitalists curtail investment as their profits decline, workers are laid off, wages decline, the reserve army rises, and the whole process keeps repeating itself, in cycles of recession, growth, recession, etc. Replacing workers with machines or increasing the productivity of labor temporarily mitigate this process, but they cannot halt the fundamental dynamic of capitalism.

These cycles were particularly prominent in nineteenth-century capitalism, though the Great Depression of the 1930s was the most dramatic demonstration of the crisis-ridden nature of capitalism. Today the West (or North) still experiences economic crises, but not the massive depressions that shook capitalism in the 1930s (at least not yet). In the wake of the Great Depression the welfare state arose, creating social programs such as unemployment insurance and social security which gave workers some degree of security. The welfare state was based on industrial trade unions fighting for higher wages and state action favoring labor. Yet since the 1970s the welfare state has been in crisis and capitalists have searched for new ways to make profits. From a Marxist perspective the current fascination with globalization is based on a search for new sources of profit. Corporations decrease their cost of production through employing inexpensive labor in Third World countries and importing cheap foreign goods, while states cut social programs such as welfare to make available more cheap labor for the workforce.

Marx argues that the nature of capitalism follows contradictory laws which promote constant crises. He also demonstrates that the nature of capitalism is tied to particular historical contexts, and its specific shape depends on the strength of the state, the power of the working class, and other social factors. Markets require a host of social and legal institutions in order to develop; they are in no sense outgrowths of "natural" human desires. Particularly, markets require coercive social mechanisms to maintain the power of capitalists. Government and social policies, in the absence of a strong labor movement, will be favorable to corporations.

Marx shows that the rise of capitalism was not a peaceful process, but involves new sources of power and exploitation compared to previous eras in history. The distinctiveness of capitalism lies in its worldwide search for markets, new types of class struggle, and the pervasiveness of commodity production in all forms of social life.

Alienation and Capitalism

Most people do not recognize the centrality of capitalism and class struggle in shaping their lives. Marx thought that most of the theories of society and morality of his time camouflaged the true dynamics of society. Marx traces the most cherished ideals of morality and religion to human, all-too-human origins. The individual and the society do not coexist as a happy medium, for institutions often do not further people's rationality and freedom, but inhibit it.

These ideas can be seen in his critique of religion. Religion disguises true sources of suffering, and Marx calls it the "opium of the people."[28] Ideas of God and morality are human creations which serve the particular needs of a ruling class. For Marx, most people do not realize that these moral and divine beliefs are of human origin, so that images of God and morality take on a universal and seemingly natural existence. Religion especially for Marx is prototypical of alienation, in which people's creations come to dominate them. Thus, the idea of God controls how people act in the world, rather than people realizing that they themselves have fabricated the notion of God. People project their powers of creation onto a divine figure, just as they give their social power later to governments and capitalists. Throughout his work Marx deepens this idea of alienation, moving from a critique of religion to a critique of the state, the division of labor, and the class inequalities generated by capitalism. Workers need to destroy capitalist society in order to free themselves from illusions and overcome alienation.

Alienation in capitalism is manifested in other ways. Capitalism crushes our particularly human experience. It destroys the pleasure associated with labor, the distinctively human capacity to make and remake the world, and the major distinguishing characteristic of humans from animals. Marx writes that because of capitalism "man (the worker) no longer feels himself to be freely active in any but his animal functions – eating, drinking, procreating, or at most in his dwelling and in dressing-up, etc.; and in his human functions he no longer feels himself to be anything but an animal. What is animal becomes human and what is human becomes animal."[29] People are only free when they can mutually recognize each other, i.e. recognize their "species-being." When people are conscious of themselves as a species they realize that they share a human essence. Accordingly, people only live authentically, in accord with their nature, when they act as a species-being, a social being. Through changing the world, people create their species-being, which in turn changes them. This is accomplished primarily through socially organized labor. The proletariat, much like Hegel's bondsman, has a historically subservient position which allows him to truly experience oppression and the potential for a rich freedom, while also giving him a distinctive experience of changing the world through labor. Under capitalism, capital replaces the lord, and capital enslaves the proletariat.

Marx's view of experience, and capitalism's distortion of it, are evident in some of his more lyrical passages from his work written when he was a young man of twenty-six, the 1844 Paris Manuscripts. Marx speaks poetically about how communism will emancipate our senses, so that the opposition of individual experience and social demands will be transcended, and we will feel fulfilled in society. Marx's debt to romanticism is clear here. The realization of our authentic human capacities requires that all of our senses, not just thinking, be fulfilled. Our senses have been formed throughout history. Yet under capitalism all that matters is what can be bought and sold, so that we approach life with an eye towards what we can get out of it. Such an approach corrupts the role of the senses in human gratification. Music must not be understood in terms of how much money it can make, but a musical ear must be developed to appreciate music; an eye for form must be developed to appreciate beauty. Each of the senses must be cultivated in a way that is appropriate for the objects that they consider.[30] This is another way in which humans are distinguished from animals, for people can create according to the laws of beauty and not simply follow functional demands. One of the worst features of capitalism is that it reduces the many-faceted and diverse nature of the human senses to the criteria of profit.

Marx's ideas about the centrality of experience and identity are central to his critique of democracy. The proletariat has its own institutions which distinguish it from the bourgeoisie, based on the distinctive history, social position, and experience of the working class. However, this sensitivity to the different experience of groups is lacking in Marx's analysis of colonialism, and the history of non-Western peoples. It demonstrates the problems associated with any linear and progressive theory of history, even the master–slave dialectic. Before turning to Marx's theory of imperialism, we will first examine his understanding of democracy.

Marx and Democracy

In the contemporary US political conflicts abound. Republicans and Democrats seem to be at one another's throats, attacking each other over any issue which seems to give them an advantage. Many citizens are cynical about the possibilities of progressive political change, if they are not downright hostile toward politics and the government. These attitudes are evident in a trend toward low voter turnout over the years. Moreover, voting rates are stratified according to income and education levels. The more money people make and the more education they have, the more likely they are to vote. How would Marx analyze these phenomena?

Many critics view Marx as opposed to democracy, as he ostensibly advocated a huge state dominated by a single communist party. Such an interpretation of Marx does make sense, as he supported the nationalization of industry by the state and at least in one instance wrote of "the revolutionary dictatorship of the proletariat."[31] Yet Marx's analysis is more complicated than this, as he sees the very existence of the state as indicative of a class-divided society, as governments have no real independence of their own. Further, Marx states that the working class must develop its own institutions outside of the state, until it can attain power. Alongside the official government, workers "must establish simultaneously their own revolutionary workers' governments, whether in the form of workers' clubs or workers' committees."[32] Workers must create a distinctive proletarian public sphere. With these ideas in mind, we can now move on to a more in-depth discussion of Marx's view of democracy.

Marx begins his analysis of politics and democracy by placing them in the context of class struggle. The political realm is not an autonomous arena where citizens and/or politicians arrive at their judgments independently; rather, their views reflect the classes that they represent and the intensity of class struggle. Though there is a lot of noise in the political realm, true power and change resides in the economic sphere. The government is largely dominated by the bourgeoisie, as they use the law and the courts to protect their property rights (failing this, they turn to the police and the army). The state is the "executive committee of the bourgeoisie" – it rules with the economic interests of the bourgeoisie in mind.[33] Most people's cynicism about politics is thus justified, unless they are wealthy, as their interests are not represented by political parties under the thrall of the bourgeoisie.

The seemingly strong political rights of a democracy in a class-divided, capitalist society reflect the power of the bourgeoisie. Marx writes that "the so-called *rights of man* . . . are simply the rights of a *member of civil society*, that is, of egoistic man, of man separated from other men and from the community."[34] The US bill of rights thus guarantees our right to be isolated, competitive individuals with few concrete ties to one another. Civil society is the realm where this competition takes place. Civil society is essentially the economic realm, for "the anatomy of civil society is to be sought in political economy."[35] The state arises on the foundation of this civil society, as the arena where a seemingly common interest can rule. But the government can never be neutral and reflect the common good, for it mirrors the wishes of the dominant class.

The biases of the state are shown in periods of social crisis. Executive committees do not always rule with one voice, and sometimes they do not unanimously agree on politics. Marx, too, sees this possibility and sometimes writes of splits among different factions of the bourgeoisie, who advocate different policies. In such cases the bourgeoisie does not rule effectively. When the proletariat is strong and threatens the bourgeoisie, the latter is quick to disband political freedoms, from the rights of freedom of the press to freedom of assembly, to protect its social power and property rights. Marx makes this judgment in his famous analysis of the rise to power of the dictator Louis Bonaparte (1808–73) in France in 1851. Splits between a landed and financial bourgeoisie lead to different political views and create the space where a dictator can arise and dominate the government. The bourgeoisie acceded to a dictator who abolished political rights rather than see their social power confiscated by the working class. A similar analysis could be made of the rise of Hitler and Nazism in Germany in the 1920s and 1930s.[36]

Real democracy is not based on constitutions or representative institutions, for these can be discarded at any time. Rather, democracy means overcoming the dichotomy of public power embodied in the government and social power embodied in civil society – essentially, it means socialism, the overcoming of class inequality. When socialism is victorious, true human emancipation will occur, rather than a limited political emancipation. People must be able to exercise social power as equals to truly practice democracy.

Marx views the short-lived Paris Commune of 1871, formed in the wake of revolts against Napoleon III in the context of the Franco-Prussian War of 1870–1, as a good example of what a true democracy might look like. He states that the Paris Commune had the following political structure:

1   It abolished the armed forces as a group separate from the people.
2   Its political functions were given to delegates recallable at any time, not to seemingly independent representatives.
3   There was an absence of monetary privileges for the delegates.
4   Legislative, executive, and judicial power was united in the same organ, abolishing the sham independence of these different branches of government.
5   The local Commune was the basis of national organization. This decentralized form of political rule overcame the pernicious centralization of political power that capitalism brought with it.[37]

Capitalism requires a state machinery over and above the people to maintain its authority. The Commune smashed this state government and represented the direct rule of the people. With his writings on the Commune

Marx argues that the proletariat will put in place a completely different type of political organization after overthrowing capitalism. Marx does not even call the Commune a state, for the latter presupposes a split between civil and political society, which the Commune eliminated. The working class must create a new form of political organization which corresponds to its rule.[38]

Marx thus advocates a decentralized form of participatory democracy that has many affinities with his anarchist rivals and the republican tradition of Aristotle through Rousseau. He supports a proletarian space, a public sphere, where workers can develop the qualities necessary to govern society. Like the anarchists, Marx distrusts the state and thinks that strong local organizations are necessary to create the collective experience of rule that a true democracy requires. True socialist democracy depends on social equality and collective participation rather than constitutional guarantees and representative institutions. Drawing on the republican tradition Marx argues that freedom and community are interdependent, and freedom can only be realized in conditions where people control their activity. They must cultivate and experience freedom and democracy in order to truly practice it. He radicalizes the republican tradition by locating the cultivation of democracy in the workplace, through the experience of free labor. Marx recognizes the limits of purely political change that only alters laws without changing the social conditions of particular groups. People have to transform the social world themselves if change is to be effective and lasting.

Marx on the Disciplinary Society

Marx realizes that there are connections between knowledge and power, as can be seen in his critique of capitalist democracy. He argues that the dominant knowledges in a society usually justify the power of the ruling class. These ideas are not true in any absolute sense, but are rather ideologies, as we have seen. They offer partial, imperfect, and often illusory understandings of society. Marx also recognizes that different groups develop varied knowledges and understandings of the world because of their differing objective relationship to the mode of production. Thus, workers develop a different understanding of the world than do the bourgeoisie. Indeed, Marxism represents the workers' viewpoint.

Logically, this argument can be expanded to other groups. For example, women and the colonized should be able to develop their own knowledges based on their social position, their unique vantage point from which they can understand society. For instance, some contemporary feminists have adopted this perspective. They argue that women's particular social position in a patriarchal society gives them a unique vantage point from which to understand gender exploitation within the family and society. But Marx does not take this step, despite some critical comments on gender relations. He is concerned with understanding and changing the mode of production. For Marx, the colonized and women are not as directly connected with the mode of production as is the proletariat, and their distinctive viewpoints can be subsumed under the category of class, a questionable assumption at best, but one that I think inhibits his understanding of these diverse groups.

Marx realizes that elements of a disciplinary society arose within the workplace, as laborers' actions were minutely governed and watched by foremen and owners. But he does not extend this insight about possible disciplinary effects into other contexts. He does not address how dominant moralities construct ideals of "normal" sexuality and how they defined mental illness. In large part this was because the new experience of capitalism dominated his world, and the spread of capitalism throughout the globe sometimes seemed to Marx to be an inevitable process. Further, the working class appeared to be the agent of liberation from exploitation and oppression. But there are also theoretical reasons for Marx's lack of attention to these issues. He thinks that his perspective provides insights into the *ordre naturel*, that it mirrors the objective processes of economics and history. Marx's positive evaluation of science leads him to argue that the problems of society can be traced to its lack of rationality, the non-scientific basis of its economy and institutions. Marx's view of rationality is complex, as he is sensitive to conflict and contradiction, given his debt to dialectics and Hegelian heritage. But Marx tends to embrace the belief that history is progressive, despite conflicts and contradictions, and that science grants us objective truths.

Marx's orientation is reinforced by his materialism and his emphasis on production. Issues that cannot be immediately related to the production process or class struggle are of little interest to him. He has few comments about the manner in which power and knowledge can marginalize people in ways other than economic oppression, as in the ostracism of homosexuals and the institutionalization of the mentally ill. This focus on the economy means that Marx does not pay sufficient attention to cultural differences among peoples and to the problems of cultural imperialism. But Marx is not consistent on this score, as he often emphasizes the importance of studying societies in their concrete historical context, and occasionally addresses issues of the cultural destruction wrought by capitalism. These themes are illustrated in his analysis of Empire.

Marx and Empire

In Marx's discussion of colonialism his Eurocentric views are most pronounced. They are inseparable from his theory of capitalism. Marx believes that capitalism is the first mode of production which expands throughout the world because of its own internal dynamics based on the pursuit of profit, rather than through military plunder so that leaders can expand their riches. Accordingly, Marx develops a theory of imperialism, the expansion of Western capitalist countries into the non-Western world. But Marx has a deficient theory of imperialism and colonialism. He simplistically transfers his sophisticated analysis of Europe to non-European societies. Marx terms this non-Western social formation the "Asiatic mode of production," and he sees it as an unchanging, static, non-dialectical area of the globe.[39] According to Marx, non-Western peoples lack a history. In his words, "Indian society has no history at all, at least no known history. What we call its history, is but the history of the successive intruders who founded their empires on the passive basis of that unresisting and unchanging society."[40] Marx's statement regarding French peasants' inability to form a strong, cohesive class is true of his view of non-Westerners: "They cannot represent themselves, they must be represented."[41] In the case of the colonized this means that the colonizer has the power to depict their history as he sees fit.

Not only does Marx deny non-Western peoples their own cultural and historical integrity, but he sometimes falls into stereotypes of European civilized superiority and non-Western inferiority. This results in Marx's endorsement of European colonial expansion as a necessary step in the progress of the world and its advance toward socialism. The oppressive Asiatic mode of production needs an external agent to overthrow it, which appears with European colonialism. As Said points out, Marx used documents supplied by the colonialists to develop his theory of imperialism, having no real knowledge of the history of native peoples (though the case of Ireland is an interesting exception, as we will discuss below). Said also states that Marx was writing for a European and North American audience, which he took for granted.[42]

Marx's Eurocentric biases are demonstrated in many of his comments about non-Western peoples and religions. He sees an inferior "Oriental mind" behind many non-Westerners' attitudes. He refers to the "fanaticism of Islam," collapsing its adherents into a mob.[43] He calls nineteenth-century China "a living fossil" destined to be overthrown by Western progress. Consequently, Chinese opposition to Western imperialism is simply a defensive reaction against modernization.[44]

His comments on British imperialism in India are especially apt in this context. For Marx, the political unity of India and its modern means of transport are the result of British actions. Marx recognizes that British imperialism destroyed Indian culture, separating India "from all its ancient traditions, and from the whole of its past history."[45] Indian agriculture is also disrupted by European invaders. But in "blowing up [the] economical basis of the Oriental mode of production," European imperialism "produced the greatest, and, to speak the truth, the only *social* revolution ever heard of in Asia."[46] Marx writes that "whatever may have been the crimes of England she was the unconscious tool of history in bringing about that revolution."[47] As Avineri states, "Marx's sole criteria for judging the social revolution imposed on Asia are those of European, bourgeois society itself."[48]

These outrageous Eurocentric comments are crucial, if not damning, criticisms of Marx's theory. Though I do not want to dismiss these criticisms, a close reading of Marx reveals that his theories are more complex than this interpretation. Marx criticizes European imperialists for their brutal treatment of native peoples, sometimes coming close to advocating wars of national liberation against colonialism, especially in the case of Ireland. In his discussion of British imperialism in India, Marx seems at times to have a sense of the autonomy and integrity of native industry. Finally, Marx states on at least one occasion that his theory applies to Western Europe only and that there may be different roads that countries will travel to modernity.

Marx scathingly criticizes the bourgeoisie for its monetary gluttony, brutality, and destruction of native industry. Marx indicts British colonialism in India, stating that it was based on plunder and murder as hideous as the slave trade. Justified by a Christianity that saw colonialism as civilizing the savages, British oppressors lived like sybarites in India at the expense of natives.[49] The British exploited the Indians both financially and physically. As Marx states, the British taxed Indians so that it crushed "the mass of the Indian people to the dust, and ... its exaction necessitates a resort to such infamies as torture."[50] Imperialism brutalized Europeans and natives. When many Indians took up arms against the British in 1857, European newspapers accused the Indians of murderous atrocities against Europeans. Marx would have none of this. Indian violence was only the "reflex" of British violence against them, for torture was an important part of British rule. British elites defined their atrocities as examples of military prowess, and applauded "atrocities" when committed by natives against their French rivals, or by the bourgeoisie against workers in European countries.[51]

The European bourgeoisie will stop at nothing to gain profits. Marx accuses the Europeans of introducing opium into China, selling and spreading it in order to make money.[52] Marx called this a "free trade in poison."

The British destroyed local Indian agriculture, forcing farmers to cultivate poppies for opium. British industry then sold it in China, maintaining a monopoly on the opium trade. The British government was a complicit partner in this trade, all the while hypocritically denouncing the drug trade.[53] The costs of British imperialism actually outweighed the benefits. Only a few elite groups benefited from it, including East Indian bond holders and various branches of British administration. Marx is especially scathing in his criticisms of British aristocrats, who he thinks would rather plunder foreign peoples than engage in skilled work in Britain.[54] In sum, the costs of British imperialism essentially resulted in a tax on the working classes of Britain and India.

European imperialism destroyed internal native industry, often not replacing it with anything else. Marx states that India had been "the great workshop of cotton manufactures, since immemorial times," but that Britain demolished it, in part through imports.[55] British landlords in India "had it in their power to undermine, and thus forcibly convert part of the Hindoo self-sustaining communities into mere farms, producing opium, cotton, indigo, hemp, and other raw materials in exchange for British stuffs."[56] Marx also at times seems to recognize that Indians have a very rich culture, in many ways superior to that of Europe. He writes of the Indians "whose country has been the source of our ancient languages, our religions, and who represent the type of the ancient German in the Jat and the type of the ancient Greek in the Brahmin."[57] In such a context expulsion of foreigners is just. Marx states: "dispassionate and thoughtful men may perhaps be led to ask whether a people are not justified in attempting to expel foreign conquerors who have so abused their subjects."[58] Indians will not enjoy the fruits of their own labor until a socialist revolution occurs in Britain, or "the Hindoos themselves shall have grown strong enough to throw off the English yoke altogether."[59]

Despite Marx's comments about the "Oriental mind" he attributed their seeming static history to a structural principle. These nations lacked extensive private property, so that the expansion of wage labor and the concomitant bourgeois–proletariat social relations integral to capitalism could not develop. This lack of private property was compounded by a strong central government which financed public works, faced by small villages which formed a self-enclosed world. Marx states: "The village isolation produced the absence of roads in India, and the absence of roads perpetuated the village isolation."[60] Such a society was not very dynamic. The over-centralization of these governments resulted in part from the necessity of artificially fertilizing the soil through irrigation.[61]

While Marx's many comments seem to indicate that he thought he had derived a universal theory of history and society, at other times he is more circumspect. In a letter to the editor of a Russian journal Marx writes that his model of economic history is only applicable to Western Europe. He argues, in reference to Russia, that this nation is trying to emulate the capitalist countries of Western Europe. If Russia desires to go down this path its peasants must be converted into wage laborers, and then it "will experience its [capitalism's] pitiless laws like any other profane people."[62] But Marx argues that he is absolutely *not* positing this process as an inevitable law, for any good theory of a people must explore "the historical circumstances in which it finds itself."[63] He points to his example in *Capital* of ancient Rome, where proletarians did not become wage laborers in the modern sense, but sided with Roman elites and contributed to the promotion of slavery, much as poor whites did in the antebellum US. Marx says that in these cases "there developed a mode of production which was not capitalist but based on slavery."[64] Thus, the existence of a proletariat does not necessarily produce capitalism, and "events strikingly analogous but taking place in different historical surroundings led to totally different results." Marx calls for an attention to historical circumstances and an avoidance of "a general historico-philosophical theory, the supreme virtue of which consists in being super-historical."[65]

Marx thinks that if conditions warrant it certain countries might not follow the classic European line of capitalist development. Thus, even though China is an agrarian country, Marx notes that "among the rebelling plebes there have emerged people who point to the poverty of some and the richness of others, who demanded and demand a redistribution of property, even the total abolition of private property."[66] Marx states that European reactionaries might soon find written on the great Chinese Wall, "République Chinoise. Liberté, égalité, fraternité!"[67] Marx also argues that the village community of tsarist-dominated Russia, a "form of the primeval common ownership of land," could lead to Russian communism if Russia and the West had simultaneous revolutions.[68]

The Issue of Ireland

The complexity of Marx's views on colonialism becomes even more pronounced when he discusses Ireland. Dominated as a colony by England, the Irish were often regarded by the English as an inferior "race," akin to the British racist views of other subject peoples. Marx does not view the Irish in this way. Rather than viewing colonialism as a secondary phenomenon in the struggle for socialism, he sees the Irish demands for national liberation as a key element in any British proletarian revolution. British workers will not cut their ties to the ruling class until Irish independence forced them to rethink their social relations.[69]

Colonialism allows English and Irish proletarians to be split into two hostile camps, as they see one another as competitors. The British worker views his Irish counterpart as lowering his standard of living. He also derives a sense of superior satisfaction and privilege from his relation to Irish workers, which ties the British proletarian to the ruling class. This antagonism is the major reason why the English working class has not revolted, although the material conditions for revolution existed in England.[70] Indeed, for English workers "the national emancipation of Ireland is not a question of abstract justice or humanitarian sentiment, but the first condition of their own social emancipation."[71]

Thus, Marx calls for the British working class, and the English more generally, to own up to "the great crime which it has committed against Ireland over many centuries."[72] Often applauding the "Irish people," he advocates Irish self-government and independence from England, along with an agrarian revolution which would redistribute wealth in Ireland.[73] Irish revolution is "not only a simple economic question but at the same time a *national* question."[74] Marx attributes this to the fact that English landlords controlled much of Ireland's land and were hated as oppressors. Ridding Ireland of English landlords and redistributing land is "a *question of life and death* for the majority of the Irish people," and agrarian revolution is inseparable from national independence.[75]

Marx castigates English elites for ruling Ireland "by the most atrocious reign of terror and the most damnable corruption."[76] The English bourgeoisie and aristocracy desire to turn Ireland into a massive pasture in order "to supply the English market with meat and wool at the cheapest possible prices." They also wish to eliminate as much of the native population as possible "by eviction and forcible emigration" so that English capital can do what it will in a context of "security."[77]

Marx thus views the Irish conflict as the result of a legitimate struggle for independence on the part of the Irish people. He recognizes that nationhood and identity are intertwined in the Irish case, and that colonial peoples must struggle to establish their own distinctiveness apart from the colonizer.

Marx on Gender and Cultural Identity

Though Marx does not develop a sophisticated theory of different types of cultural identity, he and Engels do have some interesting comments about the role of women in society. In *The German Ideology* Marx argues that in the earliest manifestations of the division of labor, in the family, the wife and children are the slaves of the man. Marx states that this is the first type of property, for it allows the male to dispose of the labor power of his wife and children.[78] In *The Communist Manifesto* Marx and Engels contend that the bourgeois family is based "on capital, on private gain." Family relations are founded on class position. People marry one another in the ruling class in order to enhance their economic position. In the bourgeois family women control the household while men provide the income by working outside of the home. This relationship is romanticized. For Marx, romantic relations cannot escape the clutches of capital. Since capital means exploitation, women are oppressed by men within the family. The notion of a family where the woman is in control of the household does not exist among the proletariat, as women work outside of the home because of the family's need for money.[79]

Let's explore these ideas in a bit more detail, by turning to the writings of Engels. In *The Origin of the Family, Private Property, and the State* Engels argues that family relations are inseparable from power relations. He concentrates on the power that men have historically held over women in the family. With the rise of civilization the paternal family, headed by the male, becomes dominant. Monogamy is based on unequal power relations, the subjection of woman by man.[80]

Engels states that throughout Western history most marriages have been arranged by parents, especially among the ruling classes. Only in modern times does the idea become dominant that the inclinations of two equal people should decide marriage. Among the bourgeoisie completely voluntary marriages are still absent, with subtle arranged marriages predominant. Wealthier people marry those of their own class, often with economic considerations in mind. Only among oppressed classes does truly voluntary marriage take place.[81]

Yet among all modern families the law does not adequately recognize the economic oppression of women. With the rise of the private sphere women were pushed out of public work and they became enslaved by man. Because of the man's superior economic position, "he is the bourgeois; the wife represents the proletariat."[82] This power differential extends into morality. A double standard for men and women regarding adultery exists, as it is almost expected that men will have affairs, while women are branded as immoral if they engage in extra-marital affairs.

Engels argues that the position of women will change dramatically when they have economic equality under socialism. Private housekeeping will be transformed into social industry, and society will help raise all children. Fully free marriage will only occur with the abolition of classes, so economic motives for wedlock disappear and the only motive bringing people together will be mutual affection. The power of men over women will vanish as their economic power disappears. Marriages will be able to be dissolved when couples no longer feel that they love one another, and few economic consequences will result from the end of a marriage.[83]

Much has happened to the family since the nineteenth century, as women have fought for equality with men and many countries have instituted child-care for working women. Yet many of Engels's statements still ring true. We will discuss many of these themes in chapter 7 on the thought of Perkins Gilman. Despite unprecedented divorce rates many people romanticize the nuclear family, seeing it as a realm of love, a "haven in a heartless world" untouched by money and power. Of course such arguments are false, as money and power greatly effect marriage. For example, people marry predominantly those individuals of their own class background. The sociologist Arlie Hochschild shows that women are still responsible for the "second shift" of child-care and housework, even if they work outside of the home.[84] Men are often still able to be the bourgeoisie within the home, with women as the proletariat.

Marx: An Assessment

Despite these critical comments about women, Marx does not develop a complex theory of the psyche, or of identification processes that might make for a more complex understanding of power relations. Further, Marx's discussion of imperialism raises fundamental questions about his social theory. For the most part, Marx sees European societies as superior to those that they were colonizing, not only technologically but also as having a higher level of civilization. His theory shows the inherent problems of evolutionary approaches to society which structure them in a hierarchical way, so that some societies are superior and more advanced than others. Such a perspective undercuts the integrity of other cultures. Marx demonstrates how a theory of knowledge tied to progress can exclude many views of the world as either irrelevant or just wrong. Thus, the histories and beliefs of entire cultures, particularly outside of the West, were not extensively studied by Marx.

Marx creates a historical salvation narrative, with the proletariat as the embodiment of good, that he disguises as scientific. Notwithstanding Marx's claim that he is developing a materialist, economically based theory of society, he produces a normative framework which allows him to evaluate different cultures in a hierarchical manner, as he especially compares the "rational" West with the "irrational" non-West. In the wake of anthropological investigations of non-modern cultures, it is apparent that almost all people can give good reasons for their conduct, for what is considered rational is tied very closely to cultural and social contexts, and varies from society to society. These considerations certainly mean that any philosophy of history based on a notion of inevitable rational progress must be rejected.

Marx's concentration on labor and economics inhibits him from analyzing other factors in structuring social life, from gender and race to administrative surveillance and culture more generally. Marx often investigates societies as self-contained wholes. While this allows him to make connections between phenomena as disparate as class and religion, as we have seen, it also raises some problems. Marx tends to compare entire societies with one another (the English with Indians, for example), and he sometimes argues that one is superior to the other (though he is not entirely consistent on this score, as we have seen). If Marx had seen cultures and societies as more permeable, open to reciprocal influences, he might not have made such hierarchical judgments. The task for a social science now is to "study social differences without essentializing and positioning them as inferior or subordinate."[85]

Marx's analysis of democracy also has difficulties. Marx has a limited view of the relationship of civil society to democracy. Many contemporary theorists now argue that civil society is much more than a market economy, as it is the realm where voluntary organizations, from unions to church groups, can arise. Such groups need a space to develop mutual ideas and solidarity. If civil society is eliminated, so is the arena for the generation of sources of solidarity and mutuality. Communist dissidents such as Václav Havel remind us that this is exactly what happened under communist and other authoritarian regimes, as the free, public spaces which allowed people to develop common ideas and beliefs were thwarted by these governments.[86]

I think these are strong criticisms of Marx's perspective. Yet Marx's view of colonialism also raises some interesting issues that should be retained in present day social theory. Marx refuses to romanticize non-Western cultures; he recognizes that they too suffered much internal oppression, from inter-tribal warfare to class, gender, and racial domination, and a simple-minded cultural relativism can blind Westerners to the injustices that exist in the non-West. Marx's rethinking of the lord–bondsman dialectic, if applied to colonialism, also opens up some interesting ways of thinking, as it combines changing types of historically determined economic and cultural oppression in a sensitive and sophisticated manner. Marx does not always heed his own call to explore cultures in their particular historical context, but that does not mean that this invitation should be rejected. Too often, contemporary sociology is satisfied with general statements about cultures and societies, and cultural critics are quick to criticize the West without exploring the complex internal dynamics and concrete historical circumstances of the countries and cultures they are discussing.

Our present concern with gender, sexual orientation, and race as sources of identity and social stratification can blind us to the continued importance of class, not only in shaping our economic life chances, but in subtly influencing the very ways that we act in the world and view our society. Marx shows that class denotes a certain experiential reality. Many recent studies have documented this fact, discussing a distinctive working-class culture that is different from middle-class or "bourgeois culture." For example, Pierre Bourdieu analyzes the social advantages of a person being born into the middle and upper classes. He states that such a person is endowed with a certain "cultural capital," which is inscribed in her very type of personality, ways of bearing, voice, grace, linguistic competence, and the like. Many of these advantages subtly accrue to those born in the upper classes. Much of Bourdieu's work shows how cultural capital is not evenly distributed among different classes, and the ways in which cultural capital helps reproduce the class structures of modern societies. Class mobility is difficult not only because of the lack of material resources, but also because of the difficulties faced by individuals in the working and poorer classes in assimilating the cultural capital associated with the upper classes. Accordingly, Bourdieu argues that sports are one of the few means of upward mobility for people in working and poorer classes. Sports represents for boys (and increasingly for girls) what beauty has always represented for girls, a market of cultural capital based on physical capital.[87]

From a Marxist view, the obsession with difference (whether it be based on gender, race, or sexual orientation) that we now see among groups reflects the competition of civil society and does little to critique capitalism. In a perverse way, seemingly radical demands for minority emancipation reflect the logic of a competitive marketplace, and make solidarity harder to achieve. It also leads people away from the problems created by capitalism. The philosopher Richard Rorty writes that many contemporary US leftists "specialize in the 'politics of difference' or 'of identity' or 'of recognition.' This cultural left thinks more about stigma than about money, more about deep and hidden psychosexual motivations than about shallow and evident greed."[88] Rorty is certainly sympathetic to these cultural themes of the left, as he is a major figure in the postmodern turn of much recent philosophy. Moreover, these cultural issues can be glimpsed in Marx's work, as we have seen. But Rorty, like Marx, fears that a focus on ideas and beliefs can blind us to the important economic practices that are profoundly influencing us.

I wish to close with several ways that Marx can help us understand our contemporary world, in addition to those delineated above. His idea that theory is closely related to practice, and that intellectual and social power cannot be separated from class, remains convincing to me. Marx views economics as the root cause, the true reality, of many of our actions and beliefs. He is often right, as it makes sense, for example, to understand political discussion about policies in terms of which class they will benefit. Yet, as I have mentioned earlier, this view means discarding entire realms of phenomena as unimportant, or derivative. Rather than seeing the economy, or any other one factor, as the sole source of our actions, another strategy might be to pluralize and contextualize this type of explanation. For example, Marx's theory of ideology exemplifies the idea that a more fundamental economic reality is responsible for the "superstructure" of surface appearances, as we saw in his analysis of religion. It seems to me that this perspective must be rejected in its strong sense, for religion is a means of political struggle (as Eugene Genovese demonstrates in his studies of American slavery) and a profound source of spiritual meaning which is not fading away.[89] Yet religion also does sometimes hide a deeper reality and camouflage economic interests, as in the US Christian right's justification of the accumulation of wealth and the free market through its interpretation of scripture. Religion or any other social institution should be studied as a complex, contradictory phenomenon embedded in particular historical circumstances.

Marx's ideas about alienation still resonate with much contemporary experience. So many jobs are dull and repetitive, even in the emerging dot.com economy. People feel most fulfilled when they can be challenged by their work and participate in the workplace, and have their ideas heard and respected. The quality of an individual's life is tied to the quality not only of the job she does, but to the community in which she lives. Many communities lack the resources and economic power to control their own fate. Alienation is still a major problem of capitalism. Overcoming it requires a radical restructuring of many aspects of the contemporary workplace, and revamping communities as well, perhaps through the redistribution of wealth from richer to poorer locales.

Marx's approach to alienation can provide insights into contemporary mass media and mass culture. Thinkers such as Max Horkheimer and Theodor Adorno of the Frankfurt School, writing in the Marxist tradition, argue that mass culture follows the same logic as mass production. The fashioning of cultural products is similar to factory-made items – both are commodities, made to be bought and sold for a profit, and so take on standardized and uniform characteristics. I see most television shows and films following a logic of predictability and calculability, where sequels and new shows/movies use the same formulas to attract and keep audiences. Just as in other realms of production, the culture industry is not controlled by the workers. This culture industry creates mass-produced concepts which do not encourage people to think critically about their lives, or conceptualize alternatives to capitalist society.[90]

Marx also demonstrates some distinctive features of our modern life. While one must be sensitive to hierarchical judgments when comparing the present and the past, it is important to keep in mind the distinguishing characteristics of our social world. Modern society is distinctive because of the rise of capitalism and industrialism, its rapidly increased scope and pace of change relative to other historical eras, and the emergence of new types of institutions, such as business corporations and a state concerned with social welfare, which use rational knowledge such as social statistics and econometric models of forecasting to understand the social world and ensure their continued existence. In our global world, Marx alerts us especially to the role of capitalism in structuring our lives. While other factors influence globalization, its dominance by global corporations must be a central factor in understanding its dynamics and consequences. Contemporary globalization is capitalist globalization, defined by a search for markets, low wages, and profits. Marx warns us that it is not a benign process that will automatically benefit everyone, but will profit the rich much more than the poor, and will create new struggles over social wealth and power.

Notes

1   Steven Seidman, *Contested Knowledge: Social Theory in the Postmodern Era* (Cambridge, MA, 1994), p. 27

2   See Christopher Lasch, *The True and Only Heaven: Progress and Its Critics* (New York, 1991); Claude Nicolet, *L'Idée républicaine en France: essai d'histoire critique* (Paris, 1982), pp. 462–3; and Nicole and Jean Dhombres, *Naissance d'un pouvoir: science et savants en France (1793–1824)* (Paris, 1989).

3   Seidman, *Contested Knowledge*, pp. 30–1.

4   Karl Marx, "Theses on Feuerbach," in *The Marx–Engels Reader*, ed. Robert Tucker (New York, 1978), p. 145.

5   Karl Marx, "Inaugural Address of the Working Men's International Association," in *The Marx–Engels Reader*, ed. Robert Tucker (New York, 1978), p. 517.

6   Cornel West, *The Ethical Dimensions of Marxist Thought* (New York, 1991).

7   Quoted in Franz Mehring, *Karl Marx: The Story of His Life* (Ann Arbor, MI, 1962), p. 247.

8   James Joll, *The Anarchists* (New York, 1964).

9   Ibid, p. 79.

10   Ibid, p. 101.

11   Ibid, pp. 104–6.

12   G. W. F. Hegel, *The Phenomenology of Mind* (New York, 1967), pp. 228–40.

13   Kenneth H. Tucker, Jr., *Anthony Giddens and Modern Social Theory* (Thousand Oaks, CA, 1998), pp. 99–102. Karl Marx, "The German Ideology: Part I," in *The Marx–Engels Reader*, ed. Robert Tucker (New York, 1978), p. 155.

14   Ibid, p. 156.

15   Marx and Engels, "Manifesto of the Communist Party," in *The Marx–Engels Reader*, ed. Robert Tucker (New York, 1978), p. 475.

16   Karl Marx, "Marx on the History of His Opinions," in *The Marx–Engels Reader*, ed. Robert Tucker (New York, 1978), p. 4.

17   Ibid, p. 5.

18 Marx and Engels, "Manifesto of the Communist Party," p. 474.

19 Ibid, p. 475

20 Ibid.

21 Ibid, p. 477.

22 Ibid.

23 Ibid, p. 475.

24 Ibid, p. 476.

25 Ibid, p. 479.

26 Ibid, p. 482.

27 Ibid, p. 489.

28 Marx, "Contribution to the Critique of Hegel's Philosophy of Right: Introduction," in *The Marx–Engels Reader*, ed. Robert Tucker (New York, 1978), p. 54.

29 Marx, "Economic and Philosophical Manuscripts of 1844," in *The Marx–Engels Reader*, ed. Robert Tucker (New York, 1978), p. 74.

30 Ibid, pp. 87–8.

31 Marx, "Critique of the Gotha Program," in *The Marx–Engels Reader*, ed. Robert Tucker (New York, 1978), p. 538.

32 Marx and Engels, "Address of the Central Committee to the Communist League," in *The Marx–Engels Reader*, ed. Robert Tucker (New York, 1978), p. 507.

33 Marx, "Manifesto of the Communist Party," p. 475.

34 Marx, "On the Jewish Question," in *The Marx–Engels Reader*, ed. Robert Tucker (New York, 1978), p. 42.

35 "Marx on the History of His Opinions," p. 4.

36 See Marx, "The Eighteenth Brumaire of Louis Bonaparte," in *The Marx–Engels Reader*, ed. Robert Tucker (New York, 1978).

37 David Fernbach, "Introduction," *Karl Marx: The First International and After: Political Writings, Vol. 3* (New York, 1974), pp. 35–6.

38 Ibid, pp. 37–8.

39 Shlomo Avineri, "Introduction," *Karl Marx on Colonialism and Modernization* (New York, 1969), pp. 5–6.

40 Marx, "On Imperialism in India," in *The Marx–Engels Reader*, ed. Robert Tucker (New York, 1978), p. 659.

41 Marx, "The Eighteenth Brumaire of Louis Bonaparte," p. 608.

42 Edward Said, *Culture and Imperialism* (New York, 1993), pp. 66, 146.

43 Marx in Avineri, *Karl Marx on Colonialism and Modernization*, p. 53.

44 Ibid, p. 442.

45 Marx, "On Imperialism in India," p. 655.

46 Ibid, p. 657.

47 Ibid, p. 658.

48 Avineri, "Introduction," *Karl Marx on Colonialism and Modernization*, p. 29.

49 Marx in Avineri, *Karl Marx on Colonialism and Modernization*, pp. 82–4.

50 Ibid, p. 334.

51 Ibid, pp. 224–6.

52 Ibid, p. 181.

53 Ibid, pp. 347–8.

54 Ibid, pp. 82–3; Avineri, "Introduction," *Karl Marx on Colonialism and Mod-*

ernization, p. 18.
55 Marx in Avineri, *Karl Marx on Colonialism and Modernization*, p. 106.
56 Ibid, p. 398.
57 Marx, "On Imperialism in India," p. 663.
58 Marx in Avineri, *Karl Marx on Colonialism and Modernization*, p. 234.
59 "On Imperialism in India," p. 662.
60 Ibid, p. 661.
61 Ibid, pp. 655–6.
62 Marx in Avineri, *Karl Marx on Colonialism and Modernization*, p. 469.
63 Ibid.
64 Ibid, p. 470.
65 Ibid.
66 Ibid, p. 49.
67 Ibid, p. 50.
68 "Manifesto of the Communist Party," p. 472.
69 Fernbach, "Introduction," p. 28. See also "Letters on Ireland," both in *The First International and After*, pp. 165–7.
70 Ibid, p. 169.
71 Ibid, p. 170.
72 Ibid, p. 162.
73 Ibid, pp. 161, 163.
74 Ibid, p. 165.
75 Ibid.
76 Ibid, p. 166.
77 Ibid, p. 168.
78 Marx, "The German Ideology," pp. 159–60
79 Marx and Engels, "Manifesto of the Communist Party," p. 487.
80 Friedrich Engels, "The Origin of the Family, Private Property, and the State," in *The Marx–Engels Reader*, ed. Robert Tucker (New York, 1978), pp. 737–9.
81 Ibid, p. 750.
82 Ibid, p. 744.
83 Ibid, p. 750.
84 Arlie Hochschild, *The Second Shift* (New York, 1983).
85 Steven Seidman, "Empire and Knowlege: More Troubles, New Opportunities for Sociology," *Contemporary Sociology* 25 (May, 1996), p. 315.
86 Václav Havel, et al., *The Power of the Powerless: Citizens Against the State* (Armonk, NY, 1985).
87 Pierre Bourdieu, "Sport and Social Class," in *Rethinking Popular Culture: Contemporary Perspectives in Cultural Studies*, ed. Chandra Mukerji and Michael Schudson (Berkeley, CA, 1991), p. 366; Tucker, *Anthony Giddens and Modern Social Theory*, p. 68.
88 Richard Rorty, "The American Road to Fascism," *New Statesman*, May 8, 1998, p. 28.
89 Eugene Genovese, *Roll Jordan Roll: The World The Slaves Made* (New York, 1976).
90 Max Horkheimer and Theodor Adorno, *Dialectic of Enlightenment* (London, 1979).

CHAPTER FOUR

Durkheim: Modernity and Social Solidarity

When I first encountered Emile Durkheim as a junior in college, I was so fascinated by his writings that I stayed up until four in the morning reading him. Admittedly, I often stayed up late as a college junior, but this was an exceptional occurrence. I read excerpts from his great work, *The Elementary Forms of the Religious Life*. Durkheim stated that all societies possess a sacred character, even if they are not founded on a religious basis. I was intrigued by his notion that we need symbols to worship and that these symbols derive from our collective life, define our identity, and become sacred, no matter how secular we think we are. These ideas were brought home to me by a comment of a friend some years ago. In a small corner of my apartment was placed a picture of my family and some other mementos that I had gathered over the years. My friend noticed this and said, "Oh, there's your worship area." I had never thought of this collection of pictures and objects in this way, since there was nothing religious about them, but his comment made me realize how sacred these various objects were to me. My friend was a Durkheimian without even realizing it!

I was struck by Durkheim's contention that people are social creatures to their core, that personalities, ideals, and behaviors are shaped by social relations. Durkheim theorizes that social solidarity – the beliefs and institutions that hold society together – defines people's existence and moral sensibility. His sociology is animated by the belief that modern morality had to be based on individualism *and* community. This is a key issue in our time, as it was in Durkheim's. In the wake of new social movements of the 1960s through the 1990s, from feminism to gay liberation, people celebrate a diversity of identities. A major right is the right to be different. Yet how can so many different people live together? Durkheim's analysis of moral community and structural differentiation supplies a powerful answer to this question.

Durkheim is often considered to be the founder of functionalist sociology, which contends that society is similar to a living organism, in that each part performs a function that helps to stabilize the whole. I think Durkheim must also be understood as a theorist who raises fundamental issues about the nature of democracy, and the role of a critical rationality and moral culture of citizenship in creating a good society. He draws on the republican tradition of active citizenship, emphasizing the importance of publicly engaged social criticism. For Durkheim, cultural and social traditions inform people's identities and their moral evaluations of society. These ideas have been resurrected in contemporary times under the banner of communitarianism. Many communitarians uncritically celebrate the idea of an integrated community which gives people moral guidelines to follow. Durkheim's approach is more nuanced. Durkheim, drawing in part on romanticism, does not dismiss tradition as invariably opposed to reason, but argues that all human thinking is situated in historical and cultural contexts. He discusses the importance of moral solidarity based on human rights and cultural diversity, which tie the individual and the community together in complex ways. I will discuss these issues in more depth in the conclusion to this chapter.

Other ideas of Durkheim's I find troubling. A medical, scientific vocabulary pervades his work, as he utilizes words such as "normal" and "abnormal" to describe social behavior. Durkheim often sees Western cultures as evolutionarily superior to what he called "primitive" societies. His comments about the inferiority of women are outrageous. Durkheim sometimes describes groups that are not central components of his social theory, such as women, as irrational, consumed by passions and emotions, and outside of the contours of rational modernity. While many of these ideas can be traced to the Eurocentric and patriarchal ambience of his time, they demonstrate a lack of critical reflexivity about his own assumptions. His self-understanding as an objective scientist blinds him to his biased assumptions. Yet Durkheim's work, when read closely, is quite sophisticated and not always consistent about a number of issues, not only concerning gender and evolution, but also the relationship of reason to tradition. His theoretical approach locates beliefs and practices in particular traditions, opening up these traditions to new ideas, such as critical perspectives on race and gender.

This chapter explores Durkheim's sociology and criticisms of his work. I examine his major writings on methodology, suicide, social solidarity, religion, and education. As this variety of topics demonstrates, Durkheim, like Marx and Weber, is a thinker of enormous range and interests. I explore Durkheim's attempt to find the bases for a non-religious morality in contemporary societies, and his analysis of the importance of democratic interaction in a public sphere for generating such a morality. I then address the relationship of his sociology to the rise of a disciplinary society, the implicit influence of the colonial context on his work, and his approach to cultural identity.

Durkheim and His Time

Durkheim was born in France on April 15, 1858, to a family with modest resources. His father was a rabbi, and Durkheim inherited his stern manner and devotion to duty. A gifted student, he was admitted to the elite École Normale Supérieure, which gathered together the best young male minds in France and prepared them for careers in teaching, research, business, and politics. Durkheim's classmates included the future great philosopher Henri Bergson, who was to become his rival for intellectual influence among French academics, and Jean Jaurès (1859–1914), the eventual leader of the socialist party, and one of the most beloved figures in the history of the left in France. These students were more or less cut off from the rest of the world, left to take classes and debate among themselves. Here Durkheim's personality became more forceful, as he gained both friends and enemies among his classmates.

By most accounts, Durkheim had a very serious and intimidating presence, as he dominated most situations that he encountered. His severe appearance was embodied in a thin, pale torso topped by a huge head, from which he emitted logical and cold argument. He inspired great loyalty and biting criticism. For example, one critic, a follower of Bergson, wrote that Durkheim's "eloquence, truly comparable to that of a running tap, was inexhaustible and ice-cold: it would not have profaned the inside of a mortuary; indeed it would have substantially assisted the refrigeration of the corpses."[1]

Durkheim went on to become an influential professor at the Sorbonne. His lectures on education were the only required courses in the university, and he served on many important committees that affected academic and university policy. Durkheim embraced the academic life. He did not involve himself extensively in political squabbles, for he distrusted politicians as ideologues who would sacrifice scientific objectivity for political expediency. He did, however, become engaged in the defense of Alfred Dreyfus (1859–1935), a Jewish army officer accused and convicted of passing military secrets to the Germans in the late nineteenth century. The Dreyfus Affair was a *cause célèbre* in *fin-de-siècle* France, as it symbolized conflicts between those who favored a democratic republic and conservatives who advocated a traditional, authoritarian regime based on military and aristocratic rule. France was the only full-fledged democratic republic on the European continent in the late nineteenth century, and many powerful groups, from the military to the clergy, were hostile to it. The Affair broke into the public domain as evidence surfaced that Dreyfus was framed by his fellow officers. Intellectuals such as Jaurès and the novelist Emile Zola (1840–1902) rallied to Dreyfus's defense, while Dreyfus's accusers were supported by the military and much of the Catholic Church. Dreyfus was eventually freed from prison in 1906, after it became clear that he had been railroaded by the military authorities.[2]

Durkheim joined this public argument in support of Dreyfus. While he did not directly address the current of anti-Semitism that underlay many of the accusations against Dreyfus and his supporters, he defended Dreyfus on the foundation of the rights of man and individual freedom, which Durkheim saw as the basis of a democratic republic. He thought that reason and science should guide people's actions, and he feared that the traditional arguments invoked by the army and the church threatened reason's autonomy. Durkheim contended that a shared respect for individual rights must be the basis of social solidarity, rather than any biologically determined notion of Frenchness, which excluded those who were different, such as Jews.[3]

Durkheim has often been painted as a political conservative, but in reality he had socialist sympathies. He could be seen carrying the socialist newspaper *L'Humanité* very prominently when strolling around the Sorbonne.[4] Nevertheless, Durkheim defended the French World War I effort against Germany, writing some unfortunate pamphlets on what he considered to be the inferior and warlike mentality of the Germans. The Great War led to Durkheim's demise, though he was not killed in the fighting. Many of his best students died at the front, and Durkheim was crushed by the death of his son, Andre, at the Marne battle in 1917. Shortly thereafter, Durkheim suffered a stroke and died.

Durkheim's Social and Intellectual Context

Durkheim wrote in the late nineteenth and early twentieth centuries when Western Europe, particularly France, was undergoing profound economic and social changes. Europe experienced a dynamic of revolution and reaction, beginning with the French Revolution of 1789, extending into the European-wide democratic revolts of 1848, and culminating in the Paris Commune of 1871, in which thousands of French workers and radicals were executed after taking power in Paris in the wake of the French defeat in the Franco-Prussian War of 1870–1. After 1875 the pace of French colonialism increased, as did that of the other European powers. Between 1876 and 1915 France increased its territory by about 3.5 million square miles, coming to dominate large parts of northern Africa and Indonesia. French colonization of Algeria in particular was brutal.[5]

While fighting abroad, French elites had to contend with class struggle at home. Industrialization and the development of capitalism produced intense class conflict. In late nineteenth- and early twentieth-century France labor strikes increased dramatically. They were often led by radical workers known as revolutionary syndicalists organized in trade unions united in the Confédération Générale du Travail (CGT). Labor militants fought a recalcitrant employer class who only grudgingly gave rights to workers. While France's capitalist system was developing slowly, it was also the only democratic republic in Europe. However, the CGT saw the state as an arm of the employers and syndicalists called for the overthrow of capitalism. Right-wing movements such as the quasi-fascist Action Française also advocated the demise of the French Republic. In sum, the French Republic was on a precarious footing.[6]

Durkheim formulated his sociology in this context. He became the unofficial philosopher of the French Third Republic, as many of his ideas took root in French institutions. He helped formulate the republican secular educational alternative to the Catholic, clerical educational system that had dominated France before the late nineteenth century. The French Republic wished to create good democratic citizens, and Durkheim's emphasis on an education which promoted discipline, attachment to shared group beliefs, and the common good of the Republic fitted well with this agenda.

The emerging social sciences entailed a new role for intellectuals. According to Durkheim, modern intellectuals should consider themselves opinion leaders who can help guide popular sentiment. As academics and scholars rather than aristocratic notables, intellectuals should educate rather than dictate beliefs to the public. In Durkheim's words, "our action must be exerted through books, seminars, and popular education. Above all, we must be *advisers, educators*. It is our function to help our contemporaries know themselves in their ideas and in their feelings, far more than to govern them."[7] Intellectuals would foster the replacement of egoism with a new "moral individualism" in which people recognize that self-realization and the rights of man are inseparable from the increased social interdependence demanded by an egalitarian democracy and expanding division of labor.[8] A public enriched with a scientific worldview and informed by moral individualism, accompanying a rationally organized industry bolstered by a free civil society and a reformist republican state, promised future prosperity.

Durkheim argues that sociology could contribute dramatically to this new society. He was influenced by Comte's and Saint-Simon's versions of social science. Durkheim takes up their call for a science of society based on positivism. Society can be understood and engineered through comprehending the laws underlying social life. Applications of science and technology to social life will guarantee continual economic expansion, and the growth of science provides a model for future social progress. But Durkheim also owes much to Kant and Rousseau, and their attempts to combine social morality and individual rights. Like these thinkers, Durkheim sees no conflict between individual rights and the common good. Rights are tied to public and private commitments to the public good and personal autonomy, which have to be grounded in institutions. Durkheim moved beyond these thinkers, however. He contends that Kant in particular does not recognize the social basis of reason and morality. For Kant, freedom occurs when culture is thrown off and people can reason together as autonomous individuals unencumbered by the "prejudices" of their cultural traditions. According to Durkheim this approach is wrongheaded. People owe their capacity for moral reasoning to the cultural traditions in which they are embedded. There are no isolated individuals existing outside of particular societies and cultural traditions. The very idea of moral individualism, according to Durkheim, is the result of European cultural traditions, and is not inherent in the human condition.[9]

Tocqueville and Durkheim

Durkheim contends that democracy and freedom have to be established on cultural traditions and social institutions. Durkheim's thought is not usually tied to Tocqueville, but I see them both as theorists of the social, cultural, and intellectual conditions necessary for democracy. Both are deeply concerned about issues of citizenship, democracy, and morality, and draw on the republican tradition for many of their insights. Tocqueville sees democracy arising simultaneously with equality, the major social trend in the West.

Tocqueville argues that democracies can only thrive, and indeed survive, if people participate in government and identify with their representative institutions. While a democratic government requires the separation of political powers and guarantees of the rights of those with minority opinions, he also develops a theory of democratic liberty, grounded in the republican tradition. Republicanism demands that citizens exercise the capacity to collectively apprehend and act towards the common good, the public interest. Mere understanding of democratic principles is not enough, however. A democratic style of life is the only way to assure that a good republic will flourish and survive over time. Democracy calls for more than just representative institutions, as it also involves concomitant changes in "the laws, ideas, customs, and morals" of a people to be effective.[10] Local participation in government and voluntary organizations gives citizens the means to actively take hold of their republic, and shape it according to their collective will through a public sphere.

Tocqueville fears that a form of democratic despotism can emerge if citizen participation withers and local sources of opposition to the centralization of power erode. By centralizing power in the federal government, despotism promotes a passive, egoistic, and atomized citizenry who have no ties to one another. In such a context people feel no attachment to the public good, and indeed selfishness and "general indifference" become "public virtues."[11] Despotism is possible in a democracy when people are obsessed with their private lives, especially the desire for personal wealth, and care little about collective life. Equality and the desire for riches are seemingly strange bedfellows, but neither links citizens in a common purpose, and each produces little concern for participation in the public realm.

Durkheim, too, is suspicious of an individualism that knows no social boundaries, and of a capitalist society promoting the pleasures of private consumption over the duties of citizenship. Like Tocqueville, Durkheim believes that a healthy democracy involves more than representative institutions and guaranteed legal and political rights. Strong secondary, voluntary organizations, such as occupational groups, are central components of a functioning democracy. A vibrant culture of citizenship has to be part of the democratic polity, for political rights rest on communal and moral foundations. Tocqueville's arguments about the problems of sustaining republican virtue are echoed in Durkheim's concerns about creating public-spiritedness through republican social solidarity, guaranteed by occupational groups and widespread public education. Durkheim, like Tocqueville, fears that a concentration of power in institutions separated from the people creates despotism. But Durkheim combines these republican themes with a commitment to social science that differs from Tocqueville's approach. Durkheim also argues that individualism can become a collective, sacred belief in democratic societies, rather than a precursor to a depoliticized private life.

Durkheim's Sociological Theory

Let's now turn to a summary of Durkheim's major themes. For Durkheim, the crisis of modern society is a moral one. Durkheim asks, how can people in modern societies lead a meaningful life? What will be the basis of new beliefs in the modern world? Durkheim contends that many people were unable to live meaningful and productive lives, that European civilization was experiencing a malaise; his famous studies of the increase in the suicide rate that accompanied industrialization demonstrated this fact. A new morality has to be found, based on science, rationality, and a democratic community, that can replace a religious morality that no longer convinced people of its authority.

This crisis is due to a lack of social cohesion. For Durkheim, a stable set of meanings and values is a prerequisite for a people's healthy existence. If we are constantly in flux, if we have no stable set of rules to guide us, we feel lost. People must be integrated into groups in order to feel fulfilled. In fact, the development of a firm set of beliefs, sentiments, and values is distinctively human – it separates humankind from animals. Yet we have some of the animal in us, as the person is double, a homo duplex. The individual has egoistic, selfish desires, yet also possesses the capacity to create a higher source of human life, meaning, and order. This latter realm raises people above purely egoistic desires. This is not just philosophical speculation, as many studies have shown that infants deprived of social interaction become developmentally disabled, if they in fact do not perish from lack of social contact.

Much of this so far is familiar terrain. It has long been a staple of Western thought that the passions and reason conflict with one another, and that reason must control emotions. Durkheim's distinctive contribution is his location of reason in society. Reason, individualism, all of our ideals, derive from the existence of social life, which informs individual actions and ideas. This is a controversial notion, but it is at the heart of Durkheim's sociology.

For Durkheim, society is greater than the sum of its parts, for it has a unique reality. Society surpasses every individual in richness and complexity. Ideals such as freedom and equality have an existence beyond particular individuals. These ideals and sentiments originate in society, and they inform and influence individual actions and beliefs. Durkheim is concerned with order in the midst of disorder. He sees the basis of order in society, not in the individual.

Durkheim attempts to discover how different societies provide meaning for their members. He is interested in uncovering the social glue that holds societies together, and how different types of social cohesion, or social solidarity, originate, develop, and maintain themselves. These questions are the proper subject-matter of sociology.

Because society is a unique reality with its own special characteristics it can be studied scientifically like any other object. In his famous 1895 book, *Rules of Sociological Method*, Durkheim defends a strong positivistic sociology. Though positivism is a complex term, its meaning can be summarized as the belief that natural and social sciences share similar methodologies, that observations of the world can be understood in a straightforward manner, and that social and natural reality is based on natural laws that science can discover.[13] A scientific, positivist sociology must separate itself from theology and philosophy in order to advance knowledge and offer practical guidance for public policy. The sociologist must approach her subject-matter like a natural scientist. She should be free from preconceptions and biases, and strive to find the universal laws underlying social reality.

The nature of social reality encourages such a scientific approach, for it consists of social facts which can be measured by the sociologist. Durkheim defines three characteristics of social facts: they are external to the individual, they influence and constrain the behavior of people, and they are general throughout a given society or group. Examples of social facts include language, law, religious practices, and the division of labor. These phenomena are not created by individuals acting alone, but confront them as pre-existing realities. One knows that social facts exist when they are violated. For instance, the social reality of the law becomes apparent when one violates the law. Sometimes the lawbreaker feels guilt, or he is caught and punished. The law has an independent existence apart from the individual. Only social facts can cause other social facts. In *The Division of Labor in Society* Durkheim argues that the legal structure of a particular society (a social fact) depends on the degree of development of the division of labor (another social fact) within that particular society. Sociology should concern itself with the study of social facts. Durkheim does not believe that a scientific sociology differed from the natural sciences, except in its object of study (society). In the social sciences, as in their natural counterparts, objective data can be collected and explained in causal form.

Yet Durkheim also develops a culturally sensitive sociology, especially in his later work. By the time Durkheim published *The Elementary Forms of the Religious Life* in 1912, he contends that people understand reality, rationality, and truth in diverse ways in different historical circumstances. As human products, societies are necessarily open to change. In Durkheim's words, "Man is a product of history; there is nothing in him that is either given or defined in advance."[14] This approach requires a sensitivity to historical context. History and ethnography, the close observation of particular cultures, are better methods than those based on mathematics for studying the different moralities embedded in different cultures. Thus, a strict scientific positivism has limitations. This methodological tension is apparent throughout his work, and we will return to it throughout the chapter.

Suicide

Now let's turn to some of Durkheim's specific studies. Durkheim the scientist is apparent in his famous work on suicide. Durkheim noted that suicides had increased in Europe in the nineteenth century and become a topic of public discussion. He embarked on his study of suicide in a context where many researchers were interested in the effect of modern society on people's mental constitution and equilibrium. A popular diagnosis of mental problems in Durkheim's time was known as neurasthenia, an increase in nervousness and mental exhaustion. George Beard (1839–83), an influential neurologist, viewed modern civilization as contributing to an enormous increase in neurasthenia, if not creating it altogether. Beard saw five factors contributing to the growth of neurasthenic disorders: an increase in steam power, the rise of the telegraph, the emergence of the periodical press, the expansion of scientific knowledge, and the increased mental activity of women. Though it was not clear how these aspects of neurasthenia fit together, all of these phenomena apparently made people very uptight, especially middle-class women, who were often diagnosed as neurasthenic. In my view, rather than an objective assessment, this concern with neurasthenia demonstrated the fear of modernity and women's public and intellectual visibility that underlay supposedly scientific research.[15]

While Durkheim by no means escapes the anxiety associated with this ambience, he develops an interesting approach to suicide. Durkheim concentrates on suicide rates as his object of study. He thinks that psychological and neurological explanations such as neurasthenia can be useful in explaining why particular individuals commit suicide, but they are worthless as explanations of suicide rates. Durkheim is not really interested in the psychological reasons why you or I might jump out of a building and end it all. He is only interested in our social characteristics, i.e. were we married, in the military, our religious affiliation, and the like. The suicide rate is a social fact, for it varies from country to country while remaining stable within countries and groups and changing uniformly over time. For example, Durkheim finds that Protestants commit suicide more than Catholics, and unmarried men more than married men, in almost every culture that he investigates.

Durkheim accounts for the variation in suicide rates through an examination of different types of social solidarity. The degree of social solidarity explains the variation in suicide rates which can be measured. Durkheim is using social solidarity in two senses in *Suicide*. First, social solidarity refers to the extent to which the individual is attached to collective rules and ideals. Second, social solidarity is based on the degree to which individuals are regulated by the rules of society. Four types of suicide correspond to these categories, which are paired opposites: egoism/altruism and anomie/fatalism (though Durkheim only discusses fatalism in a footnote). If there are different types of suicide, they must each have a particular cause.

The egoism/altruism distinction is based on the extent to which an individual is attached to collective goals and rules. Egoistic suicide results when the individual feels too little attachment to society. Her life is meaningless, she does not feel a part of any group, she cannot believe in strong values, in sum she is unintegrated. This type of suicide occurs when the individual retreats from social interaction, reflects on her own misery, and becomes depressed. People in such a state question all aspects of their existence, and sometimes fall into a kind of Epicurean indifference.[16] It is not surprising that intellectual and academic professions are incubators of egoistic suicide, given the amount of time that people in these professions spend alone.

Altruistic suicide inhabits the other side of this dichotomy based on collective attachment to society. Altruistic suicide is based on an overintegration of the individual into social life, so that the person has no sense of an independent self apart from social norms. In this type of suicide collective life is present everywhere and there is no individual autonomy. It is often performed with enthusiasm, resulting from a sense of duty or faith. The suicides of the Samurai in medieval Japan come to mind, as they did for Durkheim. Military officers who feel a strong sense of duty are prone to this type of suicide, particularly if their honor is questioned. Altruistic suicide often results from a sense of violating one's duty of conscience.[17]

The other major dichotomous suicide pair, anomie and fatalism, is based on the degree of social regulation of the individual's passions. Anomie occurs when people's passions run free and there are no limits on their desires. This sort of suicide often takes place in the economic realm. Business and trade crises excite the passions and people have no sense of the limits of their desires. People frequently commit this type of suicide out of a sense of anger.[18] We can easily surmise that a dramatic drop in economic status might contribute to suicidal tendencies, but Durkheim thought that coming into wealth too quickly, say by winning the lottery, would also make people prone to suicide, for people lose their sense of self and equilibrium. In modern societies economic life is on the verge of escaping all regulation, allowing unmitigated greed to develop and passions to become over-excited. For Durkheim, the old adage "be careful what you wish for" certainly holds true. Beware of becoming rich too quickly!

Anomic suicide occurs when married men divorce. On the other side of this dichotomy, fatalistic suicide, people are overregulated by society, they have no hope, and feel resigned to their fate. Slavery results in this type of suicide, but it also characterizes young married men, and women without children. Durkheim did not discuss this type of suicide in detail, as he believed it is rare in modern societies.

If anomic and egoistic suicide seem somewhat similar, that is because they do indeed have affinities with one another, as both stem from the insufficient presence of society in the individual. To paraphrase Durkheim, in one of his more poetic moments, the egoist is lost in the infinity of dreams, the person suffering from anomie is lost in the infinity of desires.[19]

Durkheim thinks that a kind of golden mean of social solidarity should govern the individual. While insufficient integration surely has baneful consequences for the person, so too does overintegration. A healthy person lives betwixt these two extremes. Each person must have a sense of being in harmony with his life conditions to live a healthy existence.[20] Too much or too little social integration are Durkheim's explanations for understanding suicide rates.

Durkheim tests his hypotheses in a number of different social contexts. For example, he consistently finds that divorced people commit suicide more than others. Yet he discovers an interesting anomaly. In those countries where divorce was common, such as Germany, married men have high suicide rates, compared to those countries where divorce is less common, like France. But for married women the opposite situation holds. Where divorce is common, married women commit suicide less than men, and where divorce is prohibited, married women commit suicide more than married men.[21] Durkheim explains this discrepancy by stating that marriage regulates the passions of the male. When men are released from marriage their passions run wild, resulting in anomic suicide. Women do not have such passions because they are more "natural" and "sensual," and their mental life is less developed. Marriage does not limit their desires, because they are so few.[22]

This discussion of women surely paints Durkheim as a sexist. It demonstrates an interesting problem in his analysis, which he clearly felt uncomfortable discussing. Durkheim was not in the forefront of the women's movement, to say the least, and had to perform some theoretical gymnastics to explain the suicide rates of women compared to men. He assumes that the division of men and women into public and private spheres is based on natural, biological differences, not on patriarchal power, and thus justifies the lack of rights for women in his society. Durkheim invokes biological explanations about the nature of women and men to explain his findings. For someone committed to sociological explanation, who dismisses biological argument as irrelevant to social phenomena, this is a contradiction. But it was one that Durkheim often fell back on when trying to explain differences between men and women. We will return to these criticisms in the conclusion to this chapter.

Social Solidarity and Social Change

Durkheim, like Marx, recognizes that the market economy has unprecedented importance in the modern world. *The Division of Labor in Society* addresses the relationship between the economy and society. Durkheim is influenced by the widespread distinctions between traditional and modern societies prevalent in his time. He develops two different types of solidarity corresponding to these distinct types of social organization. The first type of solidarity, characteristic of premodern societies, he designates as mechanical solidarity. In this type of solidarity the common consciousness is strong and individuals are similar to one another, sharing the same beliefs and ideas. The individual is directly linked with society. Indeed, it is a misnomer to even speak of individualism, in the sense of autonomy, as we understand it now. These premodern societies are clan-based, each clan performing political and economic functions as well as familial ones. Rules are often repressive, imposing uniform, strict punishments on all members of society. This punishment reinforces shared beliefs and values. The type of consciousness characterizing this society is traditional and often very religious, in a fundamentalist way.

As the division of labor emerges, a new type of organic solidarity arises. In organic solidarity the collective conscience becomes diffuse and there is more room for individual and personal differences. The division of labor becomes the source of this new solidarity, as it binds people together, each having her own task or special function. The individual depends upon the different parts of society, as each person has a specific sphere of activity. There is a high degree of interdependence among distinctive institutions and persons. Societies become more complex; legal rules are based on restitution rather than strict punishment, for they must regulate new roles and occupations. Societies are rational and secular, as science becomes a more important method of understanding society and nature. These societies still need a sense of shared morality and sacredness. Individualism provides such a shared consciousness, as the rights and dignity of the individual achieve an almost sacred status in modern societies. Ideals tied to the republic and the nation also become powerful moral forces binding people together.

Law, Crime, and the Division of Labor

Durkheim wishes to study these different forms of social solidarity scientifically. He examines legal codes to measure differences between mechanical and organic solidarity. Durkheim finds law a reasonable measure of solidarity because the morality of a society eventually takes the shape of a legal code, as custom is the basis for law.

Durkheim develops an interesting understanding of crime. Criminals are necessary in any society, for they define the boundaries of acceptable and non-acceptable behavior.[23] According to Durkheim, crime is socially constructed. There is nothing inherent in an action that makes it a crime. Even killing people is seen as legitimate under some circumstances, such as war or self-defense. What is common in crimes is "that they consist . . . in acts universally disapproved of by members of each society."[24]

The socially defined nature of crime is easily seen in penal law, associated with mechanical solidarity. Penal law is concerned with punishment, not obligation, and often punishes criminals in a vengeful manner. The amount of harm a criminal commits is not often related to the intensity of the reaction against him.[25] Definitions of crimes are similar across cultures because of the underlying shared solidarity of these societies, and crime calls forth similar effects. As societies become more secular, they still retain aspects of this "religious" sensibility. A shocking crime, such as the murder of a child, offends the collective conscience, our sense of something sacred that exists above and beyond us. Contemporary discussions of the death penalty in the US can be understood in this context. Numerous studies demonstrate that the death penalty does not serve as a deterrent to murder. A majority of Americans support it, however. I believe the death penalty has popular endorsement because murder appalls the collective conscience and brings forth feelings of vengeance and revenge.

While penal law expresses mechanical solidarity, restitutive or civil law denotes organic solidarity. Restitutive sanctions refer to a compensatory award for victims of a crime, not a vengeful act of retribution. In restitutive law the collective conscience is more abstract and diffuse. Law becomes specialized as the specialization of the division of labor increases. Legal contracts express this type of solidarity, for the contract regulates the division of labor. The division of labor is composed of so many different specializations that each in itself is somewhat marginal to the collective consciousness. When a crime occurs in a specialized sphere, it does not provoke vengeance, as in mechanical solidarity.[26] Rather, such crimes call for a penalty involving some sort of return to a previous state before the injury, and some compensatory reparation. Given this analysis, Durkheim would not be surprised by the explosion of lawsuits in the contemporary US.

Contracts form the major basis of social cohesion under organic solidarity. Durkheim finds the power of contracts to bind people together emanating from society rather than from self-interest. Contracts simultaneously reinforce and express sentiments and obligations that are not expressly are based on shared social ideals such as justice, professional ethics, and individual rights. Contracts also assume that social functions are in harmony.[27]

A medical and organic vocabulary pervades Durkheim's discussion of solidarity and the division of labor. He compares society to an organism with "normal" and "abnormal" forms of the division of labor. This language rightly sets off warning bells in our age that is ever-ready to criticize problematic attempts to erase social differences in the name of some overarching norm of sameness. Yet Durkheim's problematic functionalist vocabulary is not just an attempt to normalize all that was different from the average. He draws on the biological imagery of his time, which emphasizes notions of equilibrium. Biologists regarded a healthy organism as one that adapts to and reshapes its environment in a complex ecological process. Durkheim transferred these ideas to his study of society, arguing that a healthy society balances the social forces composing it, and evolves as these social forces change.

Social Change and the Abnormal Forms of the Division of Labor

Durkheim argued that the transition from mechanical to organic solidarity occurred because of differentiation, which refers to the development of new, distinctive arrangements for performing functions. As new occupations arise, old ones lose their power. New moral norms emerge, as do new relations among the parts of the society. For example, in contemporary times the change from a manufacturing to an information economy results in new occupations around computer technology, which require new skills. Old jobs tied to manufacturing, such as in the steel industry, have been lost. More individualistic values are necessary for this new economic environment, as workers need to be able to adapt to change quickly. Societies differentiate, creating new institutions and making existing ones more complex, to meet the challenges of social change. In Durkheim's view, organic solidarity emerges alongside the differentiation of the division of labor.

Durkheim realized that the division of labor had not resulted in the shared organic solidarity that he expected. Differentiation has not proven to be a smooth process. Workers fought employers, industrial and commercial crises shook the economy, and many people seemed unhappy in their jobs. These conditions reflected what he calls the "anomic" and "forced" divisions of labor, which differed from the normal course that the division of labor should follow.

When the division of labor is not sufficiently regulated, anomie occurs.

Durkheim sees many sources of anomie. In times of rapid industrialization, when the differing interests of classes have not reached an equilibrium, and when machines replace workers, the laborer is regimented in his work. When workers are separated from their families and employers, and producers from consumers, anomie occurs. Durkheim recognizes that workers are often not in the positions that best suit them. He calls this situation the "forced division of labor," which arises when the distribution of natural talents does not coincide with the worker's social function. For the division of labor to engender solidarity each worker must be performing a task he finds agreeable.[28]

Durkheim believes that a well-functioning division of labor creates a perfect meritocracy. If the division of labor is functioning smoothly and nothing hampers rivals who are in competition for jobs, then only natural talents will determine the type of activity one does. People do not have more needs than is in their nature. People only want what they can achieve.[29]

Thus, the division of labor produces solidarity to the degree it is spontaneous, and every worker can develop his potentialities. Durkheim realizes that this is not always the case. Anomie was an example of an abnormal division of labor; the "external inequality" associated with inherited wealth was another one. Hereditary wealth guarantees some individuals unfair advantage over others, for some people can attend better schools, have more contacts, etc. because of their inherited wealth. People must have equality of opportunity, as we say today. Eliminating inherited wealth can help guarantee this equality.[30]

Durkheim's view of the problems associated with hereditary wealth sounds somewhat Marxist, for he advocates social justice. In the absence of strong governmental programs favoring equality, Durkheim fears that social inequality would reproduce itself over time and doom some people to perpetual poverty. But Durkheim is unlike Marx in many ways. Durkheim does not view modern society as separated into the bourgeoisie and the proletariat. He sees society as stratified by occupations that differ by money and prestige; individuals compete with one another to find the occupation that best suits them. He does not think that the division of labor is based primarily on class exploitation and conflict, as does Marx.

Durkheim's views on social stratification have a contemporary ring. He argues that if high levels of social mobility are possible, and people view the society they live in as at least fairly meritocratic, they will accept some degree of inequality and social cohesion will not break down, a view that many people in the contemporary West support.[31] But Durkheim contends that a meritocratic society requires strong measures to ensure its survival. Governments must redistribute wealth to make sure that everyone has a fair chance to succeed, that they start from roughly similar social conditions.

There is much that is appealing in Durkheim's analysis of the division of labor. While the tradition–modern dichotomy that he employs is problematic, I think he grasps some of the distinctive dimensions of modernity, such as possibilities for increased social mobility in a more differentiated economy. I also think that his analysis of moral individualism, which he introduces in the conclusion of *The Division of Labor in Society* under the rubric "the cult of the individual," is a particularly appropriate morality for contemporary societies. I find Durkheim's argument that economic phenomena cannot be understood apart from the moral beliefs and culture of a society thoroughly convincing. Economic relationships are subject to customary and legal regulation. For example, the economic exchanges constituting a market can only function in the context of shared respect for individual rights, the sanctity of contracts, and principles of justice. Institutions, such as an independent legal system, must be in place to guarantee these values and practices. In the contemporary era, Russia and many Eastern European countries have had difficulty transforming their economies because they lack the institutional and cultural infrastructure, the non-contractual bases of contract, necessary for a strong capitalist economy.

Durkheim on Education

Durkheim's writings on education are not often studied by sociologists, yet education is a central component of Durkheim's analysis. Education informs his approach to moral individualism, which must be cultivated and learned. Before exploring his approach to education, I will discuss his theory of human nature in a bit more depth, to convey a sense of why education of a specific type is so necessary for a democratic society. Like Marx, Durkheim is fond of paradoxical statements that attempt to reconcile seemingly antagonistic ideas. In *The Division of Labor* he states that liberty is the product of regulation.[32] Liberty is not the freedom to be left alone to do what one wishes, to follow one's self-interest; rather, it means autonomy, the rational control of one's life. Liberty involves recognizing and acting upon one's rights and responsibilities. Writing in the republican tradition of Aristotle, Rousseau, and Kant, Durkheim argues that liberty entails the conscious creation of the laws which govern oneself and, by extension, society. Blind obedience to passions is not freedom but a form of slavery, for when acting passionately the individual is controlled by irrational forces.

Unlike Rousseau, Durkheim argues that liberty is not a characteristic of "natural" man, of a time before the existence of society. In the state of nature the strongest rule and the weak have no rights. Those who can manipulate and control others dominate life. The natural world is an unequal and unjust world. For civilization to develop, society must control nature. Only in the artificial realm of laws and institutions created by people are justice and freedom possible. In a society brute strength and manipulation are circumscribed by rules, laws, and beliefs which enable individuals to freely compete with one another in a context of shared ideals and equality. Education involves learning social rules and morality. A moral education is an indispensable prerequisite for a good society. People need to learn the culture of citizenship and develop skills that a functioning division of labor requires.

At first glance Durkheim's writings on education appear to support the conservative interpretation of his work. He argues that education in the schools must be a moral endeavor, which consists of discipline and the attachment of the student to the moral regulation of a group. Clear goals must limit behavior. But Durkheim is more than a disciplinarian. Autonomy, based on the rational understanding of one's actions and beliefs, is the third ingredient in moral education. Rationally understanding a belief or a social practice can make us assent to it without feeling constrained or coerced.[33] To act morally, the individual must have knowledge and understanding of her reasons for actions. Educators must be able to explain the reasons for social rules; this rational dimension is what distinguishes secular from religious morality.[34] Thus, education invariably has a critical dimension in which rationality can be used to criticize existing social norms and practices.

Durkheim's writings about education owe much to the republican desire to cultivate good citizens and understand the general will. Like Rousseau, Durkheim thought that people must be taught to act virtuously so that they can understand and follow the general will and the common good. For Rousseau, the individual must autonomously choose to follow the common good and learn to do so through participation in educational practices which awaken her critical faculties. Education must encourage a "free-spirited and civic-minded" individual, which became Durkheim's ideal, as it was Rousseau's.[35] Education is more than the study of facts. It shapes the individual and creates good citizens. But it must do so in a critical, reflexive, and empirical manner.

Education needs to be grounded in the analysis of social, economic, and political life, alongside the study of nature and literature. Durkheim was hostile to the classical emphasis that dominated French education in his era, when rhetoric, eloquence, the memorization of Greek and Latin languages, and abstract mathematics were considered the hallmarks of a first-class education. Durkheim thinks this type of education is too abstract and formal, as it ignores the natural and social sciences and posits a universal human nature which does not take into account the diversity of cultures and histories throughout the world.

A better, more rational education allows the student to understand the moralities of past cultures and how morality changes as circumstances change.[36] Moral discipline varies over time, for human nature is not fixed once and for all. Moral rules never can be understood and implemented mechanically, but "require intelligence in their application."[37] A good education supplies this sensitivity to circumstances that is necessary to understand the complexity of moral rules in different situations. Indeed, moral rules, like institutions, cannot just serve a functional social need. They must be accepted as legitimate by the populace if they are to be effective.[38]

In his lectures on secondary education Durkheim traces the history of universities in Europe, concentrating on France. From their origins in the Middle Ages universities were never narrowly nationalistic institutions, but always places of cross-cultural learning. The vitality of universities depended on extending their knowledge base. Durkheim states: "have we not seen in the renaissance of our own universities over the past twenty years an attempt to open themselves up to the outside, to attract foreign students and teachers, to multiply the opportunities for looking at the world from a different conceptual point of view to our own, while at the same time striving to extend their influence beyond national frontiers and . . . becoming centres of international civilization?"[39]

In many ways Durkheim sounds like a multiculturalist *avant la lettre*. He writes that human nature is multiple and diverse, not singular, and education should reflect this diversity. Students must understand different cultures and historical eras to appreciate the complexity of human life.[40] This is in part because the increasing diversity of modernity demands a more flexible education, but primarily because the diversity of cultures and beliefs defines the human condition. Durkheim writes that a person "is the product of a particular heredity and social condition. A multitude of all kinds of characteristics cross and recross within him and, depending upon the way in which they are combined, these create what is truly personal in his nature, for in reality his complexity is infinite."[41]

Education has been led astray by positing a universal history originating in Greek and Roman culture. Durkheim rejects this view, stating: "Can we really believe, for example, that to study the marvelous complexity of Indian civilization would be of less educational value than studying that of Rome, that the humanity which it enshrines is somehow of an inferior quality?"[42] Education must move beyond the examples of a Eurocentric focus on Greece and Rome when looking at history, because "there are others, which are again different, commonly regarded as being 'less advanced,' but which nevertheless are worthy of investigation because they too constitute manifestations of the human spirit."[43]

There is no one moral system valid for all of humankind, as there are as many different moralities as there are societies. Durkheim took this cultural relativistic viewpoint even further, stating that the bond between parents and children is not natural, for in some societies different groups take on the function of caring for the young. Durkheim even questions social evolution, seeing social development as an uneven process, which he characterized as "an interminable process of evolution, disintegration, and reconstruction."[44] There is no inevitable progress.

Students should learn that different cultural attitudes and practices are not bizarre, but are grounded in a particular social order. In Durkheim's words, "It is only because we have got so used to it that the moral order under which we live appears to us to be the only one possible; history demonstrates that it is essentially transitory in character."[45] In sum, Durkheim sees humankind "as an infinitely flexible, protean force, capable of appearing in innumerable guises, according to the perennially changing demands of his circumstances."[46]

Education should not be primarily vocational or instrumental. Knowledge oriented toward control and prediction might increase material prosperity, but "it can in no way affect our interior life."[47] Teaching is not just the communication of facts, but, if it is effective, it transforms beliefs and feelings. That is why students must be taught the ideals of justice and moral individualism. For example, Durkheim states that there are two types of nationalism. In one, nations aggressively compete with one another for control of resources and territory; in the other, the nation attempts to increase its internal level of justice to benefit its citizens. Moral education involves teaching students an appreciation of the latter dimension of nationalism.[48]

Still, science remains the best method for approaching reality, even if our understanding is limited. According to Durkheim, "science is human reasoning in action."[49] Other disciplines should try to emulate the "exemplary rationality" of natural scientific methodology. If the experimental scientific method cannot fully account for the complexity of human behavior, objective comparisons of social interaction should still be made. Durkheim predicts that distinctions between natural and social scientific methodologies will disappear over time.

In sum, for Durkheim, drawing on the republican tradition, education transforms the person into a social being who can appreciate other cultures and his or her society and govern it adequately. Durkheim does not think that a single grand plan of history gradually reveals itself over time, as do Hegel and Marx. Rather, historical change occurs in different ways in different societies. Understanding these particular histories is of the utmost importance. The citizen learns to reason given her cultural traditions, rather than relying on Kantian superhistorical rationality. In Durkheim's perspective, secondary education should encourage critical thinking and a spirit of citizenship, where the student learns that self-discipline is a key to rational thinking.[50] Durkheim's views on education show the complex nature of his thought. He problematizes the mechanical/organic solidarity distinction of *The Division of Labor in Society*. He rejects a simple theory of progress in favor of studying cultures in their particular historical circumstances. The study of non-Western cultures should inform any European education, which must also be aware of the limitations of a mathematical orientation to understanding the social world. But his approach to social evolution is still sometimes hierarchical, demonstrating the inconsistency within his texts. Further, he does not question the goals of a scientific worldview.

Durkheim and Religion

There are at least two Durkheims, if not more. The Durkheim associated with *Suicide* and *The Division of Labor in Society* influenced the development of empirically oriented scientific society, especially in the US. Durkheim has another important legacy as a cultural theorist, an analyst of society as a collection of symbols. He has influenced contemporary sociologists and anthropologists such as Robert Bellah, Jeffrey Alexander, and Clifford Geertz, who argue that society is governed by cultural patterns and shared beliefs. Durkheim has also influenced Jürgen Habermas, who adopts the Durkheimian view that the authority of modern rationality associated with organic solidarity has to do with its continuity as well as its differences from sacred religious worldviews. Durkheim is clearest about his cultural sociology in his discussion of religion, where he develops a conception of society as essentially a collection of sacred symbols and ideals.

People first become aware of the collective nature of their lives through religion. In *Suicide* Durkheim writes: "Religion is in a word the system of symbols by means of which society becomes conscious of itself; it is the characteristic way of thinking of collective existence."[51] Religion is the prototype for the awareness of the power of collective life, similar to other overarching systems of belief, such as nationalism, or even science.

The distinctive character of religion is that the world is divided into sacred and profane realms which are opposed to one another. The sacred is surrounded by myriad rituals and prohibitions which allow it to maintain a distance from profane life. Religion, then, is "a unified system of beliefs and practices relative to sacred things."[52] Any object can become sacred. Religion brings together believers into the ceremonial organization of the church. The earliest religions were found in the totemism of the aboriginal natives of Australia.

Totemism is tied to the kinship organization of Australian aborigines.

No two clans can have the same totem. Moreover, rituals and prohibitions surround the totemic emblem of a clan. Individual members share in the sacredness of the totem attached to their clan, which imparts a kind of pan-spiritualism to the entire culture. All of nature is classified in religious categories. Everything from the sun to the moon has a totem. Sacredness is pervasive in the aboriginal world, and it underlies the totem and the clan.

The totem symbolizes the clan and the spirits associated with it. If the clan and the spirit have the same symbol, that is because the spirit is in reality society; the spirit, or God, and society are one and the same. For Durkheim, like Marx, the secret of religion is found in society. Durkheim takes this insight in a different direction than does Marx, for he investigates the ways in which the sacred is maintained and communicated to people in everyday life, even in non-religious communities. According to Durkheim, religion is society worshipping itself; religion expresses community.[53]

Individuals need to reaffirm their sense of community, their collective vitality, their shared ideals, through rituals and ceremonies, whose prototype is religion. When an Australian aboriginal native engages in religious ceremonies he realizes the difference between the sacred and the profane, between everyday life and the divine. Celebrations and reunions are regenerators of moral force in which the individual gains a sense of strength from participation in rituals and actually feels the power of collective experience. In rituals people who commune with God feel energized, but they are really experiencing the energizing effect of the community. By participating in shared ceremonies, whether religious or secular, the individual finds himself in moral harmony with his comrades and develops more confidence, courage, and boldness. Durkheim states that ceremonies and rituals "perpetually give back to the great ideals a little of the strength that the egoistic passions and daily personal preoccupations tend to take away from them. This replenishment is the function of public festivals, ceremonies, and rites of all kinds."[54]

Society consecrates certain ideas as sacred even if they are not religious. Thus, nationalism in many countries is a "sacred" idea with its own symbols, beliefs, prohibitions, etc., which people feel is a part of their very identity. Certain people also become consecrated as almost sacred by public opinion. This is certainly true of celebrities today, who seem to be granted an aura by public opinion, as refracted through the mass media. Rituals are also still important as markers in personal and collective life, such as graduation from school, marriage ceremonies, the inauguration of a president, and the like, demonstrate.

Some of Durkheim's most provocative and almost mystical ideas concern his theory of ritual, ceremony, and social change. He argues that believers communing together create a "collective effervescence," a kind of collective fusion and ecstasy which is recreated through ritual and celebration.[55] Collective effervescence is the source of new social ideals and beliefs. Durkheim states: "There are periods in history when, under the influence of some great collective shock, social interactions have become more frequent and active."[56] The French and American Revolutions, the Russian Revolution, and other events have been sources of this collective effervescence, in which new beliefs crystallize into a doctrine, become symbolized in flags and emblems, and are recreated over the years through elaborate rituals and ceremonies.

Durkheim sees religion's influence everywhere. The fundamental categories of thought originate in the division of human nature into the sacred and the profane. This dualism has social origins, though it is expressed in religious terms. The body is regarded as profane and everything associated with it (such as sensations) are also seen as profane. Rationality and moral activity attain a sacred status infused with a kind of religiosity.[57] In reality, though, these differences derive from the distinction between society and the individual.

Durkheim argues that scientific thought expresses a universal conceptual vocabulary, which applies to everyone, like religion. Indeed, religion and science have many similarities. The power of society infuses religion and science, which both attempt to connect objects with one another, classify them, and systematize them in an abstract and impersonal manner.[58] The totemic classification of nature provides the original source for the notion that knowledge is ordered by categories. The idea of force, so central to modern science, derives from the elemental religious notion of mana, or force. The concept of time comes from the periodic nature of social life; the idea of space from the "physical territory occupied by society."[59] These categories can only be learned in society. Unlike Kant, Durkheim believes that moral and scientific laws did not originate innately in the human mind. Rather, they emanate from society, for impersonal reason is another name for collective thought. There is something impersonal in us because there is something social in us, and social life informs all of our representations and acts.[60]

I find Durkheim's analysis of religion and ritual fascinating. The sacred appears to be everywhere around us, and attaches to certain people in our culture of celebrity. The power of Durkheim's explanation was vividly portrayed to me at a Lollapalooza rock concert that I attended several years ago. I chaperoned my stepson and his girlfriend, then both freshmen in high school. I noticed that the concert involved a lot of body symbolism, from tattoos to rings in various orifices, and rituals, from slam dancing to surfing the crowd. (In fact, my stepson surfed the crowd and sprained his ankle. When I asked him why he engaged in such foolish activity, from my perspective, he stated that he knew "the crowd would protect him.") These concerts clearly expressed rebellion against middle-class morality, but I saw them more as a sacred, collective expression of generational identity for young people. They had rituals, totems, and symbols, expressed in the music of the rock and rap bands, that gave form to a particular type of cultural identity, a special form of community. I saw this concert as an example of generation X worshipping itself.

Durkheim and Colonialism

Like the Durkheim scholar Mark Cladis, I think that Durkheim is better at investigating the character rather than the origins of religion.[61] Durkheim had little insight into the colonial social conditions influencing his thought. He equated progress with the rise of the nation-states of Europe, and did not address colonialism in any depth. Durkheim wrote during the era of European imperialist expansion throughout the world, and he adopts many of the ideas about contrasts between supposedly "primitive" cultures invaded by colonists and the superior, rational civilizations of Europe. Thus, his distinction between rational and irrational was not only implicitly based on differences between men and women, but also on the rational West versus the irrational East and Africa. The latter had to be civilized by the West, brought into organic solidarity. Durkheim's ideas of evolution and organic solidarity are hierarchical. He tends to see modernity as free, rational, and progressive, compared to the beliefs of other cultures.

Durkheim views the "primitive" religion of the Australian aborigines as having an irrational component, for violence is at its core, embodied in sacrificial rites. This irrationality always threatens to disrupt the social order, as the mana, or energy, that is at the center of the aboriginal religious experience bursts through all attempts to contain it. For Durkheim, this is unacceptable, as irrationality must be domesticated, placed in a rational communal form. Durkheim finds a rational kernel in this irrational experience, for religion is the first form of social solidarity that is necessary for any society to exist. Durkheim to some degree colonizes the experience of the aborigines, putting it into a new context which ignores the natives' interpretations of their·experience. The irrationality of the totemic religion blends into the irrationality of the people who practice it. The aborigines do not understand what they are doing and why they believe what they do; their ideas must be placed in the rational framework of the European to make sense.

But Durkheim also draws his distinction between the modern and the traditional from his studies of premodern Europe and ancient Judaic culture. He is not simply an imperialist who disrespected other cultures.

Rather, it is best to understand his work as not always consistent, as he struggles to break through the confines of his worldview and those of the society around him. While there is no doubt that Durkheim's evolutionary perspective is not always sensitive to the cultures of non-modern peoples, his discussion of education demonstrates that he sees modernity as reflexive, able to reflect on its assumptions and change them. It is fascinating that Durkheim connects religion and science together, viewing them as existing on a continuum, rather than completely separated from one another. I will return to these issues in the conclusion to this chapter.

Durkheim on Democracy and Critical Rationalism

A legacy of modernity is that people can understand that their particular culture is only one among many possible variants. Such a flexible worldview is necessary for a democratic culture and polity. Durkheim's discussion of moral individualism and its connections to democracy demonstrates some of his most insightful contributions to sociological theory. I view Durkheim as advocating a new flexible morality for contemporary societies, which must be diverse yet maintain ties to a common culture. Democracy has to be linked to vital cultural traditions which encourage an active citizenry.

Durkheim contends that the collective conscience of modern society is based on the cult of the individual. In the contemporary world, ideas must not tower above people in the form of God-like images, but must rather be open to human activity and interpretation. The modern world is becoming more rational and individualistic.[62] Durkheim states that the individual "is an autonomous center of activity, an impressive system of personal forces whose energy can no more be destroyed than that of the cosmic forces."[63] People are still constrained by moral rules, but modern morality allows them more choice and freedom, and demands prudential judgment. This new sensibility has to be created through democratic interaction, for the common good is not a static object existing outside of social interactions, but emerges out of the deliberations and criticisms characteristic of modern democracy.[64]

Just like the division of labor, modern forms of democracy necessitate a more rational, self-directed morality that is sensitive to diversity. Contemporary society requires a rational morality whose rules are given respect and are seen as sacred.[65] Durkheim writes: "There is at least one principle which those the most devoted to the free examination of everything tend to place above discussion and to regard as untouchable, that is to say, as sacred: this is the very principle of free examination."[66] The principle of critical rationality is today sacred, in Durkheim's view.

This new "moral individualism" can provide the basis for a secular ethics. Moral individualism has to be instituted in social practices. Durkheim carefully distinguishes utilitarian or egoistic individualism, which he detests, from an individualism "of Kant and Rousseau, of the idealists – the one which the Declaration of the Rights of Man attempted . . . to formulate." Such an individualism requires a morality that seeks "out only that which our humanity requires and which we share with all our fellowmen."[67] This moral individualism, which defines the person as sacred, derives its dignity from rationality and humanity, "which is worthy of respect and sacred."[68] It involves an ideal of universal human rights.

Two elements are essential parts of this new society and collective conscience. The first is more citizen participation and the democratization of the state and society. The second is the differentiation of the spheres of society, like the family, economy, and state, each of which has its own logic. These two – democratization and differentiated realms – intertwine with one another.

For Durkheim, a society is not simply of one piece. Within modern societies different spheres develop, each with a different ethos. The family, based on intimacy, is different from the political realm, tied to citizenship. Though these spheres intersect, there can be plurality without conflict if they remain in harmony and share certain overarching beliefs, such as the values of individualism and justice.[69]

When the logic of one sphere dominates another, the autonomy of the spheres collapses. If the economic sphere dominates, laissez-faire capitalism results, encouraging egoism; if the logic of the political sphere predominates, fascism is a strong possibility. Democratic debate over the relative importance and weight of economic versus political measures needs to take place in the context of shared moral traditions, so as to not degenerate into squabbles which do not change the status quo or effect democratic change. This is why democratization and citizen participation in government and society are so important. Participation creates a common culture and allows the different spheres to be consciously integrated with one another.[70]

Durkheim argues that his era lacked a strong sense of political citizenship. Anomie in part derived from a deficit of economic restraint, as economic values escaped the market and began infiltrating all aspects of society. Untrammeled economic activity resulted in a lack of concern for the common good throughout society. He writes: "the absence of all economic discipline cannot fail to extend its effects beyond the economic world, and consequently weaken public morality."[71]

People develop ethics based on their social customs, which need to be intrinsically satisfying or else they become corrupted by external things such as money and power. If citizens share little in common, they will become susceptible to crazes, fads, and demagogues. Durkheim worried that too much egoistic individualism might result in a surfeit of narcissistic aestheticism and/or economic greed, with "the aesthete and the consumer [becoming] the new social heroes."[72] People need a widespread public morality to go along with these diverse spheres of modernity.

A larger state accompanied the growth of moral individualism and helped integrate the spheres. As the state grew, it necessarily expanded its moral and democratic role, which outweighed and informed its legislative and executive functions. Democracies facilitate communication between the government and the public, and between different spheres. The development of a critical spirit and public debate is integral to the affairs of a democracy, for only through reflection can new and better practices be discovered.[73] All of these factors point to the state's centrality in clarifying, creating, and disseminating knowledge. Only a scientifically informed elite and public can engage in the kinds of rational communication that democracy demands.[74]

Durkheim advocates a more organic relationship between the political and social realms. Because society consists of interdependent functions, the state must help coordinate and morally unify a differentiated society. Yet the state cannot be separated from the needs and beliefs of the *conscience collective*. In a manner reminiscent of Tocqueville, Durkheim argues that a large, centralized state coordinating the activities of a mass of isolated individuals would be a "veritable sociological monstrosity. For collective activity is always too complex to be capable of finding expression in the one single organ of the state."[75] Modern governments should work for social justice, guard against tyranny, and promote moral individualism. The state must protect children, establish educational standards, regulate trade and commerce, eliminate discrimination, and provide health care and food and housing for its citizens, among many other of its responsibilities. The state needs to protect fair contracts through regulation.[76] It plays an important role in the creation, enforcement, and organization of the rights of the citizen. The government establishes ideals and rights in light of the political and cultural traditions of a given society. The contemporary state actively attempts to develop moral individualism; yet its power must be checked by secondary groups, for the state must not be allowed to become separated from the people.[77]

In Durkheim's democratic vision, moral individualism has to be grounded in social groups, which informs his image of a rich, democratic civil society composed of a great number of voluntary associations. Secondary groups such as unions and political parties, existing outside of the state, act as intermediaries between the government and the people, allowing more coherent interaction between these realms and creating favorable conditions for the development of social solidarity. As social and professional associations encourage a sensibility of social rights and duties, professional ethics can be linked to a broad public opinion aware of the requirements of social solidarity.[78] Occupational groups are necessary to ground moral individualism in everyday life. Durkheim writes that occupational groups foster a morality that "becomes a rule of conduct only if the group consecrates it with its authority."[79]

This consecration of rational morality informs the moral legitimacy of democracy. It is clear that for Durkheim democracy is the expression of the collectivity's rational and moral will arrived at through discussion, rather than a place of interest-bargaining among political groups. The moral individualism of the democratic state guarantees individual rights while facilitating rational dialogue between its citizens. Democracy works by making the people's will the laws of the state, which is why democracy has a moral superiority over other forms of government. Deliberations and discussion in the public sphere make the state more conscious of its moral and democratic responsibilities.[80]

Durkheim's analysis fits in well with the dual nature of rationalization that we have discussed throughout the text. Durkheim recognizes that organic solidarity depends on a republican state, which is based on democratic participation through occupational groups and other intermediary institutions. People must debate with one another in a public sphere, which has to be more than simple bargaining among organized interests, in order to develop a sense of shared responsibilities and a common good. As we have seen in his discussion of education, Durkheim at times advocates a kind of multicultural approach based on the historical study of different cultures, problematizing, at least implicitly, his assumptions about progress and European superiority.

Yet Durkheim's theoretical approach can also be understood in a different manner. He asserts that the transition from mechanical to organic solidarity entails an increase in freedom for the individual. Foucault's analysis of the disciplinary society disputes this assertion. For Foucault, the rise of restitutive law increases the surveillance of the public in Europe, as laws begin regulating more and more aspects of individual behavior, from people's economic transactions to their marital and sexual choices. It is no coincidence that the prison and asylum took hold in European society at this time. As the state comes to control more and more aspects of the life of its populace, it enlists social science in its efforts. From Foucault's perspective, Durkheim's sociology, especially his categories of normality and abnormality, erases difference, makes everyone conform to the same laws and social processes, and therefore contributes to the modern project of eliminating anything outside the bounds of modernity.

As Bauman states, surveillance and social control are central aspects of modernity. Surveillance demands that the educator and expert control their subjects, whether they be students or patients. The state engages in a war against forms of life that do not conform to its needs, for state experts and professional specialists believe that they know what is best for people, and they control the power to implement their ideas. Education creates docile and predictable subjects who will conform to the social demands of modern states and economies.[81] We have discussed the problems of republicanism earlier, and there is no doubt that Durkheim shares in them. Durkheim does not interrogate the relationship between knowledge generated in a democratic state and forms of power. The modern state created asylums, prisons, and other disciplinary institutions on a massive scale. To the extent that Durkheim's republicanism mandates one vision of society as right and correct, and combined with his sometimes inflexible positivism, his work contributes to this disciplinary process.

But this is not the whole story of Durkheim. There is a tension in his writings between conformity and active participation. While Durkheim does not address issues of state surveillance and sometimes advocates strong forms of community, he also recognizes that modern societies require increasing democratic, popular reflexivity, the capacity to evaluate and govern society. His work reflects a fundamental tension in contemporary societies, for trends toward state surveillance and the centralization of state power conflict with the spread of critical rationality that is a central component in citizen-based democracy. I address these issues in more depth in my assessment of Durkheim.

Durkheim: An Assessment

Criticisms of Durkheimian sociology are nothing new. Durkheim has been a controversial figure since the publication of his first major work, *The Division of Labor in Society*, in 1893. His earliest critics, often psychologists, accused him of positing a mysterious group mind, the collective conscience, as the basis of individual and social identity.[82] This idea of a group mind was a staple of Durkheimian criticism throughout the years, though it was added to by Marxist and other left-wing critics who accused Durkheim of social conservatism. This criticism became prominent in the US in the 1960s; authors such as Zeitlin argue that Durkheim is interested in social order, what holds a society together, ignoring the role of constraint and coercion in this process. In Zeitlin's view, Durkheim views society as held together by shared values, ignoring issues related to Marx's theory of ideology and class struggle. Thus, Durkheim does not investigate the extent to which shared culture upheld and reinforced the values of a ruling class. Another prominent sociological attack on Durkheim came from social psychologists, who argue that Durkheim does not see people as skilled, reflexive persons who knowledgeably and actively create the world in which they live. For Durkheim, people are rule-following creatures; he does not see them as rule-creating creatures.

There is some truth to these criticisms, especially the second one. I feel that Durkheim addresses issues of conflict in his studies of the division of labor. But he does not develop a theory of culture based on politics and struggle. Culture is not a realm of shared beliefs and values, where morality and solidarity magically arise, but a place where struggle over power among different groups take place. Culture is contested and people fight over the very definition of morality (as seen in debates around gay/lesbian issues, for example), and dominant and subordinate groups attempt to legitimize their ways of life and points of view. Controversies over popular music such as rap are examples of these cultural debates. In Lembo and Tucker's words, "people struggle to redefine the meanings of media objects in ways that are consistent with their own subcultural values."[83] Durkheim does not explore culture in such a politicized way, to his detriment.

Jennifer Lehmann contends that Durkheim's reflections on women in *Suicide* are indicative of a patriarchal viewpoint which characterizes Durkheim's entire social theory. In her view, his separation of people into a homo duplex, a rational and emotional duality of self, is part of the gender coding inherent in Western patriarchal philosophy, as rational, public man is implicitly contrasted with passive, emotional woman. Lehmann argues that Durkheim divides society into the public world of the division of labor, the state, and collective ceremonies, and the private world of the family. This is a gendered division, as public, social, rational life represents males, and the private sphere of the family, which is passionate, irrational, and biological, represents females. Durkheim sees this division as beneficial, universal, and moral, when in reality it reflects the patriarchal power of men over women. Since men are "naturally" social and women "naturally" nurturing, Durkheim makes into an absolute the public/private distinction, which he does not view as historically and socially constructed and therefore open to change. Durkheim does not reflect on his view that masculinity or femininity derive from biology; thus, for example, the possibility of men becoming more nurturing is not part of his worldview.[84]

Durkheim believed that racial problems, like class issues, would be solved by the increased rational division of labor, where people naturally reached their ability level. He does not analyze the power of racism, either in terms of the psychological privileges it gives to whites, or in terms of the economic situation of minorities and immigrants, who serve as a reserve army of workers to keep labor costs cheap, and who are forced to take the lowest-paying jobs. Durkheim does not recognize the privileges that being part of the French middle class gave him, especially over colonized peoples such as those in French Algeria. He does not interrogate how being white, middle class, and male affects his worldview. Thus, for Durkheim, racial and gender hierarchy is built into his view of progress and organic solidarity. Durkheim does not let the colonized, women, or workers speak for themselves. He speaks for them, from an ostensibly universal position.

Do these powerful criticisms of Durkheimian sociology mean that his work should be discarded? There is no doubt that Durkheim advocates many views that are simply wrong and insensitive today. Yet the above criticisms regarding race, gender, and colonialism are *tendencies* that sometimes appear in Durkheim's work, and they do not capture the totality of his work, which is inconsistent on these issues. For example, in *The Division of Labor in Society* Durkheim discusses gender in the context of the family, and race in the guise of heredity and the division of labor. Durkheim defines women as passive and relegates them to the private sphere in his analysis of gender and the family. He does not investigate the family in terms of power dynamics, assuming that women will "naturally" perform the nurturing functions of child-raising and the like. Durkheim does not see the functions of men and women changing over time, and he adopts a naturalist argument about the inherent natures of men and women to justify his argument. Yet Durkheim inconsistently contends that the solidarity of the family is not based on blood relations. He disputes the notion that the family is "naturally" the central institution for forming and maintaining social solidarity, an argument that we should heed in this era of "family values" in the contemporary US and elsewhere. Durkheim states that "artificial kinship . . . has all the effects of natural kinship." People are drawn together by "physical proximity, the need to unite to fight a common danger, or simply to unite," all of which can serve as a source of solidarity greater than the "natural kinship" of the family.[85] Further, the social solidarity provided by the family declines as modern societies differentiate and become more complex.

So the family is not biologically based, but gender differences between men and women seem to be. Durkheim dismisses biological arguments when discussing heredity and race in modern societies. While he does see heredity as a primary influence on the social structure of "primitive" societies, he argues that heredity loses its influence as individuals and their social life become more complex, and have more complicated tasks to fulfill. Biology cannot transmit behavior, only a vague disposition to act in certain ways. Racial characteristics, too, lose their influence over behavior as races intermingle with one another as societies modernize.[86]

How can these various contradictory comments be reconciled? Durkheim argues that race and heredity have little explanatory power in contemporary societies, but adopts a view of gender roles that seems based on biology. This difference is due to his functionalist assumptions. He argues that the differentiation of the division of labor entails increased specialization and complexity, and naturalistic arguments about behavior based on heredity or the blood relations of the family are inadequate for comprehending this complexity. Rather, a social explanation is called for. But Durkheim abandons this explanation when discussing women. He does not view the functions of child-rearing and male–female relationships changing over time. For some reason, they do not "differentiate" as do other relationships and their functions remain the same. Thus, he falls back on a naturalistic argument to justify continued gender inequality.

This lack of sensitivity to issues of gender can be explained in part because France lagged behind other European countries in expanding rights to women, for it was not until the mid-twentieth century that women received extensive political rights. Durkheim lived in a different social context than today, where issues of class and the division of labor preoccupied him, just as they did Marx and Weber. Yet Durkheim possesses the theoretical tools to make at least some sense of issues such as gender and race. Durkheim at his best problematizes the simple dichotomy of reason and tradition. He realizes that all societies are embedded in traditions. It seems to me that from such a perspective contemporary societies, like others, are bounded and limited by the traditions constituting them. Because they are not universal it is possible to recognize how cultural traditions might exclude, ignore, or misinterpret topics such as social power based on gender and race. Though Durkheim did not take this path, his theories might lead to some interesting analyses of racism and sexism.

Durkheim had many views I find defensible and indeed central to any democratic society. In his defense of Dreyfus against accusations of spying for the Germans, Durkheim advocates the defense of civil liberties and moral individualism against the conservatives and monarchists, who opposed the Republic. He recognizes that anti-Semitism was a threat to any democratic, good society. Modern society needs a new, reflexive, individualistic morality, which has to be continually created anew, for a return to the morality of the past is impossible. A good democracy is dependent on an activist and participatory citizenry, closely tied to their capacity to wield power in their communities. Durkheim recognized that power needed to be more equitably distributed in France to ensure a stable democracy. However, he did not extend this critique to women and the colonized, for he did not see how their civil rights were being violated.

In my view, Durkheim shows us that there are some distinctive features about industrial societies that separate them from previous forms of social organization. Modern societies demand new sources of social solidarity, for they cannot rely on religion or tradition to guarantee social cohesion.

In organic solidarity there is more room for individual variation and re-flection, and the laws and customs of modern societies must reflect these new conditions. The state and the market have to coordinate complexly differentiated functions in modernity, and this complexity cannot be wished away. In fact, this is why Marx's ideas about communism seem so farfetched today, for people cannot control all of social life in a conscious, organized way. Durkheim captures a sense of what is distinctive about modernity in his ideas of moral individualism. This allows a way out of some of the debates about community and individualism that are so pressing today.

These ideas are still prominent in many of today's social and political discussions, especially concerning the appropriate political actions neces-sary for a democratic society, encapsulated in arguments about communitarianism. Many public figures, from Tony Blair to Bill Clinton to William Bennett, think that citizens in the West need to develop a stronger sense of responsibility for others in tandem with their concern for individuality. As the contemporary sociologist Anthony Giddens ar-gues, Durkheim's ideas are very much in tune with this debate. Giddens states, for Durkheim, "a condition of freedom and individual self-develop-ment is having a community or society that allows for those qualities to be created. They are not just given in the human condition. Durkheim argued that social cohesion is made problematic by the rise of individual-ism – very much the issue being discussed again now under the banner of communitarianism."[87] Many conservative communitarians argue that a form of fundamentalist religion or traditional morality can answer the cultural disorder of contemporary societies. I think Durkheim has some excellent points to make in this context. He argues that a return to tradi-tional morality is also not the answer to these problems. A modern moral-ity must recognize the centrality of individual freedom, and ensure human rights and some degree of social cohesion. He thought that these ideas complemented rather than conflicted with one another.[88] The collective conscience was becoming less distinct and more individualized in the modern world. Communities are not all of one piece; in the modern era, any society must be founded on rational debate and democratic prin-ciples. Durkheim's perspective problematizes conservative forms of commun-itarianism which do not distinguish rational from traditional communities, and the same criteria provide a basis for criticism of various fundamental-ist doctrines that have arisen throughout the contemporary world.

Durkheim realizes that contemporary societies are to some degree be-coming more reflexive, enabling them to evaluate the traditions and val-ues that inform their lives. This new reflexivity allows them to take a self-critical position relative to our own beliefs. In our era it is possible to critique Eurocentrism, despite the fact that Europe implemented imperial-ism and colonialism. Rational reflexivity allows people to understand their social conditions in a more critical way, without relying on taken-for-granted beliefs.

I have developed an appreciation for Durkheim's thought over the years. The rise of modern societies does not just disenchant or rationalize our existence, as it does for Weber. For Durkheim, people will always need a sacred and moral center in their lives. His self-perception as a scientist sometimes leads him astray and provides justification for the conservative interpretation of his work. Yet I am impressed by his passionate commitment to justice and an egalitarian, participatory form of community, even when he defends them in problematic vocabularies of "normality" and "abnormality." Our contemporary fascination with difference sometimes overshadows the continued need for social solidarity that any society requires. Durkheim reminds us that it is intellectually naive to celebrate difference as though it could exist apart from community, for contemporary societies require both, which must be founded to a great extent on rational discussion.

Still, Durkheim does not develop his ideas of rational reflexivity as far as he could have, which might have led him to a more nuanced discussion of the crosscutting cultural influences at work in contemporary societies. He often relies on functionalist arguments to analyze society, and he does not investigate worldviews from the point of view of the groups he studies. His arguments waver between a recognition that norms and values have to be publicly debated to be legitimate, and an assumption that people follow rules more often than they create them. He devotes little attention to issues of psychic and cultural identity. His fear of aestheticism means that he neglects the artistic and emotional qualities of much social experience. Such problems are addressed to some degree by Weber, but especially by the thinkers we will explore in part three of this book, from Freud to Du Bois.

Notes

1	Steven Lukes, *Emile Durkheim, His Life and Work: A Historical and Critical Study* (New York, 1972), p. 371.

2	For Durkheim and the Dreyfus Affair, see ibid, pp. 332–49. See also Durkheim's article "Individualism and the Intellectuals," in *Emile Durkheim on Morality and Society*, ed. Robert Bellah (Chicago, 1973).

3	Lukes, *Emile Durkheim*, p. 342.

4	Mark Cladis, *A Communitarian Defense of Liberalism: Emile Durkheim and Contemporary Social Theory* (Stanford, CA, 1992), p. 289.

5	E. J. Hobsbawm, *The Age of Empire, 1875–1914* (New York, 1987), p. 59.

6	Kenneth H. Tucker, Jr., *French Revolutionary Syndicalism and the Public Sphere* (New York, 1996), pp. 18–19.

7	Emile Durkheim, "The Intellectual Elite and Democracy," in *Emile Durkheim on Morality and Society*, ed. Robert Bellah (Chicago, 1973), p. 59. See also Jaap van Ginneken, *Crowds, Psychology, and Politics 1871–1899* (New York, 1992), pp. 206–7, 213–14.

8   On Durkheim's notion of moral individualism, see Anthony Giddens, "Introduction," *Durkheim on Politics and the State* (Stanford, CA, 1986), pp. 9–11.

9   Cladis, *A Communitarian Defense of Liberalism*, pp. 15–19, 52.

10   Kenneth H. Tucker, Jr., *Anthony Giddens and Modern Social Theory* (Thousand Oaks, CA, 1998), pp. 157–9. Alexis de Tocqueville, *Democracy in America*, *Vol. 1* (New York, 1990), p. 8.

11   Ibid, p. 102.

12   Alexis de Tocqueville, *Democracy in America*, *Vol. 2* (New York, 1990), p. 137.

13   Emile Durkheim, *The Rules of Sociological Method* (New York, 1938). See also Jeffrey Alexander, *Theoretical Logic in Sociology, Vol. I: Positivism, Presuppositions, and Current Controversies* (Berkeley, CA, 1982), pp. 5–7, and Tucker, *Anthony Giddens and Modern Social Theory*, p. 37.

14   Emile Durkheim, *Pragmatism and Sociology* (Cambridge, 1979), p. 67.

15   Lukes, *Emile Durkheim*, pp. 193–9.

16   Emile Durkheim, *Suicide: A Study in Sociology* (New York, 1951), pp. 282–3.

17   Ibid, p. 283.

18   Ibid, p. 284.

19   Ibid, p. 287.

20   Ibid, p. 250.

21   Ibid, pp. 262–9.

22   Ibid, pp. 270–2.

23   Emile Durkheim, *The Division of Labor in Society* (New York, 1984), pp. 106–8.

24   Ibid, p. 73.

25   Ibid, p. 72.

26   Ibid, p. 127.

27   Ibid, p. 217.

28   Ibid, p. 311.

29   Ibid, p. 312.

30   Ibid, pp. 314–16.

31   Anthony Giddens and Christopher Pierson, *Conversations with Anthony Giddens: Making Sense of Modernity* (Cambridge, 1998), p. 56.

32   Durkheim, *The Division of Labor in Society*, p. 321.

33   Emile Durkheim, *Moral Education: A Study in the Theory and Application of the Sociology of Education* (New York, 1973), p. 115.

34   Ibid, pp. 120–1.

35   Cladis, *A Communitarian Defense of Liberalism*, pp. 6–7.

36   Durkheim, *Moral Education*, pp. 12, 19–20.

37   Ibid, p. 52.

38   Ibid, p. 38.

39   Emile Durkheim, *The Evolution of Educational Thought: Lectures on the Formation and Development of Secondary Education in France* (Boston, 1977), p. 86.

40   Ibid, p. 166.

41 Ibid, p. 274.
42 Ibid, p. 324.
43 Ibid, p. 335.
44 Ibid, p. 324.
45 Ibid, p. 329.
46 Ibid, p. 328.
47 Ibid, p. 336.
48 Durkheim, *Moral Education*, p. 77.
49 Durkheim, *The Evolution of Educational Thought*, p. 339.
50 Cladis, *A Communitarian Defense of Liberalism*, pp. 196–200.
51 Durkheim, *Suicide*, p. 312.
52 Emile Durkheim, *The Elementary Forms of the Religious Life* (New York, 1965), p. 62.
53 Ibid, pp. 121ff.
54 Emile Durkheim, "The Dualism of Human Nature and Its Social Conditions," in *Emile Durkheim on Morality and Society*, ed. Robert Bellah (Chicago, 1973), p. 161.
55 Emile Durkheim, "The Origin of the Idea of the Totemic Principle or Mana," in *Emile Durkheim on Morality and Society*, ed. Robert Bellah (Chicago, 1973), p. 181.
56 Durkheim, *The Elementary Forms of the Religious Life*, p. 173.
57 Durkheim, "The Dualism of Human Nature and Its Social Conditions," p. 160.
58 Durkheim, "Elementary Forms of Religious Life," in *Emile Durkheim on Morality and Society*, ed. Robert Bellah (Chicago, 1973), p. 203.
59 Ibid, p. 199.
60 Ibid, p. 222.
61 Cladis, *A Communitarian Defense of Liberalism*, p. 123.
62 Durkheim, *The Division of Labor in Society*, p. 408.
63 Durkheim, *Professional Ethics*, p. 57.
64 Cladis, *A Communitarian Defense of Liberalism*, p. 137.
65 Durkheim "Elementary Forms of Religious Life," p. 176.
66 Ibid.
67 Emile Durkheim, "Individualism and the Intellectuals," in *Emile Durkheim on Morality and Society*, ed. Robert Bellah (Chicago, 1973), p. 45.
68 Ibid, p. 48.
69 Cladis, *A Communitarian Defense of Liberalism*, p. 139.
70 Ibid, pp. 142, 149, 163.
71 Durkheim, *The Division of Labor in Society*, p. xxxiv.
72 Cladis, *A Communitarian Defense of Liberalism*, p. 39; see also pp. 78–9.
73 Durkheim, *Professional Ethics*, pp. 89–90.
74 See Anthony Giddens, "Introduction," *Durkheim on Politics and the State*, pp. 7–9; Lukes, *Emile Durkheim*, pp. 273–4, 353. See also J. E. S. Hayward, "Solidarist Syndicalism: Durkheim and Duguit," *The Sociological Review* 2nd series 8 (1960), pp. 17–36.
75 Durkheim, preface to second edition of *The Division of Labor in Society*, p. liv.
76 Durkheim, *Professional Ethics*, p. 69; Cladis, *A Communitarian Defense of Liber-*

alism, pp. 157–9.

77   Ibid, pp. 152–5; Durkheim, *Professional Ethics*, pp. 57–63.

78   Ibid, pp. 63, 96. See also Lukes, *Emile Durkheim*, pp. 270–4.

79   Durkheim, *The Division of Labor in Society*, p. xxxiv.

80   Durkheim, *Professional Ethics*, p. 92.

81   Zygmut Bauman, *Legislators and Interpreters: On Modernity, Postmodernity, and Intellectuals* (Ithaca, NY, 1987), pp. 42–50.

82   See Lukes, *Emile Durkheim*, pp. 302–14.

83   Ronald Lembo and Kenneth H. Tucker, Jr., "Culture, Television, and Opposition: Rethinking Cultural Studies," *Critical Studies in Mass Communications* 7 (1990), p. 98.

84   Jennifer Lehmann, "Durkheim's Theories of Deviance and Suicide: A Feminist Reconsideration," *American Journal of Sociology* 100 (January 1995); and her book, *Durkheim and Women* (Lincoln, NE, 1994).

85   Durkheim, preface to second edition of *The Division of Labor*, p. xliv.

86   Durkheim, *The Division of Labor*, pp. 246–67.

87   Giddens and Pierson, *Conversations with Anthony Giddens*, p. 55.

88   Ibid, pp. 57–8.

CHAPTER FIVE

Weber: Modernity and Rationalization

In 1741 the New England preacher Jonathan Edwards (1703–58) delivered his famous sermon, "Sinners in the Hands of an Angry God." To get the flavor of this prototypical fire and brimstone sermon, it is worth quoting some excerpts at length:

> It is true, that judgment against your evil works has not been executed hitherto; the floods of God's vengeance have been withheld; but your guilt in the meantime is constantly increasing, and you are everyday treasuring up more wrath; the waters are constantly rising, and waxing more and more mighty; and there is nothing but the mere pleasure of God, that holds the waters back, that are unwilling to be stopped, and press hard to go forward.[1]

Later Edwards adds:

> The God that holds you over the pit of hell, much as one holds a spider, or some loathsome insect over the fire, abhors you, and is dreadfully provoked: his wrath towards you burns like fire; he is of purer eyes than to bear to have you in his sight; you are ten thousand times more abominable in his eyes, than the most hateful venomous serpent is in ours.[2]

People who heard this sermon left the church in a daze, staggering about the street as if intoxicated. This sermon clearly fit in with many people's cultural understanding of the world, as they took it very seriously.

At about the same time, Benjamin Franklin (1706–90) published many of his famous maxims. Franklin offered advice about how to live, much of which has entered the American vocabulary and common sense. For example, "early to bed, early to rise, makes a man healthy, wealthy and wise" and "time is money" are only two of his more famous aphorisms.

If we fast-forward to the twenty-first century, and you live in the US, what is the first question you are most likely asked after being introduced to someone? I bet it is "what do you do?" In the US one's work often defines life. To not work is considered a dereliction of duty, a mark of immorality, which is why unemployment is often experienced by many people as a devastating loss of self-esteem. I think that this ethic pervades leisure time as well as the world of work. Perhaps vacationers take so many photographs in order to demonstrate to others that they were actually doing something productive rather than idling away their time in a hotel room, or aimlessly wandering around. Now what do these three phenomena have to do with each other?

Max Weber believed that he could supply the answer. Weber's task in his well-known work *The Protestant Ethic and the Spirit of Capitalism* is to analyze the connections between ascetic Protestant religious beliefs concerning individual salvation and the wrath of a punishing God, rational capitalism, and a strong commitment to work. Weber argues that Protestant beliefs, anchored in the thought of Martin Luther and John Calvin, promote an individualistic, emotionally repressive lifestyle grounded in the idea of labor as a calling and a mark of character, which provides the psychological and cultural resources for the rise of capitalism.

Weber is much more than the author of *The Protestant Ethic and the Spirit of Capitalism*, however. He is a complicated thinker of immense scope, who wrote on topics as diverse as architecture, music, art, and social scientific methodology, in addition to his famous studies of religion and bureaucracy. He explores the emergence and nature of modern Western capitalism; he examines the role of ideas in social change; and he investigates the "rationalization" of different types of cultural beliefs. As the social and natural worlds become more rational and less magical, they become defined by systematic reasoning and calculation. Weber analyzes the cultural, ethical, and political dimensions of this rationalized modernity, as well as its economic aspects.

Weber's ideas about the connections of morality and work still resonate today. While issues of ecological crisis and possible nuclear catastrophe separate us from Weber's time, Weber is still relevant in many other ways. His critique of socialism, his analysis of bureaucracy in political parties, and the threat to university autonomy by the state are still important issues today. The sociologist Bryan Turner, like Giddens and Habermas, is most interested in Weber's theory of the ambiguities and contradictions of the rationalization process of modernity, for it can demonstrate some of the problems that people face today in the era of globalization.[3]

I, too, read Weber as fundamentally concerned with rationalization and modernity, of which industry, bureaucracy, and individualism are component parts. Weber studies how people develop a vocation, a sense of obligation tied to abstract principles of justice and competence and performing duties for a specific office. This formation of a strong sense of vocation is tied to the rise of capitalism and the rationalization process, but the long-term changes are paradoxical and contradictory. They ultimately undermine people's beliefs in strong values, while encouraging a methodical approach to life. The emergence and maintenance of a dedication to principles, to a vocation in the context of a depersonalized, rationalized world where ultimate values are in irreconcilable conflict, form Weber's main problematic. His views on the rise of the bureaucratic modern world have much in common with Foucault's conception of the emergence of the disciplinary society.

I also believe that Weber is concerned with issues of democracy. He is best read as a critic of the more enthusiastic potential for democracy found in Marx and Durkheim, for Weber concentrates on the problems facing the democratic state and its citizens. He is much more a harbinger of the new types of discipline and the loss of freedom that modern bureaucratic societies brought with them. He implicitly discusses how our very bodies, as well as our institutions, are shaped by complexes of power.

Weber is also interested in how people can develop the capacities to govern effectively. He argues that the ideal politician must be prudent, have a strong sense of proportion, and be able to make good political decisions. He evaluates political institutions on this basis, i.e. what institutional arrangements give rise to politicians who can exercise good judgment, and this forms the basis of his qualified support of parliamentary democracy. This emphasis on the cultivation of democratic character ties Weber to Durkheim, Marx, and the republican tradition. Weber, however, more than these other theorists, believes that democracy and political rights cannot be separated from constant social struggles, and that power differentials and conflict will be a part of any political system, whether democratic or socialist.

Weber also neglects many issues. He has little to say about the ideals of domesticity and masculinity that arose during the nineteenth century. Weber also lapses into a kind of Orientalism at times, for he often views non-Western cultures in terms of Western characteristics. He defines non-Western cultures by what they lack compared to the West (such as technology, a religion oriented toward this-worldly activism, etc.). Weber does not grant non-Western cultures much status as makers of their own history. Thus, the East is defined with reference to the rationality of the West, as what the West lacks. Yet Weber's analysis of this process is complex, as he often qualifies his views and recognizes the inescapably historical nature of his arguments.

This chapter briefly discusses Weber's life and times, then moves to a consideration of his writings on methodology, rationalization, religion, bureaucracy, class, and status. I then turn to Weber's complex views on democracy and colonialism. I end with an assessment of the "paradox of rationalization," how it contributes to the rise of a disciplinary society and the conditions for democracy and freedom.

Weber and His Time

Weber was born into a wealthy German home in 1864, but his life was far from idyllic. He grew into a troubled, self-divided, hesitant man. His wife stated that he took it upon himself to stand up to the "antinomies," or contradictions, of existence, to live without illusions while still following personal ideals. Weber believed in the importance of personal heroism and the attachment to strong values, while he saw social change undermining their substance. Weber's conflicted personality can be traced in large part to his parents. His father was a hard-working merchant, later a judge and politician, in many ways an embodiment of the Protestant ethic. Yet Weber's father was also authoritarian, self-indulgent, superficial, and not religious. Weber's mother was hard-working, devoted to the poor, and very religious. Weber was attached to his mother, though he joined a fraternity in college, drank a lot of beer, and acquired dueling scars.

Let me make a short aside about dueling among German fraternity students in late nineteenth-century Germany, which makes the worst excesses of contemporary fraternity hazing seem like child's play. The *Mensur*, as the duels were known, consisted of a sword fight between two German fraternity students. The combatants, usually inebriated and surrounded by rowdy and equally intoxicated students, would don goggles and wrap themselves in protective cushions and assume the *en garde* position. A signal from the umpire would begin the fighting, and the participants would exchange five rapid clashes of long swords. After the duel, a medical student, frequently drunk himself, would attend to the wounds, often inflicting more pain on the young man than did his opponent. Interest centered on the wounds, which usually occurred on the top of the head or the left side of the face. Fraternity students cherished wounds. Their goal was to graduate from the university with as many scars as possible.

These duels did not occur because of disputes among students, but were ritualized and planned in advance. The *Mensur* was an indication of a student's honor. Aristocratic in origin, it was a way of disciplining students, teaching them about military bearing and an elaborate code of honor of manly respect. Social success and attention from prized coeds often correlated with the number of dueling scars.[4]

Portraits of Weber show him as a stern man with dueling scars on the left side of his face. Weber later dismissed the *Mensur* as simply a way for students to make a name for themselves. Yet it indicated some of the taken-for-granted aspects of his thought and his time, including the importance of military demeanor and honor among the ruling elite, which prepared them for war and colonial adventures for Germany. Weber also contended that ideals such as honor motivated people's behavior, as in the duels, and intersected with their material interests in complex ways.

Weber was something of an intellectual prodigy and became a well-known and respected professor. However, in 1898 he had a nervous breakdown, which followed a violent scene with his father. Weber accused his father of mistreating his mother and stormed out of the house. A few weeks later his father died. This understandably upset Weber. He fell into a deep depression, unable to do much of anything for years. He could not read sociology or economics, his two main academic areas of interest, and he eventually returned to his work through reading art history books. Weber was never sure of his purpose in life, for he was attracted to politics in addition to academia, and had wide-ranging scholarly interests. His life was characterized by bouts of severe depression, punctuated by spurts of energy and creativity. Weber's psychological problems were hard for him to accept, for he thought that people must possess a strong character to face the problems of modern life.

By the end of World War I Weber was in better psychological shape, and saw himself in his later years as a Jeremiah, a prophet of doom. In the period preceding the entry of Germany into World War I, Weber tried to warn Germany about the consequences of its militaristic acts. He was wide-ranging in his assignment of irresponsible behavior. He denounced the German Kaiser Wilhelm II (1859–1941), the middle class, and the workers for their irresponsible actions. Though Weber survived the war, he died suddenly in the influenza epidemic of 1920.

Weber's work responded to his particular social context. He attempted to grasp the distinctiveness of capitalism and the modern state in the context of the peculiarities of nineteenth-century German political, economic, and social development. Germany industrialized at a rapid pace in the nineteenth century, becoming an economic power in the world, but it remained conservative in many ways, as aristocrats refused to give up their privileges and landlords known as *Junkers* maintained an almost feudal control over their laborers. A democratic political culture did not accompany the industrialization of Germany.

The revolutions of 1848 that swept across Europe failed to produce a democratic outcome in Germany. Germany remained a conglomeration of principalities that were not united into a single nation, and Prussia, the dominant power in the region, was still a reactionary, militaristic state.

The failure of the 1848 movements demonstrated the inefficacy of democratic reform. The heavy-handed and autocratic tactics of the famous chancellor Otto von Bismarck (1815–98) united Germany under the influence of Prussia in 1871. Political integration in Germany was not achieved through democratic compromise among different groups, but imposed by a powerful, militaristic state and authoritarian leaders. Even though a large socialist movement developed in Germany after unification and managed to secure some welfare reforms, the state remained reactionary. The German parliament was ineffective and few democratic rights existed for the people. A large bureaucracy, rather than a democratic political culture, controlled the government. The German state increased its power as it entered into competition with other European states for colonial conquests. Between 1876 and 1915 a quarter of the world's land was redistributed as colonies among a half-dozen European states. Germany was a big part of this expansion, increasing its territory by a million square miles through colonialism, as it carved out spaces for itself throughout Africa and parts of China.[5]

Despite the lack of democracy in Germany, the German workers' organization, the German Social Democratic Party (SPD), under the influence of Engels and later socialists such as Karl Kautsky (1854–1938), became the largest socialist party, indeed the largest political party, in the world. However, it did not truly challenge the power of the German state. Weber's view of the organization and leadership of the SPD influenced his view of socialism. According to Weber, the SPD was only nominally revolutionary, as it became increasingly bureaucratic and concerned with maintaining its own power as it became larger, like any other organization. Leaders who wished to remain in control of the SPD favored the growth of bureaucratic procedures. In Weber's view, socialism would only increase bureaucracy in the future, as socialist movements would impose formal rules and organization on all of social life.

The social context of Germany influenced Weber in other ways. The success of Bismarck demonstrated that political power could be influential in its own right, apart from economic conditions. Weber saw that the growth of political and economic power of workers was possible in a capitalist society, and that it was in the long-term interests of the bourgeoisie to grant workers rights and reforms. He was struck by the spread of bureaucracy into all realms of life, from the government to the workers movement to capitalist enterprises, and the analysis of bureaucracy became a major theme in his work.

Much of the German philosophical tradition influenced Weber, in particular the work of Kant and Nietzsche, in addition to Marx. Like Kant, Weber is interested in questions of morality and science. He accepts the Kantian division between the human world of values and the natural and social world of facts. Weber argues that reason is limited in its understanding, and that the social scientist's subjective world invariably structured what she studied. These ideas inform Weber's ideal-type social science methodology. But Weber is much more interested in the history of morality and its intersection with psychological, social, and economic factors, than is Kant. Here Weber is influenced heavily by Nietzsche and Marx.

Weber is reputed to have said, "One can measure the honesty of a contemporary scholar, and above all, of a contemporary philosopher, in his posture toward Nietzsche and Marx. Whoever does not admit that he could not perform the most important parts of his work without the work that those two have done swindles himself and others. Our intellectual world has to a great extent been shaped by Marx and Nietzsche."[6] Weber is interested in Nietzsche's claim that modern peoples have experienced the death of God; this theme frames much of his sociology. Weber is concerned with how a capitalist and industrial order can exist without an overarching supernatural belief system. In the modern world people must create their own identity, their own meaning, and this process is always problematic. There is no sure foundation of belief on which people can rely, as religion has lost its hegemonic power. Therefore, modern consciousness is always a consciousness of crisis, of missed opportunities and looming problems, from economic collapse to personal depression, or of economic wealth and future happiness. Modern peoples must live with uncertainty.

Weber's ideas about rationalization owe much to Nietzsche's notion that modernity has "de-deified" nature, making the idea of God unbelievable in the scientific world. Nietzsche argues that reason destroys the idea of an overarching, supernatural belief system, but that its remnants are still with us. As Nietzsche poetically puts it, "After Buddha was dead, his shadow was still shown for centuries in a cave . . . God is dead; but given the way of men, there may still be caves for thousands of years in which his shadow will be shown."[7] Weber, too, sees that the shadows of old moralities still exist. Weber states of the fate of the Protestant ethic in the early twentieth century, "the idea of duty in one's calling prowls about in our lives like the ghost of dead religious beliefs."[8]

Like Nietzsche, Weber argues that art often fills this void. For many people, art becomes a repository of a kind of non-scientific truth. Great art balances passion and form, and is a higher form of reality. The artist moves beyond the natural word and shows people a different, better way to live, a non-religious kind of mystical unity. But Weber is less sanguine about the possibility of a "transvaluation of values," in Nietzsche's terms. Weber sees little hope for a new world of meaning and exalted values; only the occasional charismatic leader, somewhat similar to Nietzsche's "overman," can provide new purposes for life.

Marx also influenced Weber. While Weber fully understands the importance of economic factors in history, he seeks to demonstrate that other elements, such as religion, were also important in the rise of capitalism. He does not logically refute Marx's materialism with an idealistic reinterpretation of the rise of capitalism in *The Protestant Ethic and the Spirit of Capitalism*. Rather, like Marx, Weber attempts to grasp the nature of modern capitalism. He shares Marx's belief that material forces and social classes are central features of capitalist development, but he rejects any overarching theory that could explain all of society. Economics is more important in some circumstances than in others, and only specific empirical and historical study can demonstrate the relative explanatory weight of different factors. Ideas always have to be taken seriously as more than reflections of material interests, for they always inform the ways that people understand their economic lives. He distinguishes between material and ideal interests. While material interests concern "worldly goods like prosperity, security, health, and longevity," ideal interests involve issues of grace, redemption, overcoming sickness, and the fear of death. The relationship between these two types of interests is complex, as ideas help define the very interests that give meaning to people's lives. Weber writes,

> Not ideas, but material and ideal interests, directly govern man's conduct. Yet very frequently the "world images" that have been created by "ideas" have, like switchmen, determined the tracks along which action has been pushed by the dynamic of interest.[9]

Though Weber believes in the power of economic interests to determine social action, he argues that rationalization, not class struggle, is the master process of modernity. The march of the bureaucrat, not the proletariat, is on the horizon.

Science and Methodology

Ambivalence characterizes Weber's view of rationalization processes, which extends to his understanding of science. In a manner reminiscent of Nietzsche, Weber argues that science cannot justify ultimate values, even its own existence. Science cannot answer why and how we should live, nor what we should do. It cannot even prove that studying social or natural life is worthwhile. Science explains things empirically and causally, and should have no regard whatsoever for the political implications of its findings. Because science cannot tell people how to act or what values to follow, politics is out of place in the classroom. There is a difference

between analyzing political positions, as to their origins and possible consequences, and advocating a particular point of view. Indeed, not only
should the teacher not advocate a political position, she should teach
students "inconvenient facts" which contradict their political outlook.

Science cannot tell a person how she should live because the values of
the world are in irreconcilable conflict. Weber departs from this Nietzschean
sentiment, however, as he tries to hold on to an ideal of scientific objectivity. While science cannot teach people what values to believe, it can give
people critical methods of thinking and tools and training for thought.
Science can clarify thinking for the individual. For example, the teacher
can confront the student with the means–end dilemma, showing the student that the desire for a particular end may require certain means to
achieve it. Weber states that science can force the individual "to give
himself an account of the ultimate meaning of his own conduct."[10]

Weber, like Nietzsche, believes that reality is infinite. Values have no
purely objective basis, but retain an independence and immanent logic of
their own. When a social scientist observes reality in order to study it, she
chooses her data on the basis of her own subjective values. Social science
is necessarily partial, retaining an element of subjectivity in any study.
Weber states that social science searches for laws only in particular circumstances:

> Nothing should be more sharply emphasized than the proposition that the
> knowledge of the cultural significance of concrete historical events and
> patterns is exclusively and solely the final end which, among other means,
> concept-construction and the criticism of constructs also seek to serve.[11]

Social life is characterized by a plurality of causal elements, with no universal laws or absolute meaning.

Weber's methodology involves ideal-types, which simplify rather than
mirror reality in some objective way. The ideal-type methodology is a
response to those dilemmas posed by the inability of reason to fully comprehend the social world. Since social science is invariably one-sided and
subjectively based, the social scientist constructs ideal-types in order to
study reality. These concepts are not given in the data itself, but are
conceptualized by social scientists out of their own interests for specific
purposes in order to facilitate research. Weber states:

> An ideal-type is formed by the one-sided accentuation of one or more points
> of view and by the synthesis of a great many diffuse, discrete, more or less
> present and occasionally absent concrete individual phenomena, which are
> arranged according to those one-sidedly emphasized viewpoints into a uni-
> fied analytical construct. In its conceptual purity, this mental construct
> cannot be found anywhere in reality.[12]

When Weber examines the Protestant ethic he explores just those aspects of Protestantism that contribute to the rise of capitalism and modern rationality. The full complexity of the religious experience of Protestantism escapes his, and indeed any, theoretical purview. Ideal-types are used by any discipline when it attempts to explain social phenomena. For example, economists often posit an ideal image of the person as a rational economic agent in order to explain economic activity, leaving aside the many irrationalities that invariably influence human action.[13]

Weber reflects on the problems and pitfalls of attempts to maintain objectivity in social research in a more sophisticated way than does Marx or Durkheim. He is up-front about how his bourgeois background and belief in German nationalism influenced his research agenda and values. Weber might have taken this argument further, reflecting on the social position of the researcher in terms of gender and race and how it influences her research. He did not take this more radical step, as such issues remain outside of his theoretical domain.

Weber on Rationalization

Weber's complex view of rationalization distinguishes his sociology from that of Marx and Durkheim. For Weber, all cultures exhibit rationality, in that all people can give reasons which make sense for their behaviors, but only in the West does a particular type of rationality, based on bureaucracy, calculation, and the like, become dominant.

Rationalization, the master process of modernity, results in a less magical, increasingly disenchanted world, in which science becomes dominant as tradition and religion lose their power. Rationalization has two meanings that are connected with one another but analytically separable and sometimes in conflict. On the one hand, rationalization refers to the increasingly precise, formal understanding of the world through abstract concepts. Mathematical and scientific models of nature and social behavior are good examples of this type of rationalization, which involves calculating maximum results at minimum cost, finding the best means to reach a given end. On the other hand, Weber also discusses value rationality, or rational action that is oriented to the realization of values, with means and ends closely tied to one another. For example, non-violent protest often assumes that peaceful ends require non-violent means.[14] Value rationality contributes to the rise of principled reasoning, in that many different areas of social life can be brought together under one unifying idea. Systems of law and morality are based on principled reasoning and ethics.

Another way of conceptualizing this difference is the distinction that

Weber draws between substantive and formal rationalism. Substantive rationalism is directed toward values, resulting in "utilitarian and social ethical blessings" granted by a prince or other authority. This differs from formal rationalism, based on calculation.[15] While these different rationalization processes can complement each other, they can also conflict. This relationship is problematic because formal rationality can overwhelm substantive values in the name of pragmatism, or seemingly neutral values such as efficiency and productivity. For example, principled ethics sometimes conflict with the calculation of the best means to reach a given end. Principled politicians often experience this contradiction, as they are forced to compromise their ideals in order to bring about some measure of social progress, as they see it, through bargaining with politicians of different viewpoints.[16] Formal rationality is often irrational when viewed from a substantive point of view. In his book *The McDonaldization of Society*, George Ritzer draws on Weber's distinction to argue that formal rationality, embodied in standardized consumer products epitomized by the fast-food industry, undermines values of democracy and individualism in the name of efficiency.[17]

For Weber, the rise of rationalism in the West is tied to the emergence of capitalism, the Protestant ethic, bureaucracy, and science. The unique Western status of urban life also promotes rationalization, as personal identification with family and village gives way to the more abstract national and political memberships promoted by urban communities.[18] Rationalization influences the subjective experience of Western peoples, as they increasingly understand and evaluate the world in terms of strategies for the best means to reach a given end. Weber is conflicted about this rationalization process, as he believes that it promotes a more realistic and scientific view of the world, yet also creates a more cynical, bureaucratic society which destroys people's capacities to believe in the exalted moral values associated with religion.

Rationalization and Differentiation

Religious worldviews also face challenges not only from capitalism, but from newly powerful realms of art, eroticism, and science. Like Durkheim, Weber views societies as becoming increasingly differentiated, as different "life spheres" become separated from one another; however, these spheres do not cohere into a harmonious whole, as Durkheim believes.

Rationalization results in the differentiation of art, science, and ethical reasoning from religion. Each sphere develops its own particular inner logic and standards of evaluation. Science becomes based on empirical methods, institutionalized in universities and research corporations. In the contemporary West the Protestant ethic has been transformed into formal law and a personal ethics of responsibility and conviction. Legal norms arise which do not appeal to magic, sacred traditions, or revelation for their justification. Rather, legal norms develop their own internal logic, based on rational argument and precedent. Institutions also emerge in each realm which embody the rationalization process. Universities and academies arise for the advancement of science, galleries and museums for art, and the judicial system for law. The increasing specialization of these different spheres results in the emergence of professions from law to business, which encourage a rational approach to planning. But these realms do not necessarily function together smoothly, as they have different logics and decision rules which can conflict. The best art cannot be decided according to scientific criteria, nor can moral decisions be based on artistic standards. In this context, art and eroticism become increasingly important as realms of meaning that replace religion in a rationalized world. In art, harmony, musical notation, and perspective in painting are examples of these internal criteria.

Weber contends that the artistic bohemian arises with eighteenth-century romantic figures such as Beethoven. The artist emphasizes the experiential and sometimes the erotic dimensions of life, which are outside the purview of rationalization. She "reenchants" the social world as religion loses its social power. Art emphasizes the role of a unique subjectivity and sensuality in the face of scientific civilization. An aesthetic outlook toward life, exemplified in bohemian movements from late nineteenth-century Parisian artists to the hippies of the 1960s and the punks of the 1970s, can compensate for rationalization in other spheres.

For bohemians, as for romantics, art demonstrates a higher truth than reason. Romantics thought art and poetry could change the world, as art provided a gateway into another, more profound and mysterious reality. Art also takes over the realm of this-worldly salvation, especially from the routines of everyday life, and competes directly with religious salvation.[19] For many religions, such as Puritanism, this artistic approach to life is immoral. The romantic artist distracts people from their moral duties and changes moral judgments of conduct into judgments of aesthetic taste. The romantic artist represents idolatry, a deceptive bedazzlement which obscures the divine truth of the world. The religious ethic of brotherliness also stands in tension with art, for the latter encourages a preoccupation with sensuality, eroticism, and individualism, rather than shared suffering and community.[20]

It would have been interesting had Weber developed these ideas further. It is clear that we live in an increasingly fragmented cultural world. Art and eroticism in contemporary life often give people a strong sense of meaning, and rock stars are many people's cultural heroes. They can publicize causes and mobilize people around them. For example, the Irish rock star Bono has become a powerful spokesperson advocating the cancellation of Third World debt owed to industrialized nations. Evidently, when Bono speaks, people listen. Popular music and romantic love are central to many people's sense of identity. These worldly emphases often conflict with religious morality, as the moral tenets of religion encourage a brotherliness and solidarity which is lacking in the more individualistic orientations of romance. Still, this is a complicated phenomenon, and one should not overstate differences. Art can provide people with a sense of community and shared suffering, as can be seen in the history of African-American music, and in the relationship of music to social movements more generally. Weber, however, concentrates much more on religion than art is his writings.

Weber on Religion

Weber, like Durkheim, is fascinated by religion, despite being a non-believer. Unlike Durkheim, Weber studies particular religious traditions in depth, writing on the religions of India, China, ancient Judaism, and Islam, in addition to the Protestant ethic in Western Europe. Like Nietzsche, he thinks that the origins of religion lie in the attempt to make moral sense of suffering. Weber is interested in the social implications of religion, the interaction of religious ideas, rituals, and organizations with economic, cultural, and political life, in particular capitalism. Weber sees the complex interaction of ideas and material interests at work in religious traditions.

Weber examines religions in the context of his theory of rationalization. He analyzes religious traditions in terms of the extent to which they retarded or advanced rationalism, such as it existed in the West. There are two criteria for determining the degrees of religious rationalization. The first concerns the elimination of magic from religious beliefs and rituals; the second is the development of an internally consistent and universally applicable theodicy. Ascetic Protestantism is the highest religious tradition on both counts, and therefore the most rationalized.[21]

Throughout history people, especially those who are fortunate, powerful, or wealthy, have seldom been satisfied with the fact of being fortunate. They have felt compelled to justify it, to feel that they deserve their good fortune. Moreover, people feel the need to explain misfortune, suffering, and evil in this world. Religion answers these problems, as it explains the world in a meaningful way. Religious messiahs and saviors have appeared in different historical eras to redeem suffering; magicians and priests arise to explain the reasons for suffering to the masses.

Thus, what Weber calls the major world religions, including the Confucian, Hindu, Buddhist, Christian, Islamic, and Jewish religions, contribute to the rationalization of the world by systematically explaining suffering, fortune, and the cosmos, and by positing their path to salvation as universal.[22] Because a religious worldview makes the cosmos meaningful and categorizes reality according to religious criteria, it promotes rationalization. It advances methodical, systematic conduct in everyday life. Religions systematize to the extent that they orient conduct toward fixed goals of salvation, and distinguish between valid and invalid ways of attaining these aims.[23] Religious rationalization is also furthered by the hierarchy of intellectuals in churches who cure souls through acting as intermediaries of God, providing counsel to sinners, and allowing such acts as the confession of sins.[24]

Weber distinguishes ascetic from mystical religions. Religious worldviews tend to split into asceticism's effort to rationally master nature, and mysticism's attempt to reach the divine through contemplation. Followers of ascetic religions, such as Puritans, view the world as containing traces of the divine, despite its wickedness. They see themselves as tools of God, acting out God's plan in the world. Furthering God's will in this life is the path to salvation. Mysticism involves meditating on the holy; this world is absolutely meaningless, or God's aims for this world are incomprehensible, and salvation is attained by ritual and reflection, rather than intense worldly activity such as labor.[25] This is not a hard-and-fast distinction, as in practice these two types of religious orientation – the ascetic and the mystical – often shade into one another.

Religious worldviews originate in particular social strata, though they can have powerful influences on a number of different social groups. Prophets and saviors appeal to lower classes, for they try to explain and redeem undeserved suffering and the worldly success of bad people, especially evil rulers. Warriors who strive for glory and riches are attracted to religions that are ascetic and encourage this-worldly activity. Peasants are inclined to magic, as they are dependent on natural forces influencing harvest for their livelihood. Civic strata, such as artisans, merchants, and traders, tend toward religions emphasizing practical rationalism, as their way of life is detached from strict economic ties to nature.[26] They calculate the potential for profits based on their business activity.

Weber views Islam as a religion with elements of ascetic and mystical traditions. Islam is a monotheistic religion and believers see people as predestined for grace or damnation. Yet the horrible salvation anxiety (am I saved or damned?) characteristic of Puritanism did not arise in Islam, and Islam did not contribute to the rise of capitalism. Weber attributes that difference to the existence of large groups of Islamic warriors, on the one hand, and mystical sects of Sufi brotherhoods, on the other.

Islam became a warrior religion, rather than one tied to merchants. More-over, the Sufis gave Islam a strong tradition of mysticism. Urban areas were primarily outposts for troops in Islam, and no capitalist ethic developed in this religion.[27]

Weber also wrote extensively on the religions of China and India and on ancient Judaism. In each case, Weber ties the religion to social circumstances and history. In China, science and Western-style modernity did not develop, despite extensive Chinese technological capacity in the early modern era. The Chinese state remained a traditional bureaucracy, ruled by an emperor and a cultural elite, the Mandarins, who based their authority on literary rather than scientific knowledge. Cities never developed the autonomy in China that they did in the West. Villages were controlled by a strong kinship system founded on ancestor worship and the consecration of tradition.

Weber labels China a patrimonial bureaucracy, for the emperor exercised enormous personal control over his empire, unlike the more impersonal bureaucracies in the West. Mandarins and administrators were loyal to the emperor himself, not to abstract ideals of vocation and duty. There was no independent strata of lawyers, jurists, or merchants in China, because such autonomous groups threatened the total power of the emperor. The rule of law did not arise in China, which followed the authority of the emperor.

The emperor, the chief priest as well as administrative ruler, appointed officials based on educational qualifications. But a particular type of knowledge was valued. The Chinese intellectual elite, the Mandarins, developed the philosophy of Confucianism, and opposed ideals of specialized expertise. Confucianism revolved around the idea that the social and individual worlds had to exist in an ordered harmony. Its social ethic emphasized devotion to family and ancestors, literary study, and service for the community. It was not appropriate for Confucian intellectuals to practice economic activity, as the desire for wealth disrupted the harmony of the individual. In sum, Confucianism, combined with the patrimonial bureaucratic rule of the emperor and traditional village life, inhibited social change as it occurred in the West, and China remained a static society.

Indian Hinduism, too, was a contemplative religion that inhibited the formation of Western ideals. Hinduism is based on the transmigration of souls and karma, the idea of compensation in the next life. Weber ties Hinduism to the Indian caste system, which prevents people from moving from one social category to another. Only through successive incarnations can members of the lower castes aspire to reach the divine. Ideas of progress are not possible in such a social order. The caste system also prevents the rationalization of the economic realm, as it emphasizes traditional skills and the making of beautiful objects rather than profit. Occupational categories remain rigid and social mobility was non-existent.[28]

Ancient Judaism, on the other hand, is a prophetic religion, arising on the outskirts of great empires. The Jewish prophets urged believers to follow the moral law against earthly powers. This law can be understood rationally, rather than mystically. Thus, Judaic religion is free of magic and irrationality in its quest for salvation, and it is oriented to action in this world. With the rise of Christianity and especially Protestantism, the idea of acting to change the world becomes an ethical ideal. Only Protestantism mandated the methodical, ascetic attainment of a given goal of salvation, requiring the precise calculation of means. Thus, Protestantism unites formal and substantive rationality, and is a prerequisite for the rise of capitalism in Europe. Let's turn to this analysis of Protestantism in more detail.

The Protestant Ethic and the Spirit of Capitalism

Weber argues that distinctive social conditions contribute to the rise of capitalism, such as the emergence of a formally free wage labor force, the separation of business enterprise from the household, and the development of rational book-keeping methods to calculate business costs and profits. Capitalism in the West is also influenced by the legacy of the Roman Empire's system of law, which developed a calculable, formal jurisprudence, necessary to regulate contracts and business transactions in a complex market economy. But capitalism requires a type of rational spirit, which economic and political conditions did not produce. Such traits are not inherent in human nature; they must be learned. The Protestant ethic supplies the motivation and cultural ethos for capitalism.

Weber links Protestantism to capitalism, stating that this ascetic religion helped create the disciplined, calculating psychological outlook necessary to engage in capitalist work and planning. According to Weber, capitalism cannot be equated with the acquisitive impulse or greed, which have existed in diverse societies throughout history. Rather, capitalism is the pursuit of profit by means of continuous, rational, market-based enterprise. Capitalism exists when peaceful opportunities for exchange exist, and future profits can be calculated. Labor is paid in wages, which can be estimated over time.

The spirit of modern capitalism is the desire for the acquisition of money and the avoidance of spontaneous enjoyment. These are considered ends in themselves. The quest for monetary acquisition dominates life, but it is not a means to satisfy material needs. Indeed, from the point of view of individual utility or happiness, such an ethic seems irrational.[29] The capitalist spirit involves the efficient performance of a vocation, which is both a duty and a virtue. Working hard is evidence of good character.

Weber finds examples of this spirit in many places in the West, as in the colonial American Benjamin Franklin. Franklin's maxims demonstrate that increasing one's capital is an end in itself, and that if one does not engage in such remunerative activity, it is a "forgetfulness of duty."[30] Earning money and working productively in an occupation are virtues which illuminate the character of the individual. For even the wealthy individual imbued with this ethic, "he gets nothing out of his wealth for himself, except the irrational sense of having done his job well."[31]

There is something specific in Protestant beliefs that contributes to the rise of capitalism. The Protestant Reformation was not an escape from the controls of the church. Catholic control over everyday life was relatively loose, as believers experienced a cycle of sin and repentance. The Reformation meant a new form of religious self-control and accountability. The emphasis on the individual's relationship to God, and his or her responsibility for this relationship, entailed "a regulation of the whole of conduct which, penetrating to all departments of private and public life, was infinitely burdensome and earnestly enforced."[32] Protestantism, by demanding a more disciplined way of life than Catholicism, injected a religious factor into all spheres of life, obliging a constant vigilance about day-to-day activities.

Weber traces this ethic to two major religious events linked to the Protestant Reformation. The first is the idea of the calling, associated with the great Protestant reformer Martin Luther (1483–1546). Catholicism did not develop an idea of an individual's calling, "in the sense of a life-task, a definite field in which to work."[33] The calling brings "the mundane affairs of everyday life within an all-embracing religious influence."[34] The Protestant individual is "called" to fulfill his obligations in his occupation, his position in the world. The individual must live morally to fulfill his duty to God. There is no analogous idea in Catholicism, which stresses monastic isolation as the path toward salvation.

Luther's notion of the calling helps bring all of life under a single, consistent code of morality. Anyone can attain salvation in any walk of life, for the individual is carrying out God's will in his calling. While the calling provides a religious justification for the division of labor, it does not emphasize the pursuit of worldly goods as an end in itself. Weber traces this emphasis on material accumulation to the religious beliefs of John Calvin (1509–64), the forerunner of Puritanism.

Weber examines those aspects of Calvin's theology that are most consequential for economic activity. He finds three major Calvinist tenets that are important in this respect: (1) the universe only has meaning in rela-

tion to God's purposes; (2) the motives of God are beyond human comprehension; (3) the doctrine of predestination. Individuals are irrevocably
saved or damned at the moment of creation and can do nothing about it,
for people cannot influence God's judgments.

Weber delineates the psychological consequences of these beliefs. Calvinism creates an unprecedented inner loneliness, where each person cannot
rely on a priest to intervene regarding sin and salvation. This eradication
of the possibility of salvation through the church and the sacraments is
what separates Calvinism from Luther and Catholicism.

Yet followers of Calvin could not handle this situation of uncertainty
about their salvation. They wondered, indeed obsessed, about whether
they were one of the saved, or if they were destined for eternal damnation
(by the way, Calvin apparently had no doubt that he was one of the
saved). Weber contends that, over time, two responses to this situation
developed. First, the individual should never question whether or not he
is one of the elect, for doubts show that one is not among the saved. All
temptations come from the devil, and individuals have to attain supreme
self-confidence that they are saved. They have to control their sexual
desires in particular. Second, intense worldly activity is necessary to maintain this self-confidence. The world exists for the glorification of God and
this must be manifested in people's everyday acts. Weber states, "the
performance of 'good works' became regarded as a 'sign' of election – not
in any way a method of attaining salvation, but rather of eliminating
doubts of salvation."[35] Worldly activity "disperses religious doubts and
gives the certainty of grace."[36]

Calvinism requires a life of constant, coherent discipline, for there is no
possibility of a cycle of confession, repentance, and atonement. Labor
takes on added importance, becoming linked to ethical issues in an even
more pronounced manner than in Luther's doctrine. Puritans demand
that everyone approach their vocation in "a methodical fashion as the
instrument of God."[37]

The Puritan creates a conviction of his own salvation which consists of
continual and systematic self-control. The individual must think constantly
of his will and actions, control himself, and try to calculate the ethical
consequences of his decisions. Enjoyment and emotions must be brought
under control, and "the moral conduct of the average man was thus
deprived of its planless and unsystematic character and subjected to a
consistent method for conduct as a whole."[38] Weber states that the most
important result of this ascetic Protestantism was "a systematic rational
ordering of the moral life as a whole."[39]

Calvinism helps to create psychological conditions conducive to the
rise of capitalism. The calling is a command from God for "the individual
to work for the divine glory."[40] Later Protestant ministers such as the

American Richard Baxter (1615–91) preached that labor was a defense against a sinful life, and work was an end in itself. Weber states, "the religious valuation of restless, continuous, systematic work in a worldly calling, as the highest means to asceticism, and at the same time the surest and most evident proof of rebirth and genuine faith, must have been the most powerful conceivable lever for the expansion of that attitude toward life which we have called here the spirit of capitalism."[41] When consumption is limited, wealth grows. For Puritans, the accumulation of wealth came to be seen as willed by God. They enacted a prohibition only against the enjoyment of wealth. The accumulation of wealth is not a problem; only if wealth is consumed in an immoral manner is affluence questionable. For Weber, these are the psychological consequences of Calvinist ideas, and subsequent Puritan thought derives from the anxieties of believers in the face of isolation.

Over the centuries wealth has a secularizing tendency, until the Protestant ethic loses its religious overtones and becomes a more generalized cultural belief. Thus, nineteenth-century Western businessmen believed that if their morality was spotless, if the way they used their wealth was not objectionable, they could not only make money, but feel that it was their duty to accumulate, even if they were not devoutly religious.

What sort of people were attracted to this doctrine, so harsh and life-denying? There may be good theological reasons for such beliefs. The Puritan minister Jonathan Edwards argues that the love of God is not the same as self-love. People should not approach God in a utilitarian way, as an entity who can solve their problems. They should not be so arrogant as to think that God will provide for their happiness, but open themselves up to God's grace, no matter the consequences. But there are more sociological reasons for following this doctrine that we have touched on in our earlier discussion of religion. Weber argues that the "civic strata," such as merchants and businessmen, found this religious worldview appealing. The existence of these groups is based on economic calculation and the mastery of economic conditions. They have to lead an orderly, systematic life in order to be successful. Thus, they are attracted to a religion that stresses molding the world according to God's will and rejects contemplation and magic as a means to salvation. Rather, the person must prove himself before God.[42] It was the rising stratum of the lower industrial middle class, with their ideal of the self-made man, who embodied the capitalist spirit.

Weber sees the Protestant ethic as declining in modern societies as rationalization takes hold, and he does not think much of this process. The religious value system that has given capitalists their rationale for accumulation (the concept of the calling) results in a system in which individuals are dominated by their own products. The Protestant ethic helps produce an economic system that subsumes these values to the demands of capitalist expansion. Sounding much like Marx, Weber writes:

> Since asceticism undertook to remodel the world and to work out its ideals in the world, material goods have gained an increasing and finally an inexorable power over the lives of men as at no previous period in history. Today the spirit of religious asceticism – whether finally, who knows? – has escaped from the cage. But victorious capitalism, since it rests on mechanical foundations, needs its support no longer.[43]

Capitalism is no longer in need of an ultimate value system to give meaning to people. Technology and the acquisition of wealth define the essence of society.

In a great historical irony, Protestantism encourages the emergence of a rationalized, bureaucratic approach to the world, an "iron cage," thereby destroying the religious bases of capitalism. The pursuit of wealth loses its ties to ethics and becomes almost a sport, as Weber puts it. Just a few years ago the bumper sticker, "The person who has the most toys wins," was popular in the US. Consumerism and efficiency overwhelm all other aspects of social life, as bureaucracy and capitalism penetrate into every realm of social existence. Weber thinks that the rise of bureaucratic rationality is paradoxical, in that it results in a valuable ethic of individual responsibility and dedication to a vocation, on the one hand, but also compulsive ascetic, pleasure-denying behavior, on the other – plus a decline in meaning, a disenchantment of the world, as he puts it, if I may use a third hand.

Weber's thesis about the relationship between Protestantism and capitalism was controversial from its initial publication in 1904–5. Many historians now argue that the same preconditions for capitalism existed in the older Italian cities at the dawn of modernity, as well as in the states of Northern Europe, and in other cultures influenced by religious traditions such as Islam.[44]

There are other consequences to Calvinist and later Puritan thought not developed by Weber. Puritans, in their quest for salvation, not only looked to maintain their own sense of salvation, but hated and attempted to repress those people who appeared to them not to be saved. From Hawthorne's depiction of Puritan life in *The Scarlet Letter* to the hangings of suspected witches and wizards in the famous Salem witchcraft episodes of 1692, Puritanism proved to be a very intolerant perspective. Others who were not like the Puritans, or who failed to live up to their standards, were condemned not only as different, but as morally inferior and dangerous. Such evaluations about those different from the majority has characterized American intolerance to immigration, some of which still occurs today. Weber does not deal satisfactorily with issues of immigration and culture. He seems to have developed some of this Puritanical intolerance of others himself, for he did not think much of Polish immigrant workers in Germany.

In sum, Weber argues that the world religions encourage a systematic approach to social action. His studies of Protestantism demonstrate that Europeans develop a mundane ethics that penetrates everyday life. While Weber sees the decline of Puritanism as an instance of the Nietzschean problem of the death of God, resulting in the "iron cage" of modernity, rationalization encourages the capacity to think in terms of abstract principles not tied to specific religious traditions. Such a capacity to reason abstractly is also tied to Protestantism's devotion to a calling or vocation, where individuals can believe in offices and laws rather than individuals or religious doctrine. These qualities – devotion to law, individualism, and the capacity to reason in terms of principles – are prerequisites for democracy, according to Weber. They inform his discussion of the "political maturity" necessary for democratic culture, which I will discuss in more detail below.

Weber's analysis of Protestantism and religion gives us some keys to how he understood modernity. But we must also turn to his theories of class, status, and bureaucracy in order to grasp his view of society. He argues that social life was wracked by conflicts and tensions which cannot easily be resolved.

Class and Status

The US is often referred to as a classless society, but many of those who see the US as a nation without classes recognize that status distinctions play a central role in social stratification. For example, in a *New York Times* article Andrew Sullivan writes that "America is a classless society, but every neighborhood, profession, and subculture has its pecking order. That means lots of opportunities for prestige – and anxiety." The *Times* catalogues various status distinctions among different groups. Gourmets value a Viking Range, "the Lamborghini Diablo of stoves," as the ultimate status symbol. Even vegetarians have a status order "gauged by culinary austerity." "Raw foodism" is an increasingly popular diet, in which anything that has to be cooked, or that has to do with animal products in any way, must be avoided. One raw foodist states, "The goal is to be 100 percent raw. We pity meat-eaters because we know they're going to die soon. They're killing themselves."[45]

Weber was no vegetarian, but he recognizes the importance of status groups. Unlike the *New York Times*, Weber sees status tied in complex ways to class. Class and status are interrelated, but have distinctive elements which prevent them from being reduced to one another. Here Weber is criticizing Marx's view of class. He argues that class must be more clearly specified than in Marx's broad definition, and that shared class position rarely gives rise to a sense of community.

Weber defines class as economic action in a market. Classes are "stratified according to their relations to the production and acquisition of goods."[46] Classes require a market in order to exist and class position is determined by the property, goods, and skills that individuals possess. Those who share similar skills, etc., will face similar economic constraints and opportunities. Weber, like Marx, contends that ownership of property is the major defining criterion of class. But unlike Marx, Weber distinguishes several classes existing under capitalism, besides the proletarian/capitalist distinction. For example, entrepreneurial groups are different from propertyless white-collar workers, who are distinguished from factory workers, who are in turn differentiated by skill levels.

People who share similar class situations rarely feel that they share a common outlook, however. In contrast to classes, status groups are communities who feel that they share a common history and, to some degree, a common destiny. Status groups are "determined by a specific, positive or negative, social estimation of honor."[47] People in the same status group often follow similar lifestyles, as status groups "are stratified according to the principles of their consumption of goods as represented by special styles of life."[48] Status groups may evolve into a closed caste, guaranteed by laws, conventions, and rituals. This happens only when "the underlying differences . . . are held to be ethnic."[49] Ethnic conflicts concern not only the distribution of material goods, but also issues such as honor and shared history, which can become subjects of contestation.

Weber sees class as more important than status in the contemporary world, for "the style of life expected for members of a status group is usually conditioned economically."[50] On the one hand, this seems to be undoubtedly the case. Status groups are often defined by a mode of consumption. Many US teenagers define their identity in terms of the brand of clothing that they purchase. Economic conditions are frequently the reason for the formation of status groups, which wish to monopolize particular material goods or opportunities. Union seniority is one way to control economic opportunities, as is the creation of positions in a firm or industry for friends and acquaintances. Members of status groups have to constantly work at sustaining their economic exclusivity and privileges, however.[51]

On the other hand, it seems that status groups, especially when tied to ethnic identity, can override class position. In our age of identity politics, individuals of similar ethnic backgrounds are assumed to share the same culture, the same political beliefs, the same lifestyle, and the like. While many members of ethnic groups undoubtedly adopt this notion of common culture, this ideal of ethnic homogeneity can stifle debate and discussion, and inhibit more fluid and complex conceptions of identity. In any case, status groups and classes are often bound up with and contribute to social and economic inequality. Why do people accept such inequality? According to Weber, they must see social authority as legitimate, as deserving of allegiance.

Weber on Authority

For Weber, power and hierarchical authority are an inevitable dimension of all societies. He defines power as the ability to realize one's objectives even with opposition from others. Domination is more specific, for it means following a specific command issued by an authority. A key aspect of Weber's argument is that authority must be recognized as legitimate in order to be respected. Weber specifies types of legitimacy tied to different forms of authority. He distinguishes between traditional, rational–legal, and charismatic authority.

Under traditional authority people follow orders that conform to tradition and custom. People are often accountable to a heritage, which informs their actions and beliefs. Traditional authority, usually characteristic of non-modern societies, has largely given way to rational–legal authority. In rational–legal authority people follow orders because they conform to a procedure, rule, or code, which can be explained and justified by reasons if need be. This capacity to furnish reasons for actions and decisions is a decisive factor. Professionalism, tied to the possession of competence and knowledge, is an important component of this authority. Competence is circumscribed and limited, as authority is subject to certification. Competence and professionalism are not exercised for the profit of the individual, but for the larger institution. Bureaucracy is the organizational form most amenable to rational–legal authority.

Rational–legal authority has come to dominate the modern world as rationalization has proceeded. Weber recognizes that this form of authority does not provide mystery and meaning in everyday life, and contributes to the "disenchantment of the world." Weber sees charismatic authority punctuating the rationalization process, providing messages of hope and spiritual renewal for people. Charismatic authority is a message or command that has an effect because it is invested with charm and grace, and is literally irresistible. Charisma is the charm or gift given to certain figures who are seen to have an almost supernatural blessing. Great religious leaders such as Jesus and Muhammad are examples of charismatic leaders. The actions of the charismatic leader have a style that gives them an authentic and distinctive flavor. A popular, pleasant person, such as George W. Bush, is not necessarily charismatic. Rather, the charismatic leader is very demanding, maintaining a distance from her disciples. The charismatic leader may achieve something miraculous, such as defeating a strong enemy, but her main attraction is that she represents the promise of a new social order. The charismatic leader fanatically devotes herself to achieving this new order. Her message is radically personal, in that she embodies the new order and legitimizes the message by opposing existing traditions. Religious sects are most favorable to charismatic leaders, as are political parties; the Russian Communist Party, when led by Lenin or Stalin, constituted a secular religion. Many contemporary social movements have also seen the rise of charismatic leaders, from Martin Luther King, Jr. in the Civil Rights movement in the US, to Nelson Mandela in the anti-apartheid movement in South Africa.

However, charismatic authority cannot prevent the long-term rationalization process from continuing. After the charismatic leader dies, her message must be institutionalized in churches, political parties, and the like, if it is to survive over time. Weber refers to this process as the routinization of charisma, as charismatic authority becomes bureaucratized and takes on the trappings of rational–legal authority to secure its continued existence.[52]

Bureaucracy

Weber is well known for his studies of bureaucracy, which epitomizes formal rationality in its goal-oriented conduct guided by calculation and abstract rules. Bureaucracy, the most technically efficient form of organization, demands hierarchy; authority is based upon written rules and management requires expert training. It favors "precision, speed, unambiguity, knowledge of the files, continuity, discretion, unity, strict subordination, reduction of friction and of material and personal costs."[53] Bureaucracy is most developed in the modern state and in capitalism. Capitalist organizations favor bureaucracy, for business management must, through rational, calculable planning, increase precision, steadiness, and speed of operation. Weber states, "The objective discharge of business primarily means a discharge of business according to the calculable rules and 'without regard for persons.'"[54] Bureaucracy levels status-honor and minimizes personal desires that cannot be calculated (such as love, hatred, etc.). Such qualities are bad for business.

Bureaucracy also is the central organizational form of the modern state, for it demands "permanent and public authority, with fixed jurisdiction."[55]

Bureaucracy mandates the separation of public official activity from the private property of officials; only in such a context does the idea of government corruption have any meaning. The modern state centralizes the means of violence in the military and the police, and similar processes take place in law and administration. In eliminating independent sources of law, violence, and administration, the state separates people from the personal control of administrative organization. Centralizing power allows formal rationality to rule, as law, administration, and other governmental functions can be calculated and codified. The growth of the civil service, alongside the courts, transforms democracy into bureaucratic rules and laws. For Weber, "Everywhere, and in all spheres of conduct, from the factory to the university, the means of operation are concentrated in the hands of those who control machinelike bureaucracies. Marx's depiction of the complete separation of laborers from ownership of the means by which they can realize their labor is but one instance of a more universal bureaucratization process."[56] Professors are separated from the means of production and administration, which are controlled by trustees and school administrators. The military becomes professionalized, as soldiers do not "own" the military and are separated from the control of administration.

While Weber believes that bureaucracy is the most efficient form of organization, he is ambivalent about its social and personal effects. He sees the professional bureaucrat chained by his apparatus, as once established, bureaucracies are difficult to abolish. Moreover, the bureaucracy can work for anyone in control of it, whether it be a democratically elected leader or a dictator. Bureaucratic office-holders demonstrate the remnants of the Protestant ethic, as a good bureaucrat views his office as a vocation, working out of a sense of duty to the office and what it represents, rather than for a particular person. Bureaucratic activity requires training, a capacity to work long hours, and "the position of the official is in the nature of a duty," for it is not to be exploited.[57]

Bureaucracy is the organizational form best suited to the disciplinary society. In a bureaucratic social world, people come to act in a disciplined, calculating way, almost out of habit. These bureaucratic tendencies of modern states and capitalist organizations are always in tension with democracy, as they promote organized, disciplined action that checks popular sovereignty.

Weber on Democracy

I argue that Weber can be understood as a theorist of democracy, in addition to rationalization. Weber was not an idealistic democrat, however. For Weber, the nation-state is tied to bureaucratic domination and control. The state is based on the legitimate use of force over a delimited territory, for governments are ultimately founded on the control and use of violence. All politicians must be willing to use state-sanctioned violence in order to responsibly carry out their duties. Another of Weber's most trenchant and potentially disturbing arguments concerns the inherent conflict between bureaucracy and democracy. Democracy and bureaucracy are inseparable, as democratic political representation and equality demand administrative and judicial provisions to prevent privilege. The will of the people becomes subject to bureaucratic rules, as attempts to ensure that democratic procedures are not undermined by corruption and discrimination require many laws, courts, commissions, etc. Moreover, officials become entrenched in the civil service because of their expertise and qualifications. To have all of the civil service elected would create chaos, as bureaucracies demand efficiency and expert qualifications.[58]

While Weber is indebted to Nietzsche's notion that life is based on struggle, he also draws on the republican tradition of developing ideals for public service, founded on the education and cultivation of qualities of judgment through participation in institutions. For example, Weber evaluates the 1905 and 1917 Russian Revolutions in terms of their possibilities for civil justice and the rule of law. He is not interested in their geopolitical impact on Germany.[59] These democratic themes are brought out clearly in his discussion of politics as a vocation, where Weber defends freedom of speech, the autonomy of the university, and the qualities for good politicians and citizens.

Weber developed these ideas in two lectures on politics and science in Munich, Germany, in 1919, just after the end of World War I. He addressed some dilemmas faced by German professors at this time which seem to have an almost timeless quality. In the wake of the first two decades of the twentieth century, a German youth movement developed, somewhat like the various youth movements in 1960s Europe and the US. Germany in the early twentieth century was undergoing industrialization, and young adults faced a harsh new environment. They lived in a highly bureaucratized society, were channeled into a technical education fit for a bureaucratic society, and saw all kinds of hypocrisies among parents and adults, in home and in school, such as sexual double standards among adults – many men had mistresses but still held to a rigid moral authoritarianism. Many students rejected this type of life and desired an existence filled with meaning. They emphasized a return to nature, feeling over thinking, doing over reflection. Just do it. There was also a strong nationalistic sentiment among these young people, as they romanticized the German peasantry as living harmoniously with their natural environment. The German youth movement stressed returning to the life of the people, the fusion of young Germans with a mythic past, and the merging of the soul with natural surroundings.

Many professors were sympathetic to this movement, advocating its goals and taking strong nationalistic positions in classrooms. Essentially, they told their students what to believe and how to live. This trend worried Weber greatly, as he saw it as a fundamental abdication of the professor's duty to be objective. On a more practical level, he feared that the German state might close down the universities to prevent their politicization. He had little use for the German youth movement. Weber's criticisms of the movement proved prophetic, as it was later coopted by the Nazis. Both stressed a desire for a strong, emotional community, the search for a mythic German past, and the superiority of experience over intellect.[60]

Weber views modern politics as invariably tied to rationalization. In democracies the bureaucratization of political parties is the rule. Often politicians offer patronage to their supporters, which encourages a party machinery. Parties demand a party organization to attain and maintain power. Weber views politics as giving leaders a feeling of power over others and of influencing historically significant events, and he develops a characteristically cynical view of political life. He writes, "Only he has the calling for politics who is sure that he shall not crumble when the world from his point of view is too stupid or too base for what he wants to offer."[61]

Politicians are involved in struggles over beliefs and values. For Weber, a good politician passionately believes in her cause. Yet a good politician must balance this passion with a strong sense of responsibility and an understanding of proportion. She should not worship power, but use it for a just cause. A politician should have the "ability to let realities work upon him with inner concentration and calmness. Hence his distance to things and men."[62] An irresponsible politician appeals to voters' emotions and often becomes vain in her search for power. She lacks objectivity, becoming more concerned with the impressions and effects of her actions than with causes. Weber writes that such a politician aims for "the glamorous semblance of power rather than for actual power,"[63] which is reminiscent of much of the symbolic posturing that occurs in politics today.

A politician is constantly faced with warring values and must decide on the appropriate course of action. He or she simply faces in a more acute manner the ethical dilemmas that are distinctive to modernity. Weber distinguishes the ethic of ultimate ends (or the ethics of conviction) from the ethic of responsibility. The ethic of ultimate ends abolishes distinctions between means and ends, views actions as inherently right or wrong, and does not worry about consequences. An example of the ethic of ultimate ends is the Christian who "does rightly and leaves the results to the Lord."

This is reminiscent of Kant's categorical imperative, as one should only do those acts which she believes everyone else should do. Weber contrasts the ethic of ultimate ends with the ethic of responsibility, in which the politician gives an account of the foreseeable consequences of her actions and takes responsibility for them. There are dangers in both ethics: the ethic of conviction may have disastrous consequences by failing to calculate the effects of actions, while the ethic of responsibility can degenerate into unprincipled pragmatism.[64] This is a perennial dilemma for politicians.

Certain social conditions must be in place for strong democratic political leaders to emerge. Weber, though initially reluctant to support a democratic parliamentary system, became a convert during the years of World War I. Though he believes that democracies tend to promote demagogues, he views parliament as a way to control the political leader's power by establishing legal safeguards and determining peaceful means of political succession. Parliament is a training ground for leaders, who learn the politics of compromise and responsibility.[65] However, Germany, like Russia, had trouble creating a strong parliament. Weber traces this problem in Germany to Bismarck's autocratic legacy, but other factors were at work. Because Germany, like Russia, industrialized comparatively late, it lacked a strong middle class. The Russian Orthodox Church and Lutheranism were religious traditions that promoted conformity. Liberal democratic ideas did not develop in Russia because there was no social group to carry them forward.[66]

Weber is also interested in the cultural dimension of democratic life. Democracy and freedom depend on much more than material conditions. He states that democracy and freedom "are in fact only possible if they are supported by the permanent, determined *will* of a nation not to be governed like a flock of sheep."[67] A strong democratic nation is based on informed popular sovereignty. It must be "a nation of masters – and only such a nation can and may engage in world politics."[68] People must become capable of making good, rational, informed decisions if any form of popular sovereignty is to succeed. Weber ties the capacity to act in a politically mature manner to ethics, for he sees the importance of leaders, as well as citizens, developing qualities of judgment and the capacity to appraise historical events and political problems. Weber distrusts eternal, transhistorical laws because they do away with the necessity of good judgment in both public and private life, which are based on knowledge of oneself and one's circumstances. Such judgment is invariably tied to particular social and historical contexts. The major achievements of democracy, such as constitutions and a belief in human rights, depend on cultivating a common capacity to rule. Their political and social institutions must teach a democratic people how to exercise "sober judgment."[69]

For Weber, social sciences such as economics or sociology should be "concerned above all else with the *quality of the human beings* reared under those economic and social conditions of existence."[70] A good democracy requires good citizens collectively exercising their judgment in a public sphere.

Colonialism

Weber limits his arguments about democracy to the European context. He contends that a major criterion for mature political leaders was their recognition of the importance of overseas expansion.[71] There is no doubt that Weber was sometimes guilty of an "Orientalist" perspective, as he sometimes evaluated non-Western societies in terms of the Western model. Recent research has shown that all peoples possess logical thought and systematic ways of thinking, and the preconditions for capitalism were present in many different areas of the world.[72]

Weber sometimes collapses irrationality and non-modern peoples into one category. He has a strong sense of the ways that irrationality could influence seemingly rational processes, as in his studies of religious asceticism and the importance of guilt in religious belief systems. For Weber, the experience of the irrational always exists, demonstrated in the rise of charismatic leaders from time to time who inject mystery into everyday life. Yet Weber, too, moves from viewing irrationality as a category outside of reason to implicitly defining social groups and cultures in terms of irrationality. The East is defined with reference to the rationality of the West. Weber's first sentence in *The Protestant Ethic* demonstrates this bias:

> A product of modern European civilization, studying any problem of universal history, is bound to ask himself to what combination of circumstances the fact should be attributed that in Western civilization, and in Western civilization only, cultural phenomena have appeared which (as we like to think) lie in a line of development having universal significance and value.[73]

The East lacks the history, beliefs, and the like which allowed Western capitalism to flourish. Despite Weber's critical comments about rationalization, he largely understands non-Western cultures through its categories. They have little capacity for agency.

Weber argues that the combination of cities, private property, democracy, rational law, and natural science provided the West with unique features, leading to capitalism. But technology and science flourished in Chinese and Islamic cultures, though they were patrimonial and bureaucratic societies. Science was often tied to magical beliefs in those societies, rather than to a rational, disenchanting worldview. Bryan Turner argues that science and technology are frequently a response to particular ad hoc needs of various societies, such as irrigation or navigation, rather than part of some larger overall systematic worldview.[74]

Turner also contends that Weber does not recognize that the social conditions of Islam were not all that different from those characterizing Puritanism. Islam was largely an urban religion based on trade, not centered in the warrior class as Weber argues. Islam had many of the prerequisites that could have led it in a capitalist direction. Weber especially neglects how Islam was shaped by its interaction with Western colonialism, inhibiting its autonomous development.[75] While Weber ties religious traditions to political and economic factors, he does not discuss colonialism in any depth. This is a major problem with his analysis, as all worldviews during this time of European colonialism were influenced by imperialism, such as the meeting of Islam and the West. Indeed, Weber supported an expansionist, imperialistic German state throughout his life.

Yet there are difficulties in tying Weber's perspective too closely to Orientalism. In Weber's discussion of religion and rationalization it is not always clear whether he is exploring an unfolding historical logic that determines differences between the West and the rest of the world – something akin to Marx's theory of history – or whether he sees rationalization as the product of local, historically specific struggles. The latter perspective would allow rationalization to take different forms in different areas.[76] Rather than positing rationalization as some inevitable universal process, sometimes Weber seems to argue that rationalization has no singular logic, that it is bound up with particular groups, social forces, and social relations that are local and historically specific. Thus, rationalization means different things in different cultures; and it may be able to be reversed or stopped in some instances.

Weber is cautious about generalizing about an inevitable historical logic. He is aware of the singularity of the religious traditions he examines. Thus, he states that for purposes of comparative study the "rich contrasts which have been alive in individual religions . . . must be left aside."[77] In his words, "By the terminology suggested here, we do not wish to force schematically the infinite and multifarious historical life, but simply to create concepts useful for special purposes and for orientation."[78] Weber shows that Western capitalism and its associated religious traditions are one form of civilization among many others.

Further, Weber sees Western rationality as infused with irrational and destructive elements, culminating in a bureaucratized world without meaning, almost a perfect example of the disciplinary society outlined by Foucault. Such a society for Weber is by no means inherently better than others, or superior to other historical eras. Speaking of Western humankind, especially the bureaucrat, Weber quotes the famous writer Goethe (1749–1832):

"Specialists without spirit, sensualists without heart: this nullity imagines that it has attained a level of civilization never before achieved."[79]

Weber: An Assessment

The German sociologist Jürgen Habermas thinks that Weber's discussion of "the paradoxes of rationalization is still the best key to a philosophically and scientifically informed diagnosis of our time."[80] I agree with much of Habermas's assessment. The paradoxes of rationalization are not lost on Weber. Weber sees distinctive ethical dilemmas for contemporary individuals, exemplified in the tension between an ethics of responsibility and an ethics of conviction. He is also a cultural relativist, for he thinks that science cannot decide what values people should follow, that our belief systems cannot be based on any ultimate truth. In the contemporary world it seems as if there is a surfeit of competing belief systems, or warring gods. As the French sociologist Alain Touraine argues, assertions of cultural or religious fundamentalism, the idea that an authentic culture is being undermined by Western modernity and rationalization, occur throughout the world. This conflict between fundamentalism and rationalization may be the most potent and enduring problem of the twenty-first century.[81]

Rationalization is indeed paradoxical. It promotes principled reasoning, so that people can discuss and debate issues in terms of rational principles which apply to everyone, regardless of race, social position, or gender, and not engage in harangues based on emotional or traditional worldviews. Such a perspective is necessary for a functioning democracy, for it promotes dialogue and mutual understanding. Democracy must be based on reasoning from conviction rather than from emotion. This allows political decision making to be accountable, and rights and obligations specified, while being subject to continuous rational monitoring. Such a strong democracy allows non-violent distinctions between the criminal and the political to be drawn.[82]

Yet it is clear that rationalization also contributes to the disciplinary society. Weber's vision can easily be assimilated to Foucault's, for the control of our own bodies and personalities, grounded in the rise of the Protestant ethic, is the reflection of a society based on surveillance and subtle forms of domination. Knowledge becomes tied to power, resulting in rules and regulations which discipline and control people, destroying capacities for autonomy and creativity. Power can never be eliminated from society, as social groups will constantly struggle with one another for social domination.

Weber's analysis of Protestantism not only can be understood as a history of ideas, but also demonstrates new types of discipline and control over the body. Protestantism is part of the rationalization process that includes the rise of monasteries and professional armies. Monasteries introduced new diets which assisted the ascetic control not only of appetite, but of impulses and passions. The army promoted social discipline and bureaucratization. Puritans condemned dance as frivolous, transforming dance and ritual into exercise and discipline. The sociologist Norbert Elias contends that this process is characteristic of civilization, as violent and unpredictable behavior is transformed into restrained and guilt-ridden bodies. Foucault argues that an important component of surveillance is to manage and control the body, to discipline it.[83] Today, everything from exercise to diet has elements of this discipline. Recreational activities are justified as relaxing and the like so that we can return to work renewed and reinvigorated. Work is our *real* life, recreation is in its service.

Anthony Giddens insightfully ties Weber's analysis to the emphasis on economic growth so characteristic of the modern era. For Giddens, industrialization has falsely equated happiness with the creation of wealth. He designates the dominant ethos of the West "productivism," where the primacy of industry creates a social world in which work defines life. Grounded in Weber's theory of the emotionally repressive aspects of the Protestant ethic and "this-worldly asceticism," productivism marginalized other traditions and ways of life as the West developed. In Giddens's words, "Following Weber, productivism can be seen as the ethos in which 'work,' as paid employment, has been separated out in a clear-cut way from other domains of life."[84] Labor, performed by males, means that child-care, emotion-work, and the like become the domain of women in the family, and is rendered invisible in public discourse. Productivism defines a social system in which "mechanisms of economic development substitute for personal growth."[85] This obsessive desire to work and increase production has created ecological problems for society and psychological problems for the workaholic. Not that there is anything inherently wrong with hard work – only when people overdo it and lose sight of why they are working.

Despite these insights, Weber's perspective is limited in many ways. While he supported aspects of women's emancipation in Germany, he did not analyze the ideal of women's domesticity that arose during his era, despite his sensitivity to cultural values. He seems to have taken masculinity and femininity for granted. When people confronted the problem of sustaining strong beliefs in the face of rationalization and disenchantment, Weber's advice was "to bear the fate of the times like a man."[86] Feminism emerged in part to question this dichotomous separation of masculinity and femininity, and the social power that such divisions assume. While Weber sees the Protestant ethic as a key factor in the formation of modern identity, feminism too has opened up the topic of modern self-identity to an unprecedented degree, as it has made people cognizant of the interconnections between personal life and political and social issues.

Weber recognizes the power of non-rational factors, from power to charisma, in motivating behavior. Consequently, his belief in the efficacy of science and reason seems almost world-weary at times, as if they are the best tools available to humans in this disenchanted era. But Weber's sober rationalism and his theory of rationalization still have elements of a moral tale, a story that reflected many taken-for-granted European assumptions of the time, rather than a scientific treatise on society. Ideas of progress, the superiority of the West over the East, and the good middle class versus the irresponsible workers, sometimes creep into his analysis. This is not to say that Weber's sociology was in some fundamental sense wrongheaded; rather, like all of us, his worldview was to some degree shaped by the time in which he lived. There are few if any contemporary scholars who can match the breadth and depth of Weber's analysis, and criticisms of his work must be advanced with caution.

Weber, more than Marx or Durkheim, sees history as a contingent process and focuses on concrete histories and cultures in his historical sociology. He does not advocate a simple evolutionary model, though his ideas about rationalization seem to sometimes suggest such a logic. Weber by no means posited the Puritan as a hero in Western development, as some of his critics charge. As can be seen in the discussion of the rise of a disciplinary society, the Puritan also contributes to an obsessive, overly disciplined personality which is ideal for bureaucracy and social control. Weber is a more postmodern thinker than either Marx or Durkheim. He ties knowledge to power, he recognizes the links between rationality and social control, and he is suspicious of claims that conflicts between social groups can be eradicated in a morally integrated community.

Yet Weber does not recognize the possibility that societies might be able to develop non-religious ethical positions in a secular world. For Weber, rationality disenchants, it undermines strong moral beliefs. Durkheim, as we have seen, puts forward a different and I believe more persuasive argument, that all societies require a moral and sacred center to provide some shared moral beliefs for their citizens.

In addition, Weber does not discuss the complexity of cultural identity, the psyche, and social interaction with as much sophistication as he might. For example, he assumes a command model of bureaucracy, that bureaucracies advance in the modern world because of their inherent technical superiority. But in the contemporary era many bureaucracies are increasingly decentralized, with more fluid models of authority. Further, anyone who has worked in a bureaucracy knows that they are not just technical organizations, but are riveted by politics as bureaucrats attempt to create their own empires. General bureaucratic rules are adapted to local conditions and the personalities of employees, or may be disregarded completely.

Weber does not explore exactly how bureaucratic rules are followed, how a shared sense of what rules mean is developed. These rules are created and sustained in a cultural context, not by isolated individuals who have no connections with one another. People do not follow rules simply out of rote, unthinking action, or through rational calculation, but often base their practices on analogies tied to custom and precedent. Even the most mundane social interaction is different from that which preceded it, and calls for skilled improvisation on the part of people to make sense of it.[87] While Weber calls for the methodological practice of *Verstehen*, the sympathetic understanding of others as a central part of sociological analysis, he does not sufficiently explore the fluid, creative, and contingent aspects of social interaction which escape scientific categories. This fluidity of social action calls for diverse approaches to studying society and the self. People are also often unaware of the factors influencing their actions, from unconscious fears to taken-for-granted ideas about race and gender. These issues of cultural identity, the self, and social interaction are addressed by the theorists discussed in part three of this book.

Notes

1 Jonathan Edwards, "Sinners in the Hands of an Angry God," in *Jonathan Edwards: Basic Writings*, ed. Ola Elizabeth Winslow (New York, 1966), p. 158.

2 Ibid, p. 159.

3 Bryan S. Turner, *Max Weber: From History to Modernity* (London and New York, 1992).

4 Peter Gay, *The Cultivation of Hatred* (New York, 1993), pp. 9–33.

5 E. J. Hobsbawm, *The Age of Empire, 1875–1914* (New York, 1987), p. 59.

6 Eduard Baumgarten, *Max Weber: Werk und Person* (Tübingen, 1964), pp. 504–5.

7 Friedrich Nietzsche, *The Gay Science* (New York, 1974), p. 167.

8 Max Weber, *The Protestant Ethic and the Spirit of Capitalism* (New York, 1976), p. 182.

9 Max Weber, "The Social Psychology of the World Religions," in *From Max Weber: Essays in Sociology*, ed. H. H. Gerth and C. W. Mills (New York, 1958), p. 280.

10 Max Weber, "Science as a Vocation," in *From Max Weber: Essays in Sociology*, ed. H. H. Gerth and C. W. Mills (New York, 1958), p. 152.

11 Max Weber, *The Methodology of the Social Sciences* (New York, 1968), p. 111.

12 Ibid, p. 90.

13 Ibid.

14 Talcott Parsons, *Theories of Society: Foundations of Modern Sociological Theory* (New York, 1961), p. 970; Kenneth H. Tucker, Jr., *Anthony Giddens and Modern Social Theory* (Thousand Oaks, CA, 1998), pp. 128–9.

15 Weber, "The Social Psychology of the World Religions," p. 298.

16 See Weber's famous distinction between science and politics as respective vocations, in "Science as a Vocation" and "Politics as a Vocation," in *From Max Weber: Essays in Sociology*, ed. H. H. Gerth and C. W. Mills (New York, 1958).

17 George Ritzer, *The McDonaldization of Society* (Thousand Oaks, CA, 2000).

18 Turner, *Max Weber*, p. 129.

19 Weber, "The Social Psychology of the World Religions," p. 342.

20 Ibid, p. 341.

21 Anthony Giddens, *Capitalism and Modern Social Theory: An Analysis of the Writings of Marx, Durkheim, and Max Weber* (New York, 1971), p. 169.

22 Weber, "The Social Psychology of the World Religions," pp. 273–81.

23 Ibid, p. 294.

24 Ibid, p. 282.

25 Max Weber, "Religious Rejections of the World and Their Directions," in *From Max Weber: Essays in Sociology*, ed. H. H. Gerth and C. W. Mills (New York, 1958), p. 326.

26 Weber, "The Social Psychology of the World Religions," pp. 275–84.

27 Turner, *Max Weber*, pp. 47–9.

28 See Weber's works, *The Religion of China* (New York, 1951); *Ancient Judaism* (New York, 1952); and *The Religion of India* (New York, 1958).

29 Weber, *The Protestant Ethic*, p. 126.

30 Ibid, p. 51.

31 Ibid, p. 71.

32 Ibid, p. 36.

33 Ibid, p. 79.

34 Ibid, p. 127.

35 Ibid, p. 129.

36 Ibid, p. 112.

37 Ibid, p. 130.

38 Ibid, p. 117.

39 Ibid, p. 126.

40 Ibid, p. 160.

41 Ibid, p. 172.

42 Weber, "The Social Psychology of the World Religions," pp. 284–91.

43 Weber, *The Protestant Ethic*, pp. 181–2.

44 Anthony Giddens and Christopher Pierson, *Conversations with Anthony Giddens: Making Sense of Modernity* (Cambridge, 1998), p. 61.

45 *New York Times Magazine*, November 15, 1998.

46 Weber, "Class, Status, Power," in *From Max Weber: Essays in Sociology*, ed. H. H. Gerth and C. W. Mills (New York, 1958), p. 193.

47 Ibid, p. 187.

48 Ibid, p. 193.

49 Ibid, p. 189.

50 Ibid, p. 190.
51 Barry Barnes, *The Elements of Social Theory* (Princeton, NJ, 1995), pp. 131–2, 138.
52 Weber, "The Social Psychology of the World Religions," pp. 294–300.
53 Max Weber, "Bureaucracy," in *From Max Weber: Essays in Sociology*, ed. H. H. Gerth and C. W. Mills (New York, 1958), p. 214.
54 Ibid, p. 215.
55 Ibid, p. 196.
56 John Keane, *Public Life and Late Capitalism* (New York, 1989), p. 44.
57 Weber, "Bureaucracy," p. 199.
58 Ibid, pp. 181, 202–3.
59 Max Weber, *The Russian Revolutions* (Ithaca, NY, 1995).
60 George Mosse, *The Crisis of German Ideology: Intellectual Origins of the Third Reich* (New York, 1964).
61 Weber, "Politics as a Vocation," p. 128. The dilemma of the ethic of responsibility versus an ethic of conviction is based on Weber's typology of social action, especially the distinction between instrumental and value-rational action. See Max Weber, "Basic Sociological Terms," *Economy and Society* Volume 1 (Berkeley, CA, 1978), pp. 3–63.
62 Weber, "Politics as a Vocation," p. 115.
63 Ibid, p. 116.
64 Ibid, p. 126.
65 Max Weber, "Suffrage and Democracy in Germany," in *Weber: Political Writings*, ed. Peter Lassman and Ronald Speirs (New York, 1994), pp. 220–30.
66 Weber, *The Russian Revolutions*.
67 Max Weber, "On the Situation of Constitutional Democracy in Russia," in *Weber: Political Writings*, ed. Peter Lassman and Ronald Speirs (New York, 1994), p. 69.
68 Weber, "Suffrage and Democracy in Germany," p. 129.
69 William Hennis, *Max Weber: Essays in Reconstruction* (London, 1988), p. 192.
70 Weber, "The Nation State and Economic Policy (Inaugural Lecture)," in *Weber: Political Writings*, ed. Peter Lassman and Ronald Speirs (New York, 1994), p. 15.
71 Ibid, p. 25.
72 Jack Goody, *The East in the West* (New York, 1996).
73 Weber, *The Protestant Ethic*, p. 13.
74 Turner, *Max Weber*, pp. 75–89.
75 Ibid, pp. 51–4.
76 Ibid, p. 130.
77 Weber, "The Social Psychology of the World Religions," p. 294.
78 Ibid, p. 300.
79 Weber, *The Protestant Ethic*, p. 182.
80 Jürgen Habermas, *A Berlin Republic: Writings on Germany* (Lincoln, NE, 1997), p. 60.
81 Alain Touraine, *Can We Live Together? Equal and Different* (forthcoming).
82 Anthony Giddens, *The Transformation of Intimacy: Sexuality, Love, and Eroti-*

cism in Modern Societies (Stanford, CA, 1992), pp. 185–7; Tucker, *Anthony Giddens and Modern Social Theory*, p. 149.

83   Turner, *Max Weber*, pp. 117–26.
84   Anthony Giddens, *Beyond Left and Right: The Future of Radical Politics* (Stanford, CA, 1994), p. 175.
85   Ibid, p. 247.
86   Weber, "Science as a Vocation," p. 155.
87   For an insightful discussion of many of these issues, see Barnes, *The Elements of Social Theory*, pp. 199–202.

PART III

Rethinking and Expanding the Canon

CHAPTER SIX

Freud, Simmel, and Mead: Aesthetics, the Unconscious, and the Fluid Self

In what seems now like ancient history, the ex-US President Bill Clinton had a sexual liaison with an intern, Monica Lewinsky. I want to highlight two aspects of this long drawn-out affair. First, if the scandal had been about, say, money rather than sex, it would not have captured the public's imagination to the extent that it did. Second, while many critics saw Clinton as the devil incarnate, others developed theories about his compulsive womanizing. Many of these theories focused on his childhood, his problems with his parents, the lack of a strong father figure in his life, etc. Several commentators recommended that Clinton seek therapy to deal with these problems. The interest in sexuality, the focus on childhood, and the recommendation of therapy as a solution to individual problems owe much to the work of Sigmund Freud. We live in a post-Freudian world in which his theories about the centrality of sexuality and the importance of childhood in psychological development are taken for granted in European and US culture. We use many of Freud's terms in our daily discourse, albeit in imprecise ways, such as characterizing someone as on an "ego-trip," having a "death-wish," or making a "Freudian slip." We often call querulous people "defensive," or someone obsessed with details "anal." Such language did not exist before Freud.

If our sense of the Clinton–Lewinsky affair is fleeting, television commercials appear and disappear at the speed of light. Let's shift gears and turn to a set of commercials for Gap in 1998–9. During one group of commercials for Gap clothes made of leather, all of the actors dressed in black. Most striking to me was the blank, blasé expression on their faces. Another series of commercials showed young actors joyfully dancing to swing music. What I find interesting in these commercials is the degree to which self-conceptions can shift, especially when tied to a fashion statement. The blasé, cynical countenance of the actors in the one series of commercials is an attitude I find widespread in US urban life, especially among adolescents and young adults. However, the adolescent is then given permission to be wildly happy, as long as it is sanctioned by a Gap ad. While I think the contemporary media can powerfully shape identities, this example also demonstrates that social experiences now have an artistic quality that contributes to how we conceive of ourselves. Such themes – from the analysis of fashion and experience, to the blasé outlook to fluid, artistic, and changing identities and the fleeting nature of modern experience – predate contemporary mass media. They were explored by the sociologist Georg Simmel at the turn of the century.

Now let's turn to a third example. During the 1999 Seattle demonstrations against the World Trade Organization many protesters adopted unusual names, such as the Radical Cheerleaders and the Black-Clad Messengers, and dressed in some pretty wild costumes. Several members of the Humane Society dressed as human butterflies on stilts and cardboard sea turtles, and members of the group Dyke Action marched topless. The "Raging Grannies" performed protest songs in granny outfits.[1] While much of the mainstream media used these examples to trivialize these demonstrations, I think they spotlight a dimension of cultural identity and the public sphere neglected by Marx, Weber, and Durkheim. The Seattle demonstrations brought together disparate groups of feminists, environmentalists, and labor, among others. Social movements now are more manifold and fragmented than in the nineteenth century, with a diversity of groups raising myriad issues in a range of public spheres. Further, the ads discussed above and these demonstrations show that art now intersects with personal experience in myriad ways. The formation of personal and cultural identity is not just a rational process, but involves aesthetic and emotional moments. The artistic and emotional components of identity and social movements have also become part of a variety of contemporary public spheres, which are not just arenas of rational debate but spaces where new identities can be expressed and created. These themes were implicitly addressed by Freud, Simmel, and the American sociologist George Herbert Mead in their theories of the formation of cultural and personal identity. While Freud emphasized the emotional core of the self, Simmel saw aesthetics, deriving from everyday social interaction, as an important ingredient in individual and cultural experience. Mead argued as well that the formation of individual identity had an aesthetic component, though he emphasized the rational dimensions of the self more than did Simmel or Freud.

The fast pace of the early twentieth-century Western world, with its massive technological expansion, a new urban, consumer culture, and a popular press appealing to the masses, contributed to this sense of the innovating, unstable self. For example, the philosopher Henri Bergson critiqued science as stifling the unique life force, the *élan vital*, of human existence, that could not be understood in scientific categories. The rise around 1910 of Post-Impressionist art such as Cubism severed any notion of a simple relationship between the artist and his object of study, as paintings combined a multiplicity of perspectives, implying that the self should be understood in an equally fragmentary way.[2]

Though Durkheim in his theory of collective effervescence and Weber in his studies of charisma document the importance of non-rational elements in social life, neither they nor Marx develop sophisticated theories of personal and cultural identity. The complex process of self-formation in a changing social context is addressed by Simmel and Mead. Freud, too, discusses the difficulty of forming a coherent identity, dissecting the complexity of the psyche. These theorists develop a sophisticated view of the relation of knowledge, culture, and power. Nietzschean themes are especially prominent in Freud and Simmel. Freud shows the complicated interplay of unconscious elements and institutions such as the family in the formation of identity, and the subtle power relations characterizing individual motivation and social interaction. Simmel highlights the fluid and transient nature of much social life, demonstrating how individual identity brings together multiple experiences. It must be created as a work of art; society, too, must be understood aesthetically, for a scientific approach to the study of social life is limited. Mead's thought is influenced more by Darwinism than by Nietzsche. While also discussing the intersection of personal and social identity, he develops a more complex theory of democracy than either Simmel or Freud. Democracy demands the psychological characteristics of flexibility and tolerance, which must be grounded in processes of self-development.

Sigmund Freud

Freud (1856–1939) does not develop nearly as sophisticated a theory of society as do Marx, Weber, and Durkheim, but he explores elements of the psyche neglected by them. He raises fundamental questions about the relationship of the individual to society and the intersection of public and psychic life. He explores the complexity of individual and social identity in ways that demonstrate the centrality of conflict and gender in self-development. While Freud does not author a convincing explanation of social life, he speculates about society as his theories of the psyche becomes more complex.

A very ambitious and somewhat vain man, Freud compared himself to Copernicus and Darwin, who forced people to accept limitations on their sense of uniqueness. Copernicus demonstrated that the earth is not the center of the universe; Darwin showed that humans are not a distinctive species; and Freud argues that conscious mental life does not capture people's real motivations. For Freud, the person is not the master of his psychic house. The image of people as rational, self-interested agents, characteristic of the worldview of the Enlightenment *philosophes*, has been reborn in contemporary economics and some versions of rational-choice sociology. Freud demonstrates the naiveté of such perspectives, for they do not take into account the irrational and unconscious factors animating beliefs and behavior.

Freud was born to a middle-class merchant father and his third wife in Freiburg, Moravia. He moved to Vienna with his family in 1860, where he lived until forced to leave by the Nazis, relocating to Britain in 1938. Freud married Martha Bernays in 1886 and they had six children. One of Freud's daughters, Anna, became a renowned psychoanalyst in her own right. She was analyzed by Freud himself, a bizarre event given the unconscious conflicts between parent and child that lie at the heart of Freud's theories.[3]

An excellent student, Freud developed a taste for science, entering the University of Vienna medical school, where he received his medical degree in 1881. He was interested in biological issues, writing some controversial papers on the medicinal qualities of cocaine as a possible anesthetic for minor operations of the eye (he later repudiated his writings on cocaine, recognizing its dangerous, addictive qualities). Freud became interested in psychology in part because there was more chance for advancement in that field compared to other types of medicine. He studied with the French physician J. M. Charcot (1825–93), who treated mental illness, in Paris from 1885–6. While in Paris, Freud became interested in the causes underlying hysterical behavior. Like many others, such as Charcot, Freud initially searched for biological, physiological explanations of neurotic symptoms. However, by the mid-1890s Freud moved to a purely psychological level of explanation for mental disturbances.

Psychoanalysis arose because Freud was dissatisfied with existing cures for neuroses, which were usually based on some form of electro-shock therapy or hypnosis, which had only short-term benefits. He developed the fundamental basis of psychoanalysis – the "talking cure" through which the patient shares his or her deepest emotions with the therapist – through his work with Dr Joseph Breuer (1842–1925). Breuer stumbled upon the talking cure by listening sympathetically to a female patient's discussion of her problems. She transferred her affections to Breuer, demanding love from him in return. Breuer freaked out at this occurrence, his wife made a scene about the patient, and he broke off therapy, leaving with his spouse for a long vacation. Freud thought that Breuer reacted badly to this situation. He extended these ideas about therapy, developing them into psychoanalysis.

Psychoanalysis

Freud developed his theories in *fin-de-siècle* Vienna. A hypocritical "Victorian" morality ruled the city, as many men of supposedly high, rigid moral principles sought pleasure in sexuality, from prostitutes to adultery. Given this deceitful facade of bourgeois morality it is not surprising that Freud drew on Nietzschean themes. Freud writes that Nietzsche's "guesses and intuitions often agree in the most astonishing way with the laborious findings of psychoanalysis."[4] For Freud, like Nietzsche, people are not a pretty species. We compete and attempt to dominate one another. Knowledge and instincts, ideas and desires and bodies, cannot be separated. People are unaware of the powerful forces at work in their psyches. Rationality is a fragile truth-teller in the face of our unconscious desires. Individuals assume that they are rational, denying their egoism; they do not realize that their behavior masks a will to control and often hurt other people. Freud, like Nietzsche, sees little use for religion; unlike Nietzsche, he believes in the power of science as a gateway to truth.

Freud views unconscious desires connected to sexuality and its repression as the central causal factors in the formation of personal and gender identities. Freud also develops themes of the interplay of the unconscious, desire, and fantasy.

Psychoanalysis introduces three new principles concerning the make-up of the psyche which distinguish it from other psychological theories. First, mental processes are essentially unconscious. Psychic activity not only consists of conscious thinking but fundamentally involves wishing and feeling, which represent unconscious infantile desires that are repressed in adulthood. Second, impulses and instincts, which Freud terms libido, are the elemental drives of the human organism. They are sexual in nature and their repression causes mental disorders. Third, repression is recreated within every generation and every individual. This repression is fragile, however, and the possibility exists that unchecked sexual impulses might shatter individual and even social life. Only the sublimation of libido can prevent social chaos and individual illness. Sublimation refers to the channeling of sexual gratification into socially approved goals. Sublimation is the basis of civilization, as its transformation of sexual instincts has contributed to the highest cultural, artistic, and social achievements of humanity.[5]

Sublimation is a difficult process because people's psychic structure is based on finding pleasure and avoiding pain, which Freud names the pleasure principle. Pleasure involves lowering the amount of stimulation of our psyche through the release of the sexually charged libido, which strives for consummation; it rules the unconscious. The frustration of libido results in neurosis, for an inhibited sexuality becomes more powerful as it is repressed. Freud constructs a tripartite theory of the mind in order to understand these processes, dividing the psyche into the id, ego, and superego. The id is pure libido, controlled by the primal search for pleasure. The superego is the conscience, personified in psychic images of society and parents. A sense of guilt emerges in the superego, which is often irrational, tied to unconscious fears of the loss of parental approval and physical harm. The ego attempts to negotiate between the demands of the pleasure principle of the id and the guilt of the superego. A most delicate mediator, the ego develops a reality principle as it seeks a diminished pleasure in adapting to the needs of reality. Maturity is based on the transition from the pleasure to the reality principle, which requires a rational accounting of desires, adjusting gratification to social demands. Only fantasy eludes the purview of the reality principle.[6]

These ideas inform Freud's famous theory of the Oedipus complex. In order to mature properly and develop an appropriate gender identity, a boy must renounce his desire for his mother and psychically identify with his father. The boy makes this identification because of his fear of the power of the father, especially concerning fantasies about castration by the father. This renunciation of the desire for the mother by the son and the acceptance of the authority of the father is the basis of civilization. It allows libido to be sublimated into socially positive ends such as art and culture. Nevertheless, socialization is not a happy process, for the superego tends to irrationally and viciously punish the ego for imagined moral transgressions, as well as real ones. The path to maturity, exemplified in sublimation, also involves repression, ambivalence about sexuality, and unattainable desires which haunt the person into adulthood. Morality is a kind of self-alienation, as the individual internalizes parental authority while raging against this very authority. The Oedipal complex results in males who develop relatively strong egos and control their emotions. Adulthood means a genitally-centered sexuality, as the pleasures of sexuality turn away from the infant's notion that the entire body is pleasurable. He learns to renunciate his desire for his mother in favor of the future procurement of another female.[7]

Freud does not devote as much reflection to female development. He tends to see females as stunted males who, because they do not undergo the Oedipal transition, do not develop strong egos, have little capacity for holding strong values, and are more emotional and sensual, but more sexually passive, than males. Girls must forsake their attachment to their mother in favor of the father, and eventually they replace their longing to please their father with the desire to have children. Though Freud views the relationship of the infant to the mother as a pivotal one for psychological development, he concentrates on the male-centered drama of the Oedipus complex.

Dreams

People's often contradictory wishes are demonstrated in dreams. Dreams have a meaning, reflecting a distorted version of psychic desires and conflicts. During sleep the ego relaxes, which allows dreaming, which is "the (disguised) fulfillment of a (repressed) wish."[8] In the dream the ego becomes one with the sexual impulse, which has no morality. The libido's striving for pleasure rules the dream. Thus, dreams often express taboo topics, from incest to wishes for revenge and death against those closest to us. Freud states, "Dreams have their origin in actively evil or in excessive sexual desires, which have made both the dream-censorship and dream distortion necessary."[9] Dreams take people back to their earliest repressed memories. Elaborate and intensive interpretation by the therapist is necessary to uncover their meaning underneath their distorted and seemingly incoherent surface.

In his later work, such as *Civilization and Its Discontents*, Freud shifts from a focus on the conflict between id, superego, and the ego to more social and species-wide concerns. He posits a contradiction between the life instinct, or Eros, the desire for unity, and the death instinct, or Thanatos, which wishes to return to a non-organic state. With his version of Thanatos Freud describes a truly independent aggressive instinct which he believes accounts for the prevalence of sadism and masochism in everyday life and the destructive impulses which are released in wars.

Civilization and Its Discontents

Like the poet Schiller (1759–1805), Freud thinks that hunger and love rule the world. Hunger concerns the instincts that preserve the individual; love strives after "objects" (people or symbols, not things) to preserve the species. But such desires are satisfied only episodically. Social life is characterized by pain and suffering, when all people want out of existence is happiness and the avoidance of pain. This pleasure principle rules human desires, for people wish to satisfy their needs, preferably quickly. Yet suffering is the human condition. Freud states that three things make us suffer: our bodies, the natural world, and our relations with other people. This last factor might be the cause of most people's suffering.[10] To paraphrase the philosopher Jean-Paul Sartre, hell is other people.

Civilization is both the source of our frustrations and the means by which we can protect ourselves against suffering. Civilization protects humankind against nature and adjusts people's relations with one another. The decisive step in civilization occurs with the institution of the power of the community over the individual, which allows the principle of justice to become a dominant social value. Civilization promotes sublimation, but it also inhibits demands and desires, for it restricts the individual's instincts.

Freud is interested in "how [civilization] arose, and by what its course has been determined."[11] He sees the origins of civilization as tied to the family, which permits continual genital satisfaction. Love becomes part of family life, for men are unwilling to be separated for long periods of time from women, while females become attached to children. The compulsion to work in the face of a hostile external nature also is important in the emergence of culture.

Sexuality holds the key to civilization. The human community is not based on shared economic or political interests, but on strong, libidinally based identifications, such as the child with the parent, or the people with the leader. Such identifications help channel sexuality in socially approved directions, while simultaneously frustrating its most pleasurable gratifications.

Eros represents this desire to join with others in community. Yet Eros is confronted by Thanatos, which is pure aggression, the "blind fury of destructiveness."[12] This aggression is the greatest impediment to civilization. It is mitigated by the development of guilt within the individual. Guilt arises from the internalization of aggression in the superego, which is a continuation of external authority originating in the father and the community. Guilt occurs when people fear a loss of love resulting from their actions, or even their wishes. The superego is very harsh, however, punishing the individual for even desiring to do something he considers bad. Every element of aggression that is not satisfied feeds the superego, which represents hostility toward oneself rather than others.

The growth of civilization results in a heightening of guilt and a loss of happiness. Freud thinks that this is an unavoidable process, though he does advocate some measures which can mitigate this unhappiness. Freud argues that education should explicitly discuss sexuality, so that children will be aware of the aggression they will face as they grow older. He also contends that the redistribution of wealth can make people's lives better and healthier, though he is far from a socialist. He thinks that Marxists underestimate the hostility and envy that are inevitably part of human nature and that will outlast the demise of capitalism.[13]

Education should be based on scientific principles. Freud thinks that people's best defense against unhappiness and aggression is their rationality, especially science. He argues that people's judgments usually follow from their wishes for happiness, and people support their arguments with illusions. Religion is a good example of this process. It is an illusion founded on wishes which cannot be verified or disproved. Ideas of God result from memories of childhood helplessness, based on the longing for the father by the infant. Religion must be combated, for it makes the intellect weak and does not encourage a realistic education for children. Freud advocates science as a corrective for religion because science is not based on illusions. Science is different from religion because its errors can be criticized and corrected, while illusions can never be corrected. Freud has great faith in reason. He states, "The voice of the intellect is a soft one, but it does not rest till it has gained a hearing."[14]

Freudian analysis has been remarkably influential in some unlikely places. For example, in the 1930s the Frankfurt School turned to Freud in an attempt to develop a more complex view of psychological processes than that found in Marx. Herbert Marcuse, one of the most prominent members of the Frankfurt School, reformulated the conservative reading which Freud gives to his own approach. Marcuse argued that Freud's findings can lead to very different, radical conclusions.

In his 1955 book *Eros and Civilization*, Marcuse contends that Freud's psychological categories can be used to understand the political and social structures of the industrial world. In modern industrial society, images of the commanding superego have shifted from parents to a depersonalized, bureaucratic authority as modern capitalist and industrialist domination solidified into a system of objective administration. Marcuse rethinks Freud's pleasure–reality principle dichotomy in this context. Marcuse develops the concept of surplus repression, or the amount of sexual repression over and above what is necessary for the survival of a given society. Akin to Marx's notion of surplus value, Marcuse argues that the amount of libido directed toward Eros and/or Thanatos varies according to the structure of society. Some societies require or demand more repression than is necessary. Marcuse believes that most repression is unnecessary and thus is surplus repression. Divergent societies demand varied levels of repression, but these differences are the result of social factors such as the control and distribution of social power, rather than biological necessities.[15]

Marcuse associates the Protestant ethic with the increases of guilt around the expression of sexuality, while also making procreation its most important function. This denial of sexuality is also a repression of life-affirming Eros; any decline in Eros necessarily produces an increase in the death instinct, Thanatos. Such an expansion in Thanatos is mainly responsible for the massive destructiveness of modern civilizations. Freeing sexuality from its repressive context will contribute to a more emancipated society.

In a later book, *One Dimensional Man*, Marcuse is more pessimistic about the liberatory potential of a freed sexuality. He states that through such mechanisms as advertising, capitalism had integrated sexuality into its very practices. Yet this is not an emancipatory development, as sexuality becomes commodified, something packaged by the mass media for public consumption, and reinforces the status quo. This version of sexuality is no longer critical, as it confirms rather than subverts the present society.

Marxists have continued to draw on Freud for inspiration, but perhaps the most interesting legacy of Freudianism concerns its influence in feminist studies. At first glance, Freud seems to be a very poor candidate for feminist analysis. However, Freud's theories of gender development, the repression of sexuality, and the centrality of children's identification with adults have played a pivotal role in feminist and other critical analyses of gender, leading to reformulations of Freud's perspective which achieve new, radical theoretical insights far from the master's own conservative conclusions.

For example, the contemporary sociologist Nancy Chodorow believes that Freud largely captures the socialization process for males. However, he misunderstands the ways that females realize a gender identity. Chodorow views the pre-Oedipal phase of childhood (the infant's relationship to the mother) as the crucial time and space of psychological development. Gender identity is rooted in the relationship to the mother because of the structure of most families, in which mothers usually have responsibility for child-rearing. Because girls never have to break away from their mother and repress their relationship with her as do boys, they are more capable of nurturing and develop more complex inner lives than do boys. Such feminine qualities are not recognized as valuable in many institutions, from the state to the economy.[16]

Judith Butler's postmodern feminism also draws on Freudian themes. Butler contends that psychological development is not a continuous and harmonious process, but is characterized by radical breaks and conflicts that fragment the psyche. To the extent that children create a unified sense of self it is based on the repression of very different and often conflicting identifications with different people, such as parents.[17] Butler substitutes the idea of fantasy identifications for the concrete identifications with the mother and the father on which so much psychological theory is based. For Butler, we identify with fantasies about the mother and father rather than with their reality, which we can never know. But fantasies do not produce a deep sense of a male or female self, only the illusion of one. To the degree that gender exists, it is because we repeatedly act in gendered ways which are socially reinforced, as in the images of men and women given to us by the mass media, especially in our bodily actions through fashion, deportment, speech, and the like.

We thus conceive our identities mythically, through fantasy – and in doing so, we believe that we truly express a male or female gender. Gendered personalities are tied to social power, for ideals of men and women "are embodied in dominant cultural representations and social practices."[18] Men act and dress in a particular, predictable manner; so do women. But there is no biological basis for these gendered ways of acting, according to Butler. She views crossdressing as a performance which breaks such stereotypes and shows gender identities to be socially constructed and fabricated.

It is amusing to imagine Freud returning today and seeing feminists use his work to advocate dressing in drag. While I think that many of the criticisms of Freud advanced throughout the years are valid – from his sexism, to the faulty empirical base which informs psychoanalysis, to his simple dichotomy of science and religion – I wish to defend Freud. I think many of Freud's arguments are still very important, and not only as a contribution to interesting versions of feminism. Freud exposes the limits of the rational-agent model so prominent in many of the social sciences, such as economics. He argues that people maintain the illusion that they are autonomous individuals who understand the reasons for their actions. For Freud, this is a psychologically naive point of view. There is no unified, consistent self, as the psyche is wracked by conflicts and identity is profoundly influenced by the unconscious. People are often not truly interacting with others in a conscious way, but projecting childhood behaviors onto others. They must do much painful psychic work to get past the deceptions governing their lives. While we might over-indulge the therapeutic impulse in the contemporary West, seeing therapy as a solution to all individual problems, the sobering worldview of psychoanalysis is a welcome antidote to the "don't worry, be happy" tendencies of our civilization.

Freud shows that people are emotional creatures as well as rational ones; that gender development is a complex and contradictory psychological process; and that sadism, masochism, and guilt haunt human civilization. The unfortunate truth of his observations have been seen in the massive human toll taken in wars throughout the twentieth century, and the continuing horrors of genocides from Bosnia to Rwanda. Freud is indeed still our contemporary, but for our purposes his theoretical approach has to be complemented by a more complex understanding of the dynamics of social interaction and society. We now turn to Simmel and Mead for a more sociological version of the psyche and identity.

Georg Simmel

Simmel (1858–1918) has received a sympathetic reception in contemporary reinterpretations of the canon. Anthony Giddens states that if he were to rewrite his classic book on Marx, Weber, and Durkheim, *Capitalism and Modern Social Theory*, he would include Simmel.[19] However, it is not clear how these new interpretations would make use of Simmel, as he seems to be merely added on to the more central narrative constructed around Marx, Weber, and Durkheim.

Simmel is often understood as a forerunner of structuralist sociological theory, for he analyzed abstract forms or structures of social interaction, investigating the invariant components of social processes such as conflict, play, and reciprocity. I think Simmel is better understood as a theorist of the complex interplay of cultural and social identity in modernity, and the importance of aesthetics in this process. Simmel raises fundamental questions about the limitations of science in understanding social life that, while similar to Weber's arguments, move beyond them. He also raises questions about the connection of gender and knowledge in a more direct way than the other theorists we have so far considered.

Simmel's Life and Intellectual Context

Simmel led a difficult life. He was not a revolutionary like Marx, nor a successful professor like Weber or Durkheim, or a founder of a school of thought and practice like Freud. Only at the end of his life did he receive a position in philosophy at the University of Strasbourg. He faced anti-Semitism in the German academy throughout his career, and his socialist sympathies and unorthodox ideas also made him suspect to the conservative German university system. Simmel made his living as a kind of itinerant speaker and scholar, well known for his provocative lectures and writings. He allowed women to attend his classes at a time when they were barred from universities as regular students. He interacted with a remarkable group of colleagues outside of the academy, such as Max Weber, the sculptor Auguste Rodin (1840–1917), the poet Stefan Georg (1868–1933), and the philosopher Henri Bergson, all of whom provided him with intellectual sustenance. He taught the famous Marxist philosophers Georg Lukács (1885–1971) and Ernst Bloch (1885–1977), and the sociologist Karl Mannheim (1893–1947), who would develop the sociology of knowledge.

A variety of intellectual perspectives influenced Simmel's theories. Like Marx, he argues that capitalism creates a culture of buying and selling that extends beyond the economy, reducing differences in quality to the same quantitative measure, money. Simmel's greatest intellectual debts are to the philosophers Kant and Nietzsche. His ideas about objective and subjective forms derive directly from Kantian philosophy. Somewhat like Kant's ideas of the categories of the mind, these forms interpret experience and organize knowledge. But for Simmel they are not eternal frames of perception, but develop over time.

He is also critical of many other tenets of Kantian philosophy. According to Simmel, Kant introduces a completely abstract and intellectual approach to the understanding of nature and humankind. Remember that for Kant both of these realms are governed by *a priori* laws of perception, which frame our experience. The natural world is determined by mathematical laws that can be precisely determined, while society functions according to its own immanent laws, such as the categorical imperative that one should only act according to rules that can be applied to everyone. Simmel thinks that Kant's reliance on laws, whether for nature or humankind, cannot grasp how people actually experience the world. Kant's approach is a "logical fanaticism which attempts to impose the form of mathematical clarity and precision upon the totality of life."[20] This type of hyper-intellectual approach to nature and humankind has dominated Western thought since the seventeenth century, manifested particularly in the cultural esteem accorded to scientific thinking. But this perspective violates the diversity of life, forcing all of social and natural life into lawlike categories. Simmel criticizes the costs associated with the dominance of this kind of science: art is not recognized as a valid approach to understanding society and the individual; the specific contributions of women to culture are hidden under the guise of scientific objectivity.[21]

To correct Kantian hyper-intellectualism Simmel turns to many Nietzschean themes, from the decline of absolute values to the fragmentation of personality. Like Nietzsche, he celebrates the diversity of life and recognizes the limits of any absolute perspective on nature and society, such as science.[22] Simmel critiques many of the assumptions characteristic of the sociological canon using Nietzschean arguments. He contends that there can be no simple positivist science of society, and that there are no secure philosophical foundations which guarantee an unproblematic understanding of the fluid and ever-changing social reality in which we live. Simmel shows that an aesthetic sensibility and a fluid, protean self are primary features of modernity that need to be central components of any account of its development. Simmel moves beyond Nietzsche in his understanding of the complexity of social relations, which cannot be reduced to the will to power. His arguments about sociability, art as form, and the different personality types in modernity, which will be discussed below, demonstrate a sociological acuity and profundity that is lacking in Nietzsche.

Simmel is interested in the transformations of culture brought about by capitalism and urbanism. He senses that a new culture has been created in the West which breaks with the traditions of the past yet lacks a secure philosophical foundation to encounter the future. His impression that contemporary societies are in flux gives Simmel's work an artistic flavor, somewhat like Nietzsche's. Aesthetic themes play a large role in his writings. Simmel's sociology approaches social life as if it were a work of art to be deciphered through multiple perspectives.[23]

Objective and Subjective Culture and Alienation

In a manner reminiscent of Marx, Simmel states that a kind of alienation characterizes modern culture, exemplified in the distinction between objective and subjective culture. Like Marx, Weber, and Durkheim, Simmel views specialization as a key component of modernity. He locates specialization in culture as well as the economy. Specialization characterizes all different types of culture, from art to philosophy to science, and they become increasingly complex. For example, as science becomes more complicated, it is more difficult for the layperson to understand. These specialized ways of understanding develop into objective forms, which emerge from biological needs and pragmatic interests, but soon take on a life of their own. Humans create activities which become autonomous from social interaction and are then used to understand and interpret it. There are many different forms, from physics to art to sociology, that emerge from our social practices, develop independently over time, and provide the lenses through which we interpret experience. These forms allow humankind to consciously shape society according to standards such as beauty and science, rather than just reacting automatically to natural needs and desires.[24]

These forms of cultural knowledge owe their longevity to their links with human associations and institutions, such as universities and colleges, the state, churches, etc. These different forms, like art and the social sciences, provide the resources for the development of subjective culture. Subjective culture is the cultural life of the individual, how she draws on objective culture in her everyday experience. As societies become more specialized, cultural forms are increasingly available to everyone. Subjective culture is "the measure of development of persons thus attained" through their use of objective forms.[25] However, as art, science, and other objective forms become more complex they develop independently of people's use, and a widening gap between objective and subjective culture occurs.[26] Culture becomes too specialized, or it develops into mass culture, providing everyone with the same mediocre products.

Simmel ties these problems to the rise of a money economy associated with capitalism. He concentrates on the cultural and psychological aspects of capitalism, rather than focusing on class relations, bureaucracy, and the like. The division of labor engenders mass production, which creates standardized cultural products. As production becomes uniform, so does consumption, and individuality becomes increasingly precarious. Money exemplifies these processes. For Simmel, money embodies constant movement and change. It provides a similar standard for all exchanges, reducing the scope of individuality and subjective culture.[27] Money, originally a means to acquire goods, becomes an end in itself, destroying all other values. For Simmel, the predominance of money encourages the domination of objective over subjective culture. People may have less ability to create a distinctive individuality from objective forms, as society appears more and more as an alien entity outside of their control. The dominance of money encourages a "blasé attitude" toward things and people, for everything can be bought and sold, nothing is special, and "the question of what something is worth is increasingly displaced by the question of how much it is worth."[28] A world-weary, "I've seen it all before" demeanor becomes the norm. This notion of alienation ties Simmel to Marx, Weber, and Nietzsche, who in different ways see culture and society frustrating the expression of individuality.

What I find distinctive about Simmel's interpretation of the "tragedy of modern culture" is his refusal to argue that this conflict will be overcome through some sort of dialectical synthesis, as does Marx in his vision of communism, or to posit a nostalgia for a return to a more simple time, as sometimes occurs in Weber's work. For Simmel, mass culture can crush individuality, but simultaneously possibilities for individual creativity expand with modernity.[29] If the old type of well-rounded, Renaissance individual is no longer possible in the modern world, a new type of fragmented, fluid personality arises that resembles a Picasso Cubist painting more than a classical Rembrandt. Simmel describes some of these new personality "types" of modernity, from the adventurer, to the stranger, to the follower of fashion. He respects the independence of these different types of social experience. His famous analysis of the stranger focuses on the distinctive experience of marginal groups and individuals. Strangers are often stereotyped, not perceived as individuals but as a group "of alien origin."[30] Yet the position of marginality gives the stranger some objective insights into the dominant culture that its indigenous members do not possess. She can see how the governing culture can marginalize the ideas of those who are different. Though concentrating on European Jewry, Simmel's argument can be applied to all those excluded by a dominant culture – racial and ethnic minorities, and women, for example – although Simmel did not develop this line of argument.

Many of the types that Simmel discusses emerge in the context of urbanism. He views changes in social space as a key dimension of modernity, focusing on the city rather than the industrial enterprise as the central modern institution.[31] Urban life requires different qualities than the small town, for it is constantly in motion and social interactions are often fleeting. People develop a blasé and cynical attitude in the context of this perpetual transformation. The attempt to mark one's individuality is increasingly difficult in urban life. People become fascinated with fashion in this context. Fashion arises in modern urban life because of its constant change and "accentuation of the present," as old authorities lose their power to dictate dress and behavior.[32] Fashion paradoxically allows one to conform to a group, while concurrently expressing one's individuality. It is based on imitation and demarcation simultaneously.

The idea of the adventure, like fashion, is a modern phenomenon. It is much like art, giving people a sense of a different and heightened experience. The adventure is one of "the great forms in which we shape the substance of life" and experience the interplay "between chance and necessity."[33] The adventure represents a continual quest for stimulation, a search for intensity and a heightening of consciousness, which are basic features of modern life, as in the popularity of extreme sports and trekking today.

Knowledge, the Self, and Art

Simmel, like Nietzsche, critiques the theory that concepts reflect reality in a simple way. Like Weber, Simmel contends that historical narratives invariably reflect a particular way of understanding human experience. They are not an objective recollection of facts. The temperament and point of view of the historian, like that of the philosopher or artist, influences his or her understanding of the past. They are "attitudes of mankind with regard to being," form-giving explanations of society and nature.[34] The study of history is rooted in the understanding of the past in order to illuminate significant events in everyday life.

Simmel's notion of the boundary represents this idea well. Humankind is always caught between determinism and richness because people themselves are fluid, changing boundaries. These borders make our lives paradoxical, for we are bounded and unbounded simultaneously. The border is like a shimmering reflection in a pond, its edges indistinct as it emerges and fades quickly. In Simmel's words, "we live continually in a border region which belongs as much to the future as to the present."[35] Life continually transforms itself into something new. It can only be understood by a social science that is flexible and tolerant of play and difference, more like an art than a natural science. Simmel states: "Life is at once flux without pause and yet something enclosed in bearers and contents, formed about midpoints, individualized, and therefore always a bounded form which continually jumps its bounds."[36] Personal identities are fluid and multiple.

There is no single overarching principle, such as Marxian class analysis, that can capture this flux of life. Simmel states that many different perspectives can effectively interpret the multiplicity of reality, from art to sociology, each accurate in its own way. The best type of sociology focuses on the complex experience of modernity, as in his essay "The Metropolis and Modern Life," and the different modern personality types, as Simmel does in his examinations of the adventurer, stranger, and other types that I discussed earlier.[37]

This focus on multiplicity informs Simmel's idea of the self, for these different personality types are not essences but manifold aspects of the individual. Like Nietzsche, Simmel sees human experience as fragmented and poetic, as the self develops in a creative fashion while crosscut by different expectations and conflicts.[38] The self is inseparable from these dimensions of creativity and flux. Simmel states that the "freedom of the human spirit" is found in its "form-giving creativity,"[39] which is multiple and changing. In his words, "Man . . . is a manifold being, which means that his relation to things is presented in the multiplicity of modes of perception in each individual, in the entanglement of each individual in more than just a single series of interests and concepts, or images and meanings."[40] Humankind, "the indirect being," must achieve a provisional unity of the self that is not given by any pre-existing essence.[41] The self is like an unplanned medieval city with many independent neighborhoods and indirect passages. There is no strong central government dictating its actions.[42]

In many ways the self resembles a work of art. Art like the self expresses but does not resolve the complex contradictions of existence, for its joy lies in its display of "the world as it is, that there is no obscure, obdurate, and unresolved reality beyond the dreamy play of phenomena, and that it [art] expresses reality at its most real, the specific and the basic essence of things and of life simultaneously." Art shapes our worldview, like language, rather than just representing it, just as the self must create a provisional psychological coherence among the individual's many different psychological tendencies and experiences. Art poses problems but does not resolve them simply, showing "those problems in their purity and . . . that they are insoluble."[43] It heightens our emotions and intellect, as when listening to a beautiful piece of music, and at its best encourages us to see the world in a new way. For Simmel, as for Nietzsche, art represents a kind of integration of human experience, the ugly and the beautiful fashioned together into a new vision of life's possibilities. Such imagery can also be applied to the self, which must integrate each individual's experience of the good, the bad, and the ugly. The self does so like a symphony conductor orchestrating a multiplicity of sounds into a coherent yet flowing melody.

Sociability

Art provides clues not only to the nature of the self but to social interaction. Impulses to art and play are enacted in society. Simmel discusses sociability as a form of social interaction involving activities such as competition and the proving of mental and physical abilities, as "the play form of association."[44] People engage in sociability for its pure satisfaction, for the "joy, relief, vivacity" it brings.[45] It is a free form of interaction where topics can change quickly because of their accidental character and lack of purpose. Sociability as play resembles the free movement of art, that complex process of distance and heightening that captures the best aesthetic experiences. Simmel writes:

> All sociability is but a symbol of life, as it shows itself in the flow of a lightly amusing play; but, even so, a symbol of *life*, whose likeness it only so far alters as is required by the distance from it gained in the play, exactly as also the freest and most fantastic art, the furthest from all reality, nourishes itself from a deep and true relation to reality, if it is not to be empty and lying.[46]

Much social interaction is like this – it is not rational, but aesthetic and playful. Sociation, from flirting to joking, develops and changes according to its own momentum and content, depending on circumstances. Simmel argues that there should be no standards outside of the sociable experience itself which should determine its content. Sociability differs between social groups and no one ideal of sociability should be imposed on all of them.[47]

I think that Simmel's view of sociability demonstrates that morality and social power are linked. If sociability is tied to its own internal standards, norms originating outside of it from another social group, whether aesthetic or moral, are illegitimate. Like Nietzsche, Simmel fears that moral judgments should not be shifted from one group to another where they are not appropriate. In his discussion of the poor Simmel sounds a Nietzschean note, stating that giving on the part of the wealthy often occurs for the selfish reason of feeling good about oneself, and creates resentment among the poor.[48] However, Simmel's approach raises some problems. What if social groups develop their own internal norms which disregard human rights, that are racist and sexist, for example? Simmel has no good answer for this possibility.

Gender

Some of Simmel's most interesting observations concern gender and culture, though sometimes he seems trite in his generalizations about men and women. He argues that women have been denied access to culture throughout history, for culture has been created and controlled by men. It is a misnomer to discuss "human culture," for culture is almost exclusively masculine. But Simmel is not so much interested in opening up male culture to women as in exploring whether women can create a distinctive culture of their own. He thinks that they can. Much of his argument rests on the notion that men and women inhabit different worlds and develop different "natures." As we saw in chapter 2, the idea of rational, public man and emotional, private woman, each with their own special nature, was widespread in *fin-de-siècle* Europe. Simmel does not escape this ambience, but develops some of these points in provocative directions.

Simmel states that the division of labor is more congruent with the "nature" of the male than the female, for men are able to specialize and create objective works which become separate from them. Women's nature, on the other hand, involves a "lack of differentiation" and "self-contained uniformity."[49] They have a more integrated nature, their ego and activity are more fused than those of males, and their psyches are more harmonious than men's.[50] Women's major achievements have been in the home, for it allows them to create an integrated cultural and social space.

While this sounds like typical stereotypical descriptions of women and men, Simmel argues that females cannot be evaluated according to male criteria. Men and women must be understood as "two existential totalities, each structured according to a completely autonomous rule."[51] Males have dominated culture by determining how the creation of cultural forms, the realization of objectivity, will take place.

Women can create a different sense of justice, morality, and knowledge than men. Simmel points to the physician, and his example has a contemporary ring. He argues that female doctors will be able to "empathize with the condition of the patient" much more than men. Through examining the feelings of the patient as well as his or her somatic symptoms a better diagnosis of illness will take place.[52] This is becoming the case in medicine, as more and more MDs recognize that the mind and body cannot be easily separated when understanding illness.

According to Simmel, women might develop a new approach to history which rejects a positivist history based on the idea "that things be photographed by ideas."[53] A female way of understanding, based on analogies, interpolations, and empathic feeling for others in the past, is actually more true to history than the old narrative, fact-based history. There are a number of psychological frames that can interpret history, none necessarily more true than another, and women might be able to develop a distinctive type of sensitive, historical knowledge.[54]

Simmel states that "a new continent of culture" might be discovered if women have a chance to develop their capacities.[55] Women should not desire to be like men, but look to create a novel culture, after which a "new synthesis – an objective culture enriched with the nuance of the female – could develop beyond this state."[56] Male and female cultures would be equivalent but follow two different rhythms, a male dualistic culture and a holistic female one. In sum, women can "possess their own world, which, from its very fundamentals, is incomparable with the world of the male."[57]

Simmel's work clearly replicates the assumptions about males and females of his time. He also has no sophisticated analysis of the ways in which men control social institutions and produce gendered forms of knowledge. Yet his arguments demonstrate that power and knowledge are related to one another, for in his view male culture has subjugated female culture throughout history. Many of his arguments intersect with feminist arguments about the two cultures, associated with Nancy Chodorow, mentioned earlier. Simmel attempts to show that so-called human culture is really male culture, hidden behind the guise of objectivity. This culture is not the end-all and be-all of knowledge. Indeed, it has come to a universal position because of its repression of alternative ways of understanding the world associated with women. A new objective culture would look very different from the current male-based one and require fundamental changes in the way people think about knowledge. It would require a recognition and respect for different points of view, a sensitivity to context and emotions. It would take empathy and aesthetic sensibilities seriously as ways of knowing on a par with conventional science. Such changes are occurring in all aspects of European and US society today, from sociology to medicine, as women reflect on their systematic exclusion from the social and natural sciences as they move into positions of power.

Much like Foucault, Simmel's discussion of gender implicitly demonstrates that power and knowledge cannot be separated, for the social power of men has denied the autonomy of women's culture. An alternative multiculturalism could develop in this context, which takes into account different ways of knowing and experiencing the world. Simmel also views art as a way of knowing and a good metaphor for understanding the complexity of the modern self and society. For Simmel, modern identities are continually changing. He grasps this process in its fluidity, unlike the more static approaches of Marx, Weber, and Durkheim. His work calls for a sociological methodology which approaches social life as if it were a literary text, encouraging the sociologist to exercise her imagination in understanding society. Simmel does not search for the invariant laws of social life. He realizes that science is limited in what it can tell us, and advocates a diversity of approaches to understanding the complexity of social life. His version of social science intersects with many of the postmodern themes of our current *Zeitgeist*.

Although Simmel does not discuss colonialism his ideas about the stranger are interesting in this context, for the stranger exemplifies the experience of marginality from a dominant culture which many minority cultures experience throughout the world. Simmel does not address issues of democracy, though he implicitly advocates open and multiple public spheres that promote dialogue and equality among different peoples. A more direct concern with the implications of democracy can be found in the philosophy of pragmatism and the sociology of Mead.

Mead and Pragmatism

We all move in and out of different situations in our everyday lives. I am sure that for most of us, coming to college was not only a rational, cognitive process, but also involved grasping the culture of the school, the dorm, and the like. We must become attentive to how students, instructors, and staff understand and interpret their social world. I remember that when I first attended college I was full of confidence, as I had considered myself to be an intellectual in high school. I was quickly deflated when I heard people in the dorms discussing Marx and Freud in a far more sophisticated manner than I had ever done. Further, I thought that my relationship with my roommate would consist of deep intellectual discussions about the human condition. However, my first encounter with him was not too encouraging. He came in late on my first night in the dorms, drunk as a skunk. He vomited all night into a trashcan between his bed and mine. Luckily, my roommate did not over-indulge in this part of college culture and he is now a successful dentist. We did even eventually get into deep discussions, though they usually concerned the female culture of the university we attended, rather than the nature of reality.

The point here is that we always encounter new and unexpected situations and must deal with them in innovative ways. People are interpretive creatures who must make sense of the world they live in. We learn to play different roles in this process. We are students, workers, children, friends, etc., and we do not act the same way in every situation. We must empathically gauge the different cultural meanings in disparate situations and act accordingly. Social interaction is often not smooth or determined. We often must innovatively solve problems with others. Living with a roommate for the first time involves compromise and at least a little sensitivity, so that two separate individuals can share the same space together.

Pragmatists philosophically and sociologically develop these insights. They see people as problem-solving creatures who face continually new issues in their everyday lives, and have to innovatively deal with them. Pragmatism is guided by the metaphor of the "creative solution of problems by an experimenting intelligence," rather than the idea that people's conduct and beliefs are determined by static, objective criteria such as their class position or the collective conscience.[58] The individual always confronts problems in a social situation with others and she has to discuss and resolve issues jointly with them. Pragmatism is tied to a particular conception of participatory, reformist democracy, a process of continual change and revision by citizens who engage in fallible and always correctable attempts to live together. Pragmatists do not attempt to reach a final utopian goal where collective problems no longer exist. Thus, democracy is more than an array of representative institutions. It demands active participation by people. Society and the state not only constrain and limit people, but can be a source of inspiration and an arena promoting the development of the self.

Pragmatists argue that people are rarely motivated by a single aim. Rather, they have many goals. Motives and goals often change and become clarified as people interact with one another in the context of particular life histories and cultures. Actions are always creative and revised over time. These ideas inform the work of Mead.

George Herbert Mead

Mead's writings have some similarities to those of Simmel. Like Simmel, Mead (1863–1931) respects art, for it often provides a better way for understanding the creativity of social interaction than does instrumental rationality. He also devises a theory of society that does not transcend individuals and determine them, as is occasionally evident in some of the claims of Marx and Durkheim; nor does he embrace a view of society as the sum of its individual parts. Rather, Mead seeks a conception of social order that is created and recreated anew through social interaction. He examines how individuals relate to one another and how self-consciousness arises in a social context. He sees this as a more rational process than does Simmel, though he develops a complex view of the psychology of the self.

Mead was born in South Hadley, Massachusetts, the very town where I teach at Mount Holyoke College – in fact, his mother was president of Mount Holyoke. Mead became a professor at the University of Chicago, forming alliances with other pragmatist philosophers, such as John Dewey. Mead's ideas became the foundation of the symbolic interactionist perspective, popularized by the American sociologist Herbert Blumer in the 1940s and 1950s. It is represented today in US sociology through the work of scholars such as Norman Denzin.

Mead's concern with the development of the self ties him to the German philosophical tradition of Kant and Hegel. Mead states that Kant's idea of the relationship of duty and experience is "formal and dead."[59] Kant has an impoverished sense of the creativity and diversity of human experience. Further, Mead contends that people have many duties and moral obligations to fulfill, not just a single moral orientation as Kant argues. Take the example of Heinz's moral dilemma, formulated by the psychologist Lawrence Kohlberg. Should Heinz steal a drug that he cannot afford to save the life of his dying wife? Some people argue that he should, others think that the druggist has an obligation to lower prices, others believe he should obey the law. This example demonstrates that obligations may not cohere, but conflict with one another. Thus, fulfilling one's duty is not clear cut and demands constant reflection and rethinking. The solution to moral problems is contingent and creative, requiring the individual to take into account many points of view. Individuals are always drawing and redrawing their boundaries in relation to others and society.

We do not simply apply pre-existing principles regardless of context, as Kant might argue. Rather, we act morally according to contingent, always changing circumstances, which we must understand. Mead adopts Hegel's criticism of Kant that the self has a history which develops through conflicting situations. Much more than Hegel, however, Mead grounds his approach in the study of everyday life. For Hegel, the real world is always subordinate to the great "Absolute Idea" of his philosophy. Mead does not agree with this view of human experience, which he sees as rich and manifold. Social action always has a creative, fluid dimension. Mead also contends that the complexity of any situation must be understood from the point of view of the individuals involved and their environment. New values and beliefs emerge through interaction. He applies this approach to moral problems and political issues as well. Participatory democracy is the best way to solve political problems and create social order. People themselves must offer solutions to difficulties.

Darwin also influenced Mead, even more than the German philosophical tradition. Darwinism represented the victory of a sophisticated experimental science over the philosophical dualism of idealism and materialism. Like Darwin, Mead focuses on the emergence of new types of behavior and action, based on evolutionary change. In Darwin's view, the organism must continually adapt to its environment. This process means that rationality, knowledge, and a sense of self are linked to behavior and natural necessities. Evolution demands constant adjustment to new circumstances, recurring solutions to problems of adaptation. As organisms evolve, new behaviors emerge. For Mead, Darwin demonstrates that mind intersects with nature, and that problem solving is founded on the struggle of the organism to survive and adapt in constantly changing circumstances. The scientific method as Mead understands it does not aim at uncovering eternal truths, but is always pragmatic and contingent. There is no "fixed form of the understanding" in science, for new problems will always arise that science will have to confront, even as it progresses.[60] Mead's behavioral concept of society and the self draws on these ideas, placing adaptation and problem solving in the context of social interaction.

Processes of interpretation should be at the center of any conception of social science. Social interaction invariably means that people define and interpret one another's actions. They respond to others based on interpretations of their conduct, gestures, and language.[61] Mead explores how people interpret their world, the particular experiential dimension of their social life. The social scientist studies a world of meaning and she must immerse herself in the social world of the people she examines. For example, social change is a process that results from historically specific interactions in group life; it is not imposed on people from outside their experience. To study such processes the researcher must become familiar with the ways of life of the people under study, and examine the group through their eyes.

Meaning is created symbolically. Through gestures and language, meanings arise in a nuanced manner. Mead explores how gestures and language come to have similar meanings for individuals of the same culture, which allows them to link their ongoing interactions to larger social categories. Language is central to this process, for it enables the production and reproduction of social life. People need to learn to cooperate in order to survive and cooperation is facilitated by a shared language. The meaning of social actions becomes embodied in language as well as other symbols.

Mead states that communication initially occurs as a gesture, which provides a stimulus for a response. The gesture stands for a possible act. A dog snarling suggests attack, and other animals or humans can anticipate such an action. For humans, gestures become significant symbols, in that they have similar meanings for many people. Shaking a fist often is a prelude to attack or an expression of anger.

For interaction to become meaningful, not just a response to a stimulus, gestures have to be embodied in language, which provides meanings which are similar for all participants. Language allows gestures to be defined, symbolized, and shared, and enables the individual to comprehend her own stimulus. When a person shakes her fist, presumably she knows why she is doing it. Thus, the significant symbol entails self-consciousness and individuals become aware that gestures have meanings. This also allows people interacting with one another to develop interpersonal relationships, to think of others as well as themselves. People internalize objective patterns of meaning which become part of thinking. Only in responding to others, taking the attitude of another toward oneself and symbolizing it in language, can a reflexive consciousness arise. Individuals learn to internalize meanings, they learn a language of gestures and acts. These meanings are social; they become normatively binding on us as rules. People can then adopt critical standards toward themselves and others, and develop rules for the use of symbols and language, which allows cultural conventions and customs to arise. To know that we should stop at a red light while driving a car requires a certain amount of cultural knowledge which must be communicated to us verbally as we grow up and learn to drive. Traffic laws are rules which we learn to obey. Communication is pivotal to the formation of identity and the self.

The Self

For Mead, the self is reflexive, in that a person can become the object of her own thought and actions. He writes, "The self has the characteristic that it is an object to itself, that characteristic distinguishes it from other objects and the body."[62] Individuals can become angry with themselves, take pride in themselves, and the like. This active process of understanding and acting on oneself also applies to other contexts, in that people continually make reality meaningful through interpreting events and actions. People do not respond to social life in a mechanistic, predetermined way.

Subjectivity is intertwined with the public symbols and meanings that are available to people. We do not express a deep-seated, true self; rather, the self is constructed through interpretations of events, objects, other people, and oneself. Mead writes, "No hard-and-fast line can be drawn between our own selves and the selves of others, since our own selves exist and enter as such into our experience only in so far as the selves of others exist and enter as such into our experience also."[63] Individuals develop their sense of self in the context of family, peers, and the media, among many other factors. Thus, people bring many assumptions and beliefs into any situation. The interpretive process is invariably a social one, in which many people must align their actions together. This is done through taking the role of the other (the role of a specific person or a group). This process of role taking shows that the individual is a social product, and that "group or collective action consists of the aligning of individual actions, brought about by the individuals' interpreting or taking into account each other's actions."[64]

Mead argues that the self only arises through interaction. The infant is spontaneous, unable oftentimes to differentiate self and other. At a young age children learn to take the role of another, often through imitating parents, siblings, and others. Mead writes: "A child plays at being a mother, at being a teacher, at being a policeman; that is, it is taking different roles, as we say."[65] In our day, with the rise of mass media, children might imitate a Pokemon character on television, or perhaps Mr T if they watch reruns of *The A Team*. Children acquire interaction skills through role playing, taking the role of another. They learn social rules that invisibly regulate behavior. Mead likes the analogy of a baseball game, where one's individuality is defined through its connection to others. How one plays a position in baseball depends on her talents, but the very position itself is socially determined. Eventually, the individual advances beyond this "game" stage and learns how to take into account the values of the society. Mead calls this taking the role of the generalized other, "the attitude of the whole community," recognizing the common meanings and moral rules of the society in which one lives.[66] The generalized other allows a coherent self to develop, even as it plays different roles.

Yet self-development is not automatically determined. Every new action or playing of a role does not just repeat the past, but involves something creative and new because of the passage of time and the newness of the situation. Every new gesture or role has an emergent quality which is different from those preceding it. Mead attempts to get at this creativity of role playing and communication through distinguishing between the I and the Me. The I is the novel, spontaneous part of the self which drives social action; it is "the [uncertain] response to that situation as it appears in his immediate experience." The Me is the social aspect of the self, where others define who one is. It is "the organized set of attitudes of others which one himself assumes."[67] The self's reflexivity is based on an internal conversation where the I interacts with those already-constituted parts of the self embodied in the Me. The self is multiple, made up of changing roles and experiences. If the interplay of the I and the Me did not exist, there would be no "conscious responsibility, and there would be nothing novel in experience."[68]

In Mead's view, evolution demonstrates that prior conditions cannot account for newly emergent ones, and that new problems and forms of consciousness and interaction are always arising. Mead's image is of a continually innovating individual who requires democratic political conditions and a flexible culture. Mead discusses these issues of change and differing experiences in terms of sociality. For Mead, sociality is "the principle and form of emergence."[69] Sociality means simultaneously existing in several psychological and cultural places at once. The individual is never completely determined and has to constantly reintegrate new experiences into a fluid identity. We continually reinterpret the past as conditions change. Mead's ideas of the I and the Me, and of sociality, attempt to encapsulate this idea of innovation, of change, of the constant interplay of identity and difference.

While Mead thinks that knowledge is always partial and provisional, he does not argue that his approach leads to cultural relativism, where there is no possibility of objective knowledge. His idea of the generalized other helps create coherence among different perspectives. Mead also discusses language as a path to scientific knowledge. For Mead, as for Hegel, language synthesizes various meanings into a relatively stable set of significations, so that people can move easily between roles and perspectives without jarring their sense of self.[70] Indeed, Mead's conception of the self is more integrated and rational than that of Simmel or Freud. Mead focuses on the development of the social self through interaction and participation in a community. This is in many ways a rational process, for people attempt to achieve goals through understanding the rules of social interaction. People consciously and rationally choose among alternative courses of action.

Yet Mead is no positivist social scientist. He does not think that there is an ultimate truth which the individual, or the scientist, can find. Mead writes that the scientific method "is a method not of knowing the unchangeable but of determining the form of the world within which we live as it changes from moment to moment."[71] The consistency and universality demanded by science does not mean that we are approaching a true reality through increasing knowledge, but more humbly that any plan of action needs to be "intelligent and generally applicable."

> Science always has a world of reality by which to test its hypotheses, but this world is not a world independent of scientific experience, but the immediate world surrounding us within which we must act. Our next action may find these conditions seriously changed, and then science will formulate this world so that in view of this problem we may logically construct our next plan of action.[72]

This view of science opens up the possibility that the human world can be understood by different types of perspectives, different forms of knowledge. Mead's views on aesthetics are important in this context.

Aesthetics

John Dewey approvingly cites the poet Shelley's (1792–1822) dictum that poets were the founders of civil society, because they emphasized a sense of imaginative projection, wholeness, and harmony which is at the heart of human existence.[73] Mead has similar ideas about art and experience. In *Mind, Self, and Society* Mead underlines the centrality of the aesthetic dimension of play in social interaction.

Play is an important stage in the child's development of a sense of self. Through play, children learn to take the role of another, to develop a sense of how different people think and act. They learn to sympathetically and empathically interpret the actions of others. Fundamental to Mead's pragmatic attitude is the idea of the "playing out" of varied courses of action, different ways of thinking. Play remains a part of later adult life, as in "our affection for familiar objects of constant employment, and in the aesthetic attitude toward nature which is the source of all nature poetry."[74]

Mead can be read as arguing that playful experience should be more or less abandoned as we mature. For example, he writes: "The essence of the self . . . is cognitive: it lies in the internalized conversation of gestures which constitutes thinking, or in terms of which thought or reflection proceeds."[75] The self is rational, but Mead is not consistent on this point. In other places he writes that experience and the self have a strong aesthetic dimension. I think this positive evaluation of aesthetics is a central component of Mead's thought, especially when he discusses how meaning arises.

In Mead's view, meaning is not only cognitive, but also aesthetic. He writes: "Man lives in a world of Meaning," and aesthetics contributes much to making existence meaningful.[76] He states that great works of art "have permanent value because they are the language of delight into which men can translate the meaning of their own experience."[77] Art is creative, demonstrating possibilities for new and more profound meanings. But the aesthetic sense is not just the possession of great artists. Aesthetic experience is inherent in everyday life. Art glimpses and makes conscious the wholeness and joy of human experience that underlies and arises through social interaction.

Aesthetics allows people to enjoy and appreciate their life experience. Art has the "power to catch the enjoyment that belongs to the consummation, the outcome of an undertaking."[78] There is aesthetic delight in the completion and achievement of a goal, even if this is only partial, for all fulfillment is tied to creativity. Aesthetic activity is meaningful in itself, it is "more than the mere adaptation of means to end, the mere successful cooperative fashioning of the goods which are enjoyed in common."[79] Aesthetics is based on shared experience. It allows people to realize their interdependence with one another. Mead discusses labor in this context, arguing much like Marx that the industrial division of labor inhibits the experience of this aesthetic sensibility at the workplace. The division of labor elevates technique over the meaning, joy, and creativity of work. The social nature of work should be celebrated and appreciated, so that there is a degree of "common delight" in labor.[80]

The artistic experience creates a feeling of a kind of flow in the skilled work of craftsmanship, imparting a "joy of creation" to anyone doing such work, whether it be fashioning a work of art or writing a research paper.[81] People share an *esprit de corps* when they work together and develop a sense of doing a common task. From the artisan who enjoys his work to a statesman stepping back and surveying the results of her good works, anyone who feels "in a Whitmanesque manner the commonalty of experience" has an aesthetic attitude.[82]

For Mead, aesthetics indicates a "rich intersubjectivity" based on the "compassionate understanding of difference."[83] People are interpretive creatures who can develop sympathetic awareness of the self and others. Mutual understanding among individuals who maintain their autonomy is the goal of interaction. Mead posits a kind of democratic communication utopia in which people can understand one another in an unconstrained manner. He assumes that a sense of individuality arises through public acts and shared speech, so there is no need to engage in deep, introspective analysis to grasp the self, and meaning more generally. Communication occurs between individuals who share symbols and traditions, which ensures that similar cultural rules and conventions exist for all participants in interaction. The generalized other is the locus of cultural order and sustains the moral authority necessary to guide conduct.

From Mead's perspective, people are intelligent; they are not cultural dopes. The relation between social life and the individual is complex, not reducible to simple formulas. His vision of community is rich in meaning. But Mead has no systematic analysis of the ways in which collective organizations and institutions, or coercive ideas, can influence and/or constrain behavior and consciousness. He has no comprehensive theory of how power works. His notion of the generalized other does not take into account the power dynamics that might subtly inform it, nor the possibility that the generalized other might be fractured by multiple, contradictory beliefs around issues such as class and gender.

Alternative Identities, Social Movements, and Public Spheres

Some of Mead's, Simmel's, and Freud's most interesting ideas involve a rethinking of the public sphere and social movements. I have interpreted the public sphere as a realm of democratic debate, and demonstrated how Marx, Weber, and Durkheim contributed to a theory of democracy and public life. Social movements such as the labor movement bring new voices into the public sphere. Mead's and Simmel's discussion of aesthetics points to a conception of the public sphere and social movements as more than spaces for rational argument, as realms of sociability and play. Freud also demonstrates that emotions can play a role in collective action, though for Freud they often involve irrationally following leaders who can play on and manipulate people's psyches. In our mass media-dominated world, these aspects of interaction have become increasingly important, as patterns of speech, dress, sexuality, and music are playful arenas of culture that are primary experiences of identity for many people. Popular culture might provide the most fruitful terrain for alternative constructions of cultural identity.[84]

Social movements can be understood as free spaces in which new ideas, symbols, and experimental ways of living can be discovered and elaborated. New social movements, like gay and lesbian movements, are as much about playing with new forms of sociability and symbolism as about developing rational programs for social change. Like some workers' movements of the past, they offer the possibility of breaking into history with something new and "turning the world upside down."[85] Social movements may be understood as "arenas for the formation and enactment of social identities."[86]

Music provides common symbolic meanings and a kind of shared cultural world and aesthetic of living – from British hippies and bike boys to contemporary rappers. Because these cultures are permeable they are constantly innovating, as groups come into symbolic and real contact with one another. Style becomes a symbolic code that expresses these new identities. For example, punk music and appearance contributed to an alternative public space for white youths, defined by style as much as by discourse; further, punks were part of a kind of surreptitious, anarchist cultural tradition that has exploded into public consciousness on occasion, from the festivals of the Paris Commune to the Surrealist art movement. Much the same can be said of rap and its relationship to African-American young people. Rap is a form of "common literacy" for many young black males, which has provided a public arena for their voice and a sense of cultural alternatives and criticism, as other areas such as conventional politics are not open to them.[87]

I do not want to uncritically celebrate popular youth culture, as there are many elements in it that I find problematic, from the sexist and violent lyrics of some rap to the bleak and nihilistically destructive tone of much punk music. The capacity of the mass media to assimilate and reconstruct these new cultural identities also seems to be increasing in power. Supposedly alternative and critical music and styles easily become commodified and packaged, sold to middle-class youth as a preformed type of fake rebellion that becomes simply another consumer choice, reducing the politics of everyday life to a fashion statement and an attitude of being cool.

But this is not the whole story of popular culture and the public sphere. I think that Mead and Simmel outline possibilities for a different type of cultural criticism that does not simply dismiss popular culture as apolitical. Their work can lead to an understanding of the intersection of cultural identity, social movements, and the public sphere. Freud, too, is relevant here, for many political protests now place sexuality and the body at the forefront of their activities, and elements of fantasy enter into demonstrations. New social movements, from feminism to gay and lesbian movements, and conservative ones such as the pro-life movement, have reconfigured the public sphere so that it cannot be conceived as a singular entity, but is better understood as a series of multiple, overlapping public spaces. These arenas are contested terrains, as a multiplicity of new types of political practice arises concerning who has the right to define identities as well as policies, from the demonstrations over AIDS policy by the group ACT-UP, to the creative and imaginative protests against the policies of the International Monetary Fund and the World Bank, to the emergence of patriot and militia movements in the US.

What I am discussing here is the politics of culture. I think that Mead's, Simmel's, and Freud's work can contribute to this new way of conceiving the public sphere. I stress that this is my interpretation of tendencies in their work. None of these theorists explicitly views culture in a strongly political sense. Despite Simmel's and Mead's grounding of aesthetics in everyday life, they do not systematically explore the interconnection of cultural power and everyday life, though some of Simmel's writings on gender and the sociology of money outline at least the beginnings of such ideas. They do not address structural issues such as the nature of capitalism, rationalization, and the division of labor with the sophistication of Marx, Weber, and Durkheim. A sociologically grounded theory of the relationship of power to social stratification, such as class, is also lacking in their approaches. These are powerful criticisms which leave large gaps in their approaches.

Yet I think that the theoretical perspectives of Freud, Simmel, and Mead can give us different and more complex visions of community, the self, art, and science than those found in Marx, Weber, and Durkheim. These theorists demonstrate that the self is not entirely rational, but that it is multiple and conflicted, intersecting with society in complex ways. Mead and Simmel argue that scientific concepts do not reflect reality in any simple way, and social science must be flexible and open in order to capture the richness of human experience. They recognize that contemporary societies are more reflexive than those of the past, but they do not uncritically celebrate rationality. Simmel's emphasis on aesthetics complements his suspicion of theories of large-scale processes that become too distant from the actual experience of people. Mead, though not as aesthetically oriented as Simmel, sees ever-changing and fluid social interaction as the basis of social life. Freud alerts us to the role of unconscious psychic processes in shaping individual and social behavior.

Simmel and Mead in particular implicitly problematize hierarchical theories of social development, such as a traditional–modern divide, for all societies are based on social interaction, informed by different social conditions and cultural traditions. They demonstrate that democracy requires an open society and a tolerant, emotionally mature individual who can sympathetically experience how different peoples understand the social world. A consideration of Simmel, Freud, and Mead can enrich the sociological tradition and contribute to new narratives of classical theory which address the central philosophical and social issues and debates of contemporary times, from the changing nature of public spheres to new conceptions of identity. Yet these thinkers often do not address the ways in which groups may develop unequal and distasteful norms and values that may be sexist, racist, and the like. In the next chapter I address some of their shortcomings concerning culture and power by exploring the influence of race and gender on culture and knowledge in the work of Du Bois and Perkins Gilman.

Notes

1   *Time Magazine,* December 13, 1999.
2   See Kenneth H. Tucker, Jr., *French Revolutionary Syndicalism and the Public Sphere* (New York, 1996), pp. 163–4.
3   See Peter Gay, *Freud: A Life for Our Time* (New York, 1988).
4   Sigmund Freud, "An Autobiographical Study," in *The Freud Reader,* ed. Peter Gay (New York, 1989), p. 38.
5   Kenneth H. Tucker, Jr., *Anthony Giddens and Modern Social Theory* (Thousand Oaks, CA, 1998), pp. 188–90; Sigmund Freud, *A General Introduction to Psychoanalysis* (New York, 1938), p. 27.
6   Ibid, p. 319–22, 365, 421.
7   See Terry Eagleton, *The Ideology of the Aesthetic* (Cambridge, MA, 1990), p. 272; Freud, *A General Introduction to Psychoanalysis,* p. 219.

8   Freud, "An Autobiographical Study," p. 28.

9   Freud, *A General Introduction to Psychoanalysis,* p. 212.

10 Sigmund Freud, *Civilization and Its Discontents* (New York, 1961), p. 24.

11 Ibid, p. 45.

12 Ibid, p. 68.

13 Ibid, pp. 60–1, 81, 91.

14 Sigmund Freud, *The Future of an Illusion* (New York, 1964), p. 87.

15 Herbert Marcuse, *Eros and Civilization: A Philosophical Inquiry into Freud* (New York, 1955), ch. 1; Tucker, *Anthony Giddens and Modern Social Theory,* pp. 190–3.

16 Nancy Chodorow, *The Reproduction of Mothering: Psychoanalysis and the Sociology of Gender* (Berkeley, CA, 1978).

17 Judith Butler, "Gender Trouble, Feminist Theory, and Psychoanalytic Discourse," in *Feminism/Postmodernism,* ed. Linda Nicholson (New York, 1990), pp. 324–33; see also Judith Butler, *Gender Trouble: Feminism and the Subversion of Identity* (New York, 1990), and Tucker, *Anthony Giddens and Modern Social Theory,* p. 201.

18 Steven Seidman, *Contested Knowledge: Social Theory in the Postmodern Era* (Cambridge, MA, 1994), p. 252.

19 Anthony Giddens and Christopher Pierson, *Conversations with Anthony Giddens: Making Sense of Modernity* (London, 1998), p. 67.

20 Georg Simmel, *Kant* (Munich, 1921), quoted in Guy Oakes, "The Problem of Women in Simmel's Theory of Culture," *Georg Simmel: On Women, Sexuality, and Love* (New Haven, CT, 1984), p. 38.

21 Ibid, pp. 36–41.

22 Donald Levine, "Simmel Reappraised: Old Images, New Scholarship," in *Reclaiming the Sociological Classics: The State of the Scholarship,* ed. Charles Camic (Malden, MA, 1997), p. 177.

23 David Frisby, "Introduction to the Texts," in *Simmel on Culture: Selected Writings,* ed. David Frisby and Mike Featherstone (London, 1997), p. 7.

24 Georg Simmel, "Subjective Culture," in *Georg Simmel on Individuality and Social Forms,* ed. Donald Levine (Chicago, 1971), pp. 228–9.

25 Ibid, p. 233.

26 Georg Simmel, "On the Essence of Culture," in *Simmel on Culture: Selected Writings,* ed. David Frisby and Mike Featherstone (London, 1997), p. 45.

27 Oakes, "The Problem of Women in Simmel's Theory of Culture," pp. 21–2.

28 Georg Simmel, "Money in Modern Culture," in *Simmel on Culture: Selected Writings,* ed. David Frisby and Mike Featherstone (London, 1997), p. 249.

29 Georg Simmel, "Group Expansion and the Development of Individuality,' in *Georg Simmel on Individuality and Social Forms,* ed. Donald Levine (Chicago, 1971), p. 291.

30 Georg Simmel, "The Stranger," in *Georg Simmel on Individuality and Social Forms,* ed. Donald Levine (Chicago, 1971), p. 148.

31 Frisby, "Introduction to the Texts," p. 12.

32 Georg Simmel, "Fashion," in *Georg Simmel on Individuality and Social Forms,* ed. Donald Levine (Chicago, 1971), p. 303.

33 Georg Simmel, "The Adventurer," in *Georg Simmel on Individuality and Social*

Forms, ed. Donald Levine (Chicago, 1971), p. 191.

34 Georg Simmel, *Schopenhauer and Nietzsche* (Amherst, MA, 1986), p. 14.

35 Georg Simmel, "The Transcendent Character of Life," in *Georg Simmel on Individuality and Social Forms*, ed. Donald Levine (Chicago, 1971), p. 361.

36 Ibid, p. 363.

37 Simmel, *Schopenhauer and Nietzsche*, p. 4.

38 Donald Levine, "Introduction," in *Georg Simmel on Individuality and Social Forms*, ed. Donald Levine (Chicago, 1971), pp. xxxvii–xxxix.

39 Georg Simmel, "How is History Possible?" in *Georg Simmel on Individuality and Social Forms*, ed. Donald Levine (Chicago, 1971), p. 5.

40 Simmel, *Schopenhauer and Nietzsche*, p. 15.

41 Ibid, p. 3.

42 Alexander Nehamas, *Nietzsche: Life as Literature* (Cambridge, MA, 1985), p. 182.

43 Simmel, *Schopenhauer and Nietzsche*, p. 104.

44 Georg Simmel, "Sociability," in *Georg Simmel on Individuality and Social Forms*, ed. Donald Levine (Chicago, 1971), p. 130.

45 Ibid, p. 132.

46 Ibid, p. 139.

47 Ibid, p. 132.

48 Georg Simmel, "The Poor," in *Georg Simmel on Individuality and Social Forms*, ed. Donald Levine (Chicago, 1971), pp. 153–4.

49 Georg Simmel, "Female Culture," in *Georg Simmel: On Women, Sexuality, and Love* (New Haven, CT, 1984), p. 70.

50 Ibid, pp. 73, 86, 88.

51 Ibid, p. 72.

52 Ibid, pp. 76–7.

53 Ibid, p. 78.

54 Ibid, p. 80.

55 Ibid, p. 98.

56 Ibid, p. 99.

57 Ibid, p. 101.

58 Hans Joas, *Pragmatism and Social Theory* (Chicago, 1993), p. 248.

59 George Herbert Mead, "Scientific Method and Individual Thinker," in *Creative Intelligence: Essays in the Pragmatic Attitude*, ed. John Dewey et al. (New York, 1917), p. 194.

60 Ibid, p. 213; see also Robert Dunn, *Identity Crises: A Social Critique of Postmodernity* (Minneapolis, 1998), pp. 190, 203.

61 Herbert Blumer, *Society as Symbolic Interaction* (Berkeley, CA, 1969) p. 139.

62 George Herbert Mead, *Mind, Self and Society from the Standpoint of a Social Behaviorist* (Chicago, 1934), p. 200; see also Dunn, *Identity Crises*, pp. 207–8.

63 Mead, *Mind, Self and Society*, p. 164.

64 Blumer, *Society as Symbolic Interaction*, p. 142.

65 Mead, *Mind, Self and Society*, p. 150.

66 Ibid, p. 154; see also Dunn, *Identity Crises*, p.208.

67 Mead, *Mind, Self and Society*, p. 175; see also Dunn, *Identity Crises*, p. 209.

68   Mead, *Mind, Self and Society*, p. 178.
69   George Herbert Mead, *The Philosophy of the Present* (Chicago, 1932), p. 85; see also Dunn, *Identity Crises*, pp. 204–5.
70   Ibid, p. 219.
71   Mead, "Scientific Method and Individual Thinker," p. 225.
72   Ibid, p. 226.
73   John Dewey, *Art as Experience* (New York, 1934), p. 347.
74   Mead, *Mind, Self and Society*, p. 378.
75   Ibid, p. 173.
76   George Herbert Mead, "The Nature of Aesthetic Experience," *International Journal of Ethics* 36 (1925–6), p. 382.
77   Ibid, p. 387.
78   Ibid, p. 384.
79   Ibid, p. 387.
80   Ibid, p. 384.
81   Ibid, p. 387.
82   Ibid, p. 386.
83   Robert Antonio, "The Normative Foundations of Emancipatory Theory: Evolutionary versus Pragmatic Perspectives," *American Journal of Sociology* 94 (1989), p. 743.
84   bell hooks, *Yearning* (Boston, 1990), p. 31.
85   Christopher Hill, *The Century of Revolution: 1603–1714* (New York, 1961).
86   Nancy Fraser, "Rethinking the Public Sphere: A Contribution to the Critique of Actually Existing Democracy," in *Habermas and the Public Sphere*, ed. Craig Calhoun (Cambridge, MA, 1992), p. 125; see also Sara Evans and Harry Boyte, *Free Spaces: The Sources of Democratic Change in America* (New York, 1986).
87   hooks, *Yearning*, p. 27; see also Greil Marcus, *Lipstick Traces: A Secret History of the Twentieth Century* (Cambridge, MA, 1989); and Kenneth H. Tucker, Jr., "Aesthetics, Play, and Cultural Memory: Giddens and Habermas on the Postmodern Challenge," *Sociological Theory* 11 (July 1993), pp. 194–211.

CHAPTER SEVEN

Du Bois and Perkins Gilman: Race, Gender, and Cultural Identity

Even in this age of divorce, single-parent households, and blended families, the ideal of "home, sweet home," the place where we can always return, still has a sentimental appeal. Charlotte Perkins Gilman disagrees with this assessment. She writes: "When we sing, with tears in our eyes and a catch in our voices, 'Home, sweet home, there's no place like home!' we do not mean, 'Housework, sweet housework, there's nothing like housework!'"[1] And who did the housework in 1907, when Perkins Gilman wrote these words? Women, as many still do today.

In the late nineteenth and early twentieth centuries, in the context of the sexism of Victorian society, Perkins Gilman addressed many issues that have become staples of twenty-first century feminism. She explores the "second shift" – that women rather than men remain responsible for housekeeping and child-rearing, even if they work outside of the home. She discusses the limited economic opportunity for women (what we now call the "glass ceiling" facing women executives, for example) and the right of women to control their own bodies. She criticizes the romantic myths surrounding the family, arguing that it is an institution wracked by paternalism and must be completely transformed to benefit women and society. Perkins Gilman's advocacy of women's education intersects with contemporary studies that point to women's lack of education as a primary cause of global gender inequality.[2]

W. E. B. Du Bois wrote in 1903 that the problem of the twentieth century would be the problem of the color line. Du Bois's words and writing proved prescient, as he addressed issues of the intersection of race and class and the problem of racial privilege that have been burning issues throughout the contemporary era. In this age of globalization and global economic restructuring, when peoples move from one country to another, no problems are more urgent than immigration and racial and ethnic discord. Issues concerning how different races and cultures can live together now have a powerful urgency.

Du Bois and Gilman bring to prominence topics of gender and race that were usually below the radar screen of the theorists we have considered. They show that these issues are often invisible to people, yet influence their worlds in powerful ways. Self-identity and cultural identity cannot be understood apart from the economic and cultural power signified by race and gender. Their analyses draw on many of the same theorists and traditions that we have considered throughout this text, from Hegelianism and Nietzsche to socialism and positivism.

Perkins Gilman and Du Bois demonstrate that many ways of thinking and acting are powerfully gendered and raced, though both also integrate class issues into their respective analyses. Du Bois, like Simmel and Mead, proposes a fluid theory of the self and criticizes positivist science. He develops an innovative theory of a black public sphere. Perkins Gilman, like Mead, reformulates Darwinism in her analysis of gender and society. She raises some radical conceptions about the constitution of the family and child-rearing. Both Du Bois and Gilman wrote outside of academia, which made them dependent on a literate public for their survival. It also allowed them to experiment with different styles, from autobiography to fiction, to express their arguments.

These theorists also demonstrate some of the theoretical shortcomings that I have discussed throughout the text. Each theorist tends to embrace a theory of progress and a sometimes uncritical view of science, though Du Bois is more complex in his understanding of these phenomena than Perkins Gilman. Each thinker also develops somewhat patronizing and elitist views of the public. Perkins Gilman occasionally embraces the racist pseudo-science of her time, reinforced by the strong evolutionary dimension of her thought.

W. E. B. Du Bois

The African-American sociologist Du Bois (1868–1963) contributed to the formation of a distinctive African-American culture, comprising those individuals brought to the US in slavery from places as disparate as Senegal, Angola, and the Congo. By 1903, the year that *The Souls of Black Folk* was published, Du Bois was among the most traveled and well-read men in the world, and the most widely published black essayist since the abolitionist Frederick Douglass (1817–95).[3] Many of his works have become sociological classics, from *The Souls of Black Folk* to *The Philadelphia Negro*, the first ethnographic and statistical account of a black community in the US. He saw that issues of race were going to shadow the world.[4]

Du Bois raises issues of race and cultural identity in his work. He also addresses the relationship between economic and cultural power. Du Bois formulates the idea of a black public sphere and its relationship to African-American culture. He develops fluid conceptions of the self and identity, raising the problem of the reflexivity and situatedness of the intellectual. He problematizes the universal viewpoint that so often influences social theory. Du Bois reconstructs modernity from the slave's point of view, drawing on images and ideas that are often outside the purview of theorists such as Marx, Durkheim, and Weber.

Du Bois and His Times

Du Bois was born in predominantly white Great Barrington, Massachusetts. He was something of an intellectual prodigy as a child, excelling in all subjects. He could not afford to attend the wealthiest schools, which were also rife with racism, so he attended the all-black Fisk University. Du Bois studied briefly with Max Weber while in Germany, and eventually became a Marxist after World War I. But Du Bois is best known as an advocate for African-American cultural, economic, and political rights. He was an important force in the founding of the National Association for the Advancement of Colored People (NAACP). He was the first African-American to receive a Ph.D. from Harvard University, but he faced racism his entire life, never teaching in a white-majority university. Du Bois eventually became disillusioned with the US and migrated to Ghana near the end of his life.[5]

Much of Du Bois's work took place in the Jim Crow era in the US. Segregation was given legal sanction in the late nineteenth-century South with the *Plessy v. Ferguson* Supreme Court decision of 1896. Railways, streetcars, buses, and schools were divided between blacks and whites. This was far from a condition of equality, however. Lynchings of blacks by whites were commonplace in the southern US. Southern whites, through various literacy tests and poll taxes, prevented blacks from voting. Unions also discriminated against African-Americans. Politicians did little to challenge the racial status quo. Though the North did not practice legal segregation, *de facto* segregation characterized black-white relations, as racism was virulent in the North as well as the South. Social Darwinism, the "survival of the fittest," justified the privileges of whites and the poor treatment of African-Americans and other minorities. Much US social science was explicitly racist, drawing on dubious biology to "scientifically" demonstrate the alleged superiority of the Anglo-Saxon race.

Within this racist context Du Bois struggled with Booker T. Washington (1856–1915), president of the Tuskeegee Institute, for leadership of the African-American community. Washington accepted segregation, doing little for black civil rights. Instead, he stated that blacks should pursue the American economic dream. African-Americans had to adopt middle-class virtues such as hard work and individualism, and pull themselves up economically through their own efforts. Blacks should emulate entrepreneurs and captains of industry, who provided models for economic and moral improvement. African-Americans needed vocational training above all, and education should be oriented toward this end.

Du Bois agreed with Washington on several points. Du Bois, too, emphasized self-help and racial solidarity among blacks. But Du Bois, following in the path of Douglass, advocated complete, equal civil and political rights for African-Americans. For Du Bois, the economic advancement of blacks could not occur without full political rights. He criticized Washington's embrace of existing American capitalism, protesting against the abridgment of economic rights and the inequality of economic opportunity facing African-Americans. Du Bois was sympathetic to the aims of the labor movement, despite its racist actions, because he saw the future of African-Americans tied to the plight of all workers. Du Bois also differed from Washington in his view of culture. Du Bois advocated a broad, liberal arts college education for blacks, so that they could understand the social and cultural forces influencing them. Vocational training would not teach blacks critical thinking and cultural self-reliance. Most importantly, Du Bois favored the creation of a distinctive African-American culture, and developed a complex view of multiculturalism that was beyond Washington's purview.

Du Bois was influenced by Marx, Hegel, and the American pragmatist tradition. Like Marx, he sees that ownership of wealth often translates into social power. He fears that capitalism debases all forms of culture, reducing social activity to a race for money. He adopts Hegel's master-slave dialectic to interpret the distinctive history of African-Americans, problematizing many of Hegel's ideas in the process (I will discuss these points in more detail below). Like pragmatists such as James, Du Bois adopts the notion that understanding and experience are closely tied together. Further, the individual self is often conflicted and divided. Though Du Bois does not discuss Nietzsche, his work addresses similar themes. Like Nietzsche, he is interested in the relationship between culture, power, and knowledge, often criticizing beliefs in any absolute truth. He sees the self as changing and fluid, and places great importance on art in the development of African-American culture.

Race and Identity

In Du Bois's two most important early works, *The Philadelphia Negro* (1899) and *The Souls of Black Folk* (1903), he discusses the interplay of race and class, "the intersection of segregation, poverty, crime, and urban blight that . . . still commands our attention and remains one of the most pressing issues facing American society."[6] In these books Du Bois often views immorality, manifested in alcoholism, prostitution, and crime, among a large section of the African-American population as contributing to their problems and poverty. He traces this moral deficit to the legacy of slavery and racism.

Du Bois develops a more structural theory of poverty and racism in his later work, focusing on colonialism worldwide. Moving beyond the US, he argues that the world was becoming divided into master capitalists (primarily white) who control most wealth; the national middle classes of many countries (European, Hispanic, and Asian) who share bonds of common interests and history; and finally the oppressed workers of all nations (primarily black, Asian, and Hispanic). According to Du Bois, racism is the major hindrance to a fair redistribution of wealth. Whites benefit economically from racism, and the profits of colonialism accruing to the West prevent social change.[7]

The Souls of Black Folk

The Souls of Black Folk was influenced by the historical milieu of Jim Crow segregation. In 1903 many whites were not convinced that blacks actually had souls. Blacks were considered to be utterly different beings. They were stereotyped by whites as either clowns or dangerous felons, who needed to be controlled by terror. These stereotypes were reinforced in popular culture; for example, blacks were portrayed in theaters by white actors who blackened their faces. Du Bois smashes this white portrayal of black culture, taking back for blacks the possession of their music and other art forms, providing a sense of the richness of their heritage.[8]

Du Bois is critical of capitalism. He sees the pursuit of wealth overwhelming all other values, especially so in the US. Du Bois worked for many years at Atlanta University in Georgia. He views Atlanta as in many ways the prototypical American city that was arising in the early twentieth century. The people of Atlanta worked for money, rather than in a calling, in Weber's terms. They found little moral meaning in their work. These beliefs influenced the black community. The preacher and the teacher, two pillars of African-American society, were declining in influence, as wealth became the standard for values and behavior. But Du Bois places his criticisms of capitalism in the context of racism. Rather than stating that blacks have to become like whites, Du Bois argues for a strong black culture which can provide the basis for a new multicultural humanity.[9]

In the opening lines of *The Souls of Black Folk* Du Bois writes that whites view him as a problem. This is typical of the stereotyping of blacks *as* a problem, rather than people *with problems*; blacks are viewed as abstractions rather than individuals. Du Bois also develops the ideas of double consciousness and the metaphor of the veil. The black and white worlds are divided by a veil that requires role playing on the part of blacks, rather than real interaction. African-American double consciousness, that of being black and American, is often conflicted, and blacks must suppress their rage at their oppression in order to assuage white anxiety.[10] *The Souls of Black Folk* explores various dimensions of African-American life, from religion, to the family, to black spirituals, in the wake of the failure of Reconstruction and the rise of Jim Crow segregation in the South. But it is much more than a chronicle of early twentieth-century African-American life. Like most intellectuals in his time, Du Bois sometimes advocates a positivist science and a belief in progress. But the thrust of his thought problematizes these issues.

In a manner reminiscent of Nietzsche, Du Bois is sensitive to the intersection of power and knowledge, and how marginalized knowledges are hidden by dominant ones. His use of the biblical metaphor of the veil in the opening chapter of *The Souls of Black Folk* gets at this issue. The veil appears in verses throughout the Bible, from Exodus to Hebrews, but its most powerful meaning revolves around the crucifixion of Jesus, when the rending of the veil marks the conversion of the Roman centurion to the truth of Jesus. But while the biblical veil is lifted to show the truth, in Du Bois the veil descends, separating the white and black worlds from one another. When Du Bois lifts the veil, he too finds new insights. However, he does not discover freedom and enlightenment, but a history of terror and oppression visited upon African-Americans.[11] The black experience, embodied in traditions from the Ethiopian kings to the mixing of African and Christian themes, has never been recognized by whites. Du Bois calls for an acknowledgment of this repressed knowledge, embodied in a distinctive African-American culture. For Du Bois, the destiny of African-Americans is not to be absorbed by the white majority, but to have their particular contributions recognized and cultivated. Black colleges, newspapers, and other organs of education are necessary for such a culture.[12]

The church has been a conserver and progenitor of this culture, for it preserves the remnants of African tribal life while mixing it with Christian and republican themes. Art is central to the African-American experience, embodied for example in what Du Bois calls "the sorrow songs" or spirituals of slavery. This music drawn from Africa is the most authentic in the history of the US. Its rhythms and intensity bring the body into music.[13] These songs are voices of exile, a music of unhappiness, death, suffering, and the longing for a better world.[14] American folklore, too, originates outside of Europe. Du Bois writes: "there is no true American music but the wild sweet melodies of the Negro slave; the American fairy tales and folklore are Indian and African."[15] According to Du Bois, art and music are part of everyday experience. For African-Americans, music is a means of preserving memories of hardship, struggle, and redemption. Paul Gilroy in his book *The Black Atlantic* builds upon Du Bois's insights. He states that black music represented, and still represents, a kind of alternative public sphere, for it signals black cultural value, integrity, and autonomy. Music reconciles art and life, promoting a sense of black community and self-development.[16]

The power of a dominant culture to repress difference is demonstrated in the taken-for-granted beliefs of whiteness. Du Bois's analysis of whiteness has a contemporary resonance, as it has become a popular topic in cultural studies and critical race perspectives. Du Bois states that the idea of whiteness is a recent invention: "The discovery of personal whiteness among the world's peoples is a very modern thing – a nineteenth- and twentieth-century matter, indeed."[17] From the universal cosmopolitanism of the Enlightenment, the European world "has discovered that it is white and by that token, wonderful!"[18] Black, yellow, and brown are defined as those skin colors which are not only different, but inferior. They must be actively repressed and hidden, redefined as bad in opposition to good as white.[19]

This perspective can illuminate aspects of contemporary race relations in the US. Whites sometimes state that they have no culture, no traditions, especially if they come from the suburbs. But what does this mean? To be white is not a problem for Anglo-Americans as being black was a problem for Du Bois. Whiteness for many Anglos is an indescribable and cultureless identity; other identities which are not white are marked by race and ethnicity. As the dominant cultural group, whites do not have to name themselves. They often see themselves as having no history or traditions, as "suburban white-bread." But whiteness has a history, grounded in the ascetic Protestantism analyzed by Weber. Because whites often see themselves as colorless, whiteness becomes a norm, a taken-for-granted way of measuring others. As the non-defined definers of others, whites often view the social world in dualistic terms, understanding themselves as either better than people of color, or romanticizing other racial and ethnic cultures as more "authentic" than their own. This subtle form of cultural power also manifests itself in economic and social institutions.

Whites benefit disproportionately from seemingly neutral institutional operations. From employment to the criminal justice system, to access to health care and home financing, whites have privileges based on their race which are invisible to them, and that do not accrue to people of color.[20]

This critique of whiteness is analogous to Du Bois's criticisms of positivist thinking. The categories for understanding the world are shaped by language and history; concepts do not reflect reality in a simple, positivist way. Ideas of race are not grounded in biology but fashioned by culture. Du Bois recognizes that positivist science can be mobilized for racist ends, as in the scientific discussions of race that posited the inferiority of blacks in the early twentieth century.[21] Science must be complemented by a more sensitive, hermeneutical approach to the social world. Du Bois developed such an approach in his discussion of democracy and African-American culture. African-American culture has to be created in an atmosphere of oppression and racism. While components of an African-American culture existed in Du Bois's time, they were fragmented and had not been given coherence or voice.

Du Bois on Democracy

Du Bois contends that literate, educated African-Americans are the major bearers of black culture. He sees the future of African-Americans as carried by their most talented members. In "The Talented Tenth" (1903) Du Bois defends the idea of a distinctive black culture, criticizing arguments that rights and duties should be understood in individual terms. Because of slavery, blacks are forced to see themselves and act as a group if they are to achieve any justice. Du Bois also thinks that every race produces a kind of "natural aristocracy," a professional elite that has a duty to help the less fortunate. African-Americans bear the same superior relation to Africans as elites did to their subordinates. Blacks are to be saved by their exceptional men, who will guide the masses away from their worst instincts. Educated and talented African-Americans have led the masses throughout their history. The best black students should be educated for leadership.[22]

This is a very elitist doctrine. Yet Du Bois also recognizes that democracy ultimately has to be grounded in the activity of the people. He writes: "Democracy is a method of realizing the broadest measure of justice to all human beings."[23] He criticizes capitalism for its undemocratic practices, calling businessmen the "tyrants of the industrial age."[24] More insidious for the prevention of democracy is the practice of benevolent guardianship for those ostensibly unable to act for themselves. Du Bois contends that African-Americans and women have both been treated as weak-minded subjects by white men who supposedly know better. But this "is simply the old cry of privilege" which must be abolished.²⁵ Democracy is based on faith in the people, that they have wisdom. Du Bois states that only the individual knows what is good for himself or herself. Democracy is inherently a messy process, for the extension of voting rights to new people, such as women, allows new points of view and new interests to be expressed, and may initially cause confusion and conflict.

Du Bois seems to be talking out of both sides of his mouth here, for he advocates trust in the democratic will of the people while simultaneously arguing for the necessity of the leadership of the talented tenth. Du Bois is not entirely consistent on this point, but I think this conflict can be partially resolved. I see Du Bois contributing to a black public sphere, a space where African-Americans can articulate and create their sense of commonalty. His controversial points about the talented tenth can be understood in this context.²⁶ Du Bois, like Nietzsche, harbored aristocratic sentiments, and he sees black intellectuals as necessary for the expression of African-American culture. The people might possess good will, but their ideas and sentiments must be made public and debated by articulate representatives, of necessity a minority of the community. He maintained a faith in education throughout his life, for articulate leaders could enlighten those who were oppressed. Like others in the republican tradition of democracy, Du Bois argues that a democratic culture requires common experiences and educational practices, which must be cultivated and developed over time. Only the vitality of an energized and educated public can guarantee democracy.

Du Bois raises the particular problem of the black intellectual who tries to write and perform in a world that does not recognize his or her intelligence. Such a person faces a double-bind. Many whites were reluctant to admit that an African-American could develop intellectual insights on a par with the great European thinkers, and that African culture should be studied alongside Greek and Roman history: Du Bois must convince the white intellectual world that he should be taken seriously. But by desiring to be an intellectual, Du Bois also takes up a problematic position in relation to uneducated blacks. He realizes that he has responsibilities to the black community as an intellectual, but also that he could replicate the colonizing viewpoint of many whites, discounting the experience and knowledge of poor blacks.

In *The Souls of Black Folk* the chapter "Of the Coming of John" deals explicitly with this issue of a college-educated black intellectual, John Jones, who returns to his roots in poor, southern, rural life to "enlighten" the community. The young man encounters much resistance from whites when he tries to teach blacks to think critically about their social situation. He also finds opposition from blacks, who see him as an elitist who does not respect them. The chapter ends with John's lynching by a group of whites after he kills a white man who raped a black woman.

Biblical imagery aside, many of Du Bois's writings not only address the conflict of the black intellectual in substantive terms, but also develop a literary style that mixes together different genres and traditions, tones and viewpoints. For example, he often begins a chapter in *The Souls of Black Folk* with a verse from an African-American spiritual. In his other writings black folklore plays an important role. Du Bois's mixture of the popular and the academic assures his readers that he is speaking with a particular, distinctive voice that can be challenged and debated. He draws on his autobiographical experiences to convey his points. Nietzsche, too, mixes styles together to demonstrate that it is always he who is writing. Neither Nietzsche nor Du Bois hides behind a distanced, abstract academic style. Both men's academic marginalization turns out to be a strength, for they can passionately and provocatively express their ideas.

The Self

There was no guarantee that black culture would survive, or that American ideals of equality and justice would ever be realized. Du Bois rejects ideas of inevitable progress or historical teleology. Such issues are important for his concept of the self. Like Marx, Du Bois draws on Hegel's *Phenomenology of Mind*, but he analyzes the plight of African-Americans. From Du Bois's philosophical perspective, reinterpreting Hegel's master-slave dialectic, African-Americans develop a more profound understanding of human experience because of their confrontation with the terror of slavery, and their labor in the world.[27] Du Bois calls this the two-sightedness of African-Americans. Yet the double-consciousness of blacks is not resolved in terms of Absolute knowledge, as in Hegel's philosophy. While striving for a kind of multicultural synthesis of European and African-American culture, the black self remains conflicted, torn, scarred. The individual, according to Du Bois, cannot overcome this twoness in any simple manner, for the self is tied to concrete historical circumstances. There is no dialectical guarantee of wholeness. The self is fluid, changing, and marked by power. It is not a synthesizing self as much as one that must be constantly reshaped in the context of terror and subjugation, incorporating and overcoming the definitions of evil that surround it. It is divided and multiple, just like the different souls in *The Souls of Black Folk*, from the Harvard-educated Du Bois to the poor blacks that he discusses. There is no God's-eye view from which to make moral judgments.

African-Americans, while they are subjected to racism, must develop their own sense of dignity and worth. African-Americans must be educated to be actional, as Nietzsche might say. Thus, Du Bois argues that the leadership of the African-American community must come from blacks themselves.[28] Colleges should teach humanistic knowledge and culture, and not be vocationally oriented. Their goals must be to produce a person capable of independent thinking and action.[29] This has consequences beyond the African-American community. Du Bois thought the future of the world "will rest ultimately in the hands of darker nations."[30] He became an advocate of Pan-Africanism and developed a strong critique of the oppression of women.

Gender and Pan-Africanism

In Du Bois's view, women, like blacks, have been subjected to a culture which defines them as passive and unable to act on their own. While many of Du Bois's writings on women in *The Souls of Black Folk* are moralistic and patronizing, by 1920, the year he published *Darkwater*, he develops a different tone. He argues that women, like blacks, have been silenced, and they must be able to make their own history and participate in the creation of culture and public policy. He writes that "women have been excluded from modern democracy because of the persistent theory of female subjection."[31] But the subjugation of women goes beyond their lack of political rights, as black women in particular have to develop a sense of identity and worth in the context of white standards of beauty. For Du Bois, "one of the mightiest revolts of the century is against the devilish decree that no woman is a woman who is not by present standards a beautiful woman."[32] Culture defines identities. It is a type of power that extends even to conceptions of the body, and such forms of cultural authority must be challenged.

Du Bois became disheartened with the slow pace of reform in the US and moved to Ghana, where he died in 1963. He became a Marxist later in his life, writing in 1948 that new leaders, a new talented tenth, should be trained economic experts willing to plan for a revolution in industry, and able to effectively carry out the redistribution of wealth.[33] In discussing the future of Africa, Du Bois demonstrates his Marxist sentiments by arguing that deleterious African customs must be slowly abolished, and that any new government should follow "the example of the best colonial administrators."[34] But he also contends that change has to come from the people themselves, and he never gives up his belief that black culture can contribute to a greater humanity. He sees African-Americans as part of a new pan-African movement. All change in Africa should be built upon "the present government, religion, and customary laws of the natives." There must be no tampering with African institutions of local self-government based on the tribe and the family, and no attempts at religious conversion.[35] He states that whites should approach Africa in terms of "uplift and prevention and not merely as alleviation and religious conversion." A respect for humanity must underlie all blueprints for social change, and whites themselves much change dramatically if social change in Africa is to succeed. For Du Bois, black culture is not an end in itself. It must be part of a new humanity, a new culture that eventually will know no color. But Du Bois despaired that this could ever occur, given the power of whiteness and the difficulties of racism faced by people of color throughout the world.

Much of Du Bois's thought can be interpreted as elitist. He tends to believe that a cultural elite must arise to lead people in a rational direction. Like Perkins Gilman, he sometimes uncritically embraces ideas of expert knowledge as a cure for mass ignorance, not recognizing how an expertise separated from democratic debate can contribute to a disciplinary society. He has no overarching theory of the dynamics of society that approaches the grandeur and scope of Marx, Weber, and Durkheim.

But Du Bois's sociological account of race, culture, and the individual provides a complex, socially and historically informed understanding of suffering, the relationship between power and knowledge, and the tribulations of a divided self. Nietzsche, too, addresses these issues, but his account remains abstract. Du Bois grounds his discussion of power, knowledge, and double consciousness in the rich experience of African-American history. Like Simmel and Mead, he sees the formation of cultural and social identity as a complex, fluid process. He discusses how the self is shaped by cultural and economic power in a more profound way than do these other theorists, however. He also focuses on colonialism and the intersection of race and class domination in a more powerful manner than the other theorists we have considered. He implicitly raises the question of the black diaspora, of the problem of transnational notions of black identity in the context of racism and oppression. Such ideas must develop within and outside of the conventional accounts of modernity, taking racism and imperialism to be central components of the black experience, and modernity itself. It requires a flexible sociology sensitive to the migrations and displacements, the terrors and struggles, of many blacks throughout the world. Yet Du Bois's work raises issues beyond those of race. It provides a good starting point for understanding the complexities of contemporary postmodern identities.

Charlotte Perkins Gilman

Perkins Gilman (1860–1935) views society through the lens of gender. Her major themes include the dominance of a male culture over a female culture, the economic subordination of women, the necessity of transforming the family in an egalitarian direction, a belief in social evolution, and a conviction that rationality can guide social change in a progressive direction.

Perkins Gilman develops many arguments similar to Durkheim and Marx. Like Durkheim, and drawing on the imagery of Herbert Spencer, she adopts biological imagery to discuss society, seeing it as a kind of organism governed by laws. She also argues that specialization and differentiation characterize the modern era and are central components of progress. Like Marx, she believes that the capacity to labor defines human existence. Social power is based on the economic control of wealth, possessed by male capitalists. Perkins Gilman's critical rationality informs her analysis of the family and capitalist society. More problematically, she also adopts tenets of progress and a narrow version of community which inform her racist views of people of color and non-modern cultures. Her criticisms of the family lead her to celebrate the virtues of expertise and specialization, without recognizing that an uncritical acceptance of these ideas can promote a closed, disciplinary society.

Perkins Gilman and Her Time

Perkins Gilman, born in Hartford, Connecticut, faced many obstacles during her life. She was neglected and felt unloved by her mother, her father having abandoned the family shortly after her birth. She had a history of depression and mental illness, reinforced by a miserable marriage and divorce. Indeed, one of Perkins Gilman's most famous works is *The Yellow Wallpaper*, a short story dealing with the experience of a nervous breakdown. She lived near the edge of poverty most of her life, making a living as a lecturer after she achieved a measure of fame in the early twentieth century. Perkins Gilman left behind a great amount of work, writing on almost all topics, from economics to the psyche, relating to women.[36] Two of her most famous works are *Women and Economics* (1898) and the feminist novel *Herland* (serialized in 1915).

Perkins Gilman came of intellectual age during the Progressive Era in the US (approximately 1900–14). The Progressive period was dominated by the new business ethic of laissez-faire, which posited that market forces should determine the production and distribution of wealth. In this culture only individual wealth and success counted. This was the era of the massive growth of industrial capitalism. A new notion arose of the rugged individual who depended only on himself, as did the "rags to riches" saga, exemplified in Horatio Alger's stories in which poor boys became wealthy through their own efforts. The central government was weak, having little to do with guiding the economy. Many politicians embraced this ideology of wealth, as political decisions were often based on deals among wealthy individuals, and bribes and corruption became rampant.[37]

The British sociologist Herbert Spencer's conception of Social Darwinism, or the survival of the fittest, became a dominant worldview at this time in the US. He adopted the positivist argument that the same laws govern society and nature, and it is impossible to change the laws of social evolution. The rigors of the market determine who is fit to succeed and who will be a loser. Society is a self-regulating system impervious to change, which the government should leave alone. Does this sound familiar? Many people have reverted to a similar kind of logic in our era of dot.com capitalism.

Great numbers of people were dissatisfied with this new culture. We have examined several of these groups throughout this book, from the labor movement to an incipient African-American movement for social reform. Perkins Gilman was influenced by the Progressive movement, another important group opposing laissez-faire. The Progressives were a coalition of urban middle-class reformers and farmers threatened by the new industrial society. They included teachers, writers, artists, ministers, and educated homemakers who brought about reforms in child labor, sweatshops, public health, and factory conditions. Progressives promoted the primary election of political candidates, the direct election of senators, a progressive income tax, trust busting and government regulation of business, conservation measures, and food and drug safety. A responsible, publicly regulated social order managed by a welfare state could ensure steady economic growth.

Many women were involved in these activities. They tended to be well-educated; opening up higher education to women was a central concern for them. They shared with men a belief in progress and a confidence that their ideas could bring about change. These women viewed the patriarchal family of their time as a kind of prison-house. Estimates of college-educated women during this era who did not marry vary wildly, from 25 percent to 60 percent, but there were certainly more divorces among college-educated women, and they had fewer children than the less educated.

The participation of women in Progressivism was in part an extension of the women's movement. Arising in the context of the movement to abolish slavery before the Civil War, the women's movement initially addressed the rights and needs of all socially disadvantaged women. After the Civil War a split occurred between those most interested in rights for black women, and reformers concerned with the questions facing white women. Black women became more interested in issues of race, while white women sought to suppress vice and increase female self-reliance. Perkins Gilman developed her ideas in the context of this latter type of feminism.

The Progressive movement drew on many of the moralistic values that had characterized nineteenth-century middle-class US life. Middle-class morality was dominated by the Protestant ethic; many nineteenth-century reformers attempted to rid public and private life of sensuality, games, and alcohol, while protecting women from "evil" men. This moralizing activity reached a pinnacle in the Prohibition of alcohol in the 1920s. These objectives were linked to the massive immigration of Europeans from southern and eastern Europe to the US, and the migration of African-Americans from the rural South to northern cities. Middle-class women saw themselves as the moral guardians of the poor and immigrants. This meant "Americanizing" the poor and immigrants, making them into respectable citizens. Most Progressives were oblivious to the racism and ethnic segregation of the US, if they did not actively support racist ideas and programs. In this impulse to moralize we can see the disciplinary culture at work, as middle-class Anglo-Americans attempted to abolish other ways of life which they defined as disorderly and inferior to their own.[38] This aspect of Progressivism also influenced Perkins Gilman.

Male and Female Culture

Much like Marx and Durkheim, Perkins Gilman argues that people are social creatures, influenced by collective economic and cultural organization, through which humanity reproduces itself. Human nature is the result of historical and social conditions: "we create conditions and they react upon us."[39] However, people often live in social institutions left over from the past that have not modernized. The family is one such institution.

Perkins Gilman is heavily influenced by the Darwinism prevalent in her time. Like Mead, her work demonstrates that Darwinism could be used in many ways, not just as a justification for laissez-faire. She constructs her arguments through analogies to the animal world and a consideration of the "progress" of the human race. The laws of social evolution "do not wait for our recognition or acceptance: they go straight on."[40] She adopts biological imagery to understand social life. She compares society to an organism, with individuals as its cells. She discusses evolution as an organic progress. It is also social, because human progress is collective, based on collective achievements in science, nutrition, and the like. The freeing of women from economic and social domination responds to and encourages "the calm, slow, friendly forces of social evolution."[41] But for Perkins Gilman, human evolution is not always linear, as local retrogressions and changes can occur. Further, the ties of blood and heredity no longer determine people's behavior, which is now conditioned by culture and social organization.[42]

Many contemporary feminists argue that men and women inhabit different cultures, and they wish to validate women's distinctive capacities. Perkins Gilman is a forerunner of this approach. She argues that men and women live in different cultural universes, which are grounded in childhood and evolutionary development. Girls and boys learn gender differences as children - notions that boys are aggressive and rational and girls are emotional and caring - which are replicated in later life. The tragedy is that men and women think that male characteristics are the most essential, valuable, and truly human qualities. The measures of the social world are masculine, from the ways that achievement is understood to what is considered significant art and literature. In her words, the "main avenues of life are marked 'male'."[43] Women are effectively prevented from participation in science, literature, and other fields because of their lack of exposure to these areas, and because men have shut them out of these institutions.

The basic female orientation is to construct and build culture and relationships, qualities which are neglected in the modern world: "the constructive tendency is essentially feminine; the destructive masculine."[44] Men have created coercive governments, a competitive capitalist economy, and an educational system which divides the world into winners and losers. They have made the horrors of combat and war things to be honored and celebrated. Women have developed traits of physical attractiveness, coquettishness, and the like to attract males, rather than cultivating qualities of rationality and independence. Men and women must come to value female traits of endurance, adaptability, giving, and social service, rather than the male characteristics of war and competition. For Perkins Gilman, the truth of life is growth, not combat and rivalry.[45]

It bothers her than many women take on the aggressive qualities of men when entering public life, for such features do little to improve humanity. Perkins Gilman does not think that men and women are necessarily inherently different, but that different qualities have been developed over time in each of them. Only among humans are females dependent on males. At one time in early human history this dependency made sense, for women had to rely on men's skills in hunting and aggression for survival. This is not a healthy situation for men or women today. Men suffer from too easy a dominance over their wives and daughters, and do not develop good qualities of leadership and compassion. They acquire the "vices of the master:" pride, cruelty, and selfishness.[46] In the contemporary world female values of cooperation and nurturance must be integrated into society to form a more balanced human nature.

Men create an individualistic, competitive culture and economy, which obscure how people actually live and produce wealth. In a manner reminiscent of Durkheim, Perkins Gilman argues that the secret of human culture can be found in the collectivity. Morality derives from public life, for ethics is synonymous with awareness of collective duties and rights. Every virtue has a societal quality, for the highest virtues are those serving the most people. Human virtue is based on altruism, the respect for "otherness." Like Durkheim, Perkins Gilman argues that what holds people together defines morality. The general needs of society form the basis of ethics. Accuracy and punctuality become virtues as business develops. Different virtues were called for in agricultural and industrial eras. In the more differentiated contemporary world, ethics are based on a "more elaborate moral organization" than in previous eras. In the European Middle Ages the major virtues were strength, courage, and sincerity. In the modern world they involve self-control, kindness, gentleness, strength, sagacity, bravery, sincerity, and cheerfulness. These virtues become part of everyday life through gradual but arduous practice. In her words, "The common, law-abiding citizen does not consider himself a hero; yet he is manifesting a high degree of social virtue, often at great personal sacrifice."[47]

Pleasure derives from participation in collective life, not from the accumulation of goods and wealth. Private property and personal ownership, which many people justify as deriving from nature, are in reality particular values that have developed historically and are now outmoded. Competition is not the best way to organize society and the economy; a cooperative culture and economy would be much better for society. She calls for a more feminine public world of cooperation, and a private world, especially the family, that is specialized and efficient. Women need to participate in politics, for men tend to see the nation as a fighting organization in conflict with other nation-states for regional or even world dominance. She thinks that women would address issues of public health, education, and morality in a more effective way than men. From a male "androcentric" point of view, it is hard to imagine nations living together peaceably, and difficult to envision societies organized along lines other than competition and combat.[48]

Religion, too, reflects this masculine dominance. Perkins Gilman was a Christian, but she rejected much organized religion. In her view, Christianity and other organized religions often teach blind obedience. They are based on the fear of death, which allows a priestly caste to become powerful. They provide reasons for death and explain suffering in terms of good and evil. She argues that "death-religions" concerned with the afterlife and conceptions of sin and hell are based on masculine notions of power and control. For Perkins Gilman, religion should be based on service in this life. These are the true teachings of Jesus. Had women rather than men developed religion, it would look much different. A woman-based religion would emphasize growth, nurturing, and concern for future generations, not the individualistic salvation anxiety so characteristic of organized Christianity, exemplified in the Protestant ethic.[49]

Like Simmel, Perkins Gilman can be accused of promoting stereotypes of men and women. However, I see her as calling for a more inclusive culture which respects and values different human qualities, such as nurturing, which should not be restricted to gender. Such a culture cannot come into being until women's role within the family is transformed.

Work and the Family

Perkins Gilman is best known for her writings on the oppression of women in the nuclear family. Many years before Betty Friedan's *The Feminine Mystique* she criticized idyllic fantasies about the home as camouflaging the oppression of women. She argues that the home and family are shrouded in romantic myths, but should be understood as an institution like any other, such as the workplace or the state. As an institution, the family is characterized by power differentials and conflicts, with a dominant father, subservient mother, and dependent children. The wife is "a private servant."[50] It is an arena where abuse as well as love often occurs. The woman's work carried out in the home is demeaning and destructive, performed in isolation. The family and the workplace outside of the home must be transformed to eliminate male dominance and female subordination.

A transformation of women's economic condition will change their social status and do much more. It will allow them to become free, creative beings. Women are restricted from their freedom of expression through labor, which is the most basic human capacity. Perkins Gilman writes: "What we do modifies us more than what is done to us."[51] Work is not only or even primarily a means to make money; labor is what is truly human: "to do and to make not only gives deep pleasure, but it is indispensable to healthy growth."[52] It has cost women dearly to be subjected to unfree labor in the home: "but in the ever-growing human impulse to create, the power and will to make, to do, to express one's new spirit in new forms, - here she has been utterly debarred."[53] Using Durkheimian terminology, but applying it to the family in a way that Durkheim did not, Perkins Gilman writes that the specialization of labor is the basis of human progress. Specialization has not come into the home, where women are expected to be mothers, cooks, housecleaners, and nurturers without training for any of these activities.

Women share in the world through the work of their men, rather than their own labor. Wives are said to be the partners of their husbands, in their shared love and responsibility for children. But a woman is not a partner in men's work, for a housewife usually knows little of her husband's profession. Instead, housewives perform domestic work and are essentially unskilled, unpaid laborers. Perkins Gilman compares the housewife to the baker - both are expected to cook effectively. But the baker is paid for his labor, and is able to develop advanced skills because of his specialized work that the housewife cannot.[54] Untrained laborers cannot bake or make shoes, but such specialized tasks are expected of women. The home is a place of unprotected, exploited labor. Housekeeping is a group of diverse and incompatible industries held together by custom. Specialized training and institutions exist for the sick, cleaning, lodging, schooling, and cooking, yet they are lumped together in the home. Since there is no freedom or equality in the home, there is no justice.

While many of us today might applaud Perkins Gilman's arguments about housework, she applies the same logic to child-rearing, which is much more controversial. She argues that most women have no training for raising children and are not good mothers. Children require the care of many others besides the mother. A woman concerned solely with her children can become almost obsessively pathological about them, living vicariously through them. Children become selfish and overly individualistic if they have too much attention lavished upon them. Social progress would be enhanced if all children had wise, communal care. Thus, the raising of a child should be a community affair (it takes a village to raise a child). Parents should be taught to care for all children, not just their own. The health of the community provides the key to good child-raising, for the community, not the home, provides security for the individual. Progress has little to do with motherhood and everything to do with collective advances in education and public health. "Maternal instinct" means nothing to Perkins Gilman. Instinct decreases and culture increases as a determinant of behavior as societies develop. Maternal instinct cannot teach a mother to administer the proper diet for her children, manufacture articles of clothing, or educate an infant. While most men qualify through training for a trade before entering it, mothers are ignorant and untrained.[55]

Perkins Gilman advocates community child-care, so that children can interact with one another and learn the importance of community values.

Children must be taught to learn, not to obey. Infants need a space to explore apart from overbearing parents, so that they acquire the tools to think rationally and empathically. Teachers must pay close attention to what a child thinks and feels, rather than concentrating on her behavior. Children should learn to reason sequentially, so that they understand the desirability of acting in communal ways. While children need love and consideration, they must also learn justice and the value of the community in which they live. For a baby to become healthy physically and intellectually, she needs "that trained hand" more than a blood relation. The attention directed toward a child should not be based on blood and heredity, but on ideals of justice and wisdom.[56]

In sum, Perkins Gilman argues that the family should be increasingly socialized. Her insight that work within the home is productive work is still often ignored in many economic and sociological studies. For example, the kitchen should "become a clean, scientific, businesslike place."[57] Housework should be a collective affair, not only performed by the husband and wife, but many families together. With a revamping of the home that eliminates the drudgery of domestic work such as cleaning, parents will actually get to know their children, seeing them as future adults, not just as beings to care for. Much like Marx, she states that work is the greatest of human endeavors, for it defines one's sense of self and creates collective wealth and culture. Like Durkheim, she contends that the specialization of the division of labor increases production and wealth. People should also get joy from serving humanity and fulfilling their duty to society. Yet most people do not recognize the fact that wealth is produced socially, and view the social world in an individualistic way.

In Perkins Gilman's view, feminism will transform the world. She writes that the woman's movement "should be hailed by every right-thinking, far-seeing man and woman as the best birth of our century."[58] As women attain economic freedom and equality, democracy will improve. Encouraging people to think outside of the small circle of their family can allow freer social interaction, a prerequisite for democracy. As women gain more economic power, divorces will naturally increase. Women will no longer tolerate abusive conditions "which used to be borne in silence, with death as the only relief."[59] In her fiction she explores male violence against women as occurring in the home. Until women are no longer dependent on men, such violence will exist. She advocates specific women's rights, such as a "woman's right to her own body and to the decision as to when she should become a mother."[60]

These ideas informed Perkins Gilman's support of socialism. Capitalist culture emphasized selling over creativity. A small minority gains wealth, often due to the laws of inheritance and the possession of natural resources. The qualities that promote getting rich, such as competition and avarice, are not socially beneficial. Society should be organized without classes, with no division between the producer and the consumer, and all sharing in social capital and labor. Socialized workplaces should become the norm, like public schools and libraries.[61]

Like the other sociologists we have discussed, Perkins Gilman sees people as social creatures. There is much plasticity in human nature, as people are shaped by history and social circumstances as well as biology. But unlike the other social theorists, Perkins Gilman emphasizes the intersection of gender and social power. She criticizes rigid distinctions between public and private life, arguing that the family is an institution like any other. The family is distinctively premodern, maintaining almost feudal conditions of dominance and submission based on loyalty that mask oppression and the abuse of women and children. Thus, the family must be transformed. Child-rearing is of equal importance to the work in the public sphere and requires the same kind of training and specialized skills as any other profession. Perkins Gilman's arguments have a contemporary resonance. Nurturing work, from child-rearing to infant care and housework, is still drastically underpaid compared to other professions. Perkins Gilman advocates the professionalization of the home, as efficient industries and trades should take over the chores of housework. The quality of family life is tied to the larger society of which it is a part. A competitive, patriarchal society will produce a male-dominated family.

Perkins Gilman recognizes the masculine dominance of knowledge and language, arguing that this supremacy distorts human nature. Nurturance and cooperation, rather than rivalry, should define human nature. The workplace is not a gender-neutral site, but a masculine one. She advocated parental leave, professional child-care, and well-funded nurseries long before such measures were enacted into law. She forces men and women to see that masculinity and femininity are social constructions, and that there is no necessarily natural way to organize the family and the economy. Just as Du Bois demonstrates that whiteness is a taken-for-granted assumption, so too is masculinity. Perkins Gilman shows that there are many different types of masculinity, and that humanity requires the integration of masculine and feminine qualities.[62]

Freud certainly would criticize Perkins Gilman's view of the family. For Freud, the libidinally charged relationships between parents, children, and siblings cannot be so easily severed without profound psychological damage. I see Perkins Gilman exemplifying the contradictions and power of classical social theory. Her critical approach demystifies the power relations that often inform the family. She recognizes the intersection of economic power and culture, for the two cannot be separated. But her evolutionary theory leads to racism, and she has no reflexivity about her racial privileges. She is fearful of "swarming immigrants" who come to the US for free education, free hospitals, free healthcare, and better jobs than they can procure in their home nations.[63] Not coincidentally for her, these immigrants are also different in color and/or ethnicity from the Anglo-Saxons who dominated the US at her time. She sees problems for democracy in this context. Democracy demands a "community of intellect," which is difficult to achieve in a society of different cultures and races.[64] Non-modern peoples, like the inferior races and ethnicities, act individually, not in terms of collective needs and understanding. They must be disciplined, in Foucault's sense, so that they can become good, productive citizens.

These tensions between a positivist science and a more flexible sociological orientation are reminiscent of Durkheim. Perkins Gilman's arguments revolve around the conflict between the centrality of human agency in remaking gender orders, and evolutionary trends toward gender equality which assume that invariant laws governing human conduct, and seem to be occurring almost automatically. Because of her theory of progressive evolution – that modern societies are superior to those above them, inhabited by a more evolutionarily progressive race – her ideal of community is exclusive and racialized, as those who are not white cannot participate in it.

The work of Du Bois and Perkins Gilman raises issues of race and gender to a prominence lacking in the other theorists we have discussed. Du Bois situates his analysis of the distinctiveness of African-American experience, racism, and the self in the context of Hegelianism, Marxism, pragmatism, and Nietzsche. Perkins Gilman draws on themes from Darwin and Marx, indirectly influenced by Durkheimian ideas as well.

Du Bois's discussion of multiculturalism and the hidden privileges of whiteness speaks to the present. Perkins Gilman's analysis of the hidden labor performed by women, the necessity of women's education, and the close connection between the family and other social institutions, also illuminates many aspects of contemporary Western society. Women still face greater pressures of dealing with work and home, caring for children and building a career, than do men. Housework and nurturing work are still often not considered to be productive labor. Women must be educated for global gender inequality to decrease. Perkins Gilman and Du Bois do not break with the philosophical themes informing classical social theory in developing their analyses, but build on these ideas and refashion them in some new directions. They demonstrate both the strengths and the limitations of much classical social theory. They imbibe the scientific climate of their time, fruitfully leading them to study social and philosophical questions empirically, so that they are not satisfied with abstract speculation about race and gender. This scientific orientation also constrains their thought to some degree. Du Bois struggles with the limitations of positivist science to understand the history and distinctiveness of African-American experience and the fluidity of the self. He sometimes relies uncritically on a belief that a scientifically educated elite is necessary to lead African-Americans to freedom. Perkins Gilman implicitly recognizes the limits of science by turning to fiction to document the experience of women. But her reliance on seemingly scientific evolutionary assumptions reinforces the racism that was so dominant in the Anglo-American society of her time.

Notes

1 Charlotte Perkins Gilman, "Why Cooperative Housekeeping Fails" (1907), in *Charlotte Perkins Gilman: A Nonfiction Reader*, ed. Larry Ceplair (New York, 1991), p. 171.
2 See Amartya Sen, *Development as Freedom* (New York, 1999).
3 Henry Louis Gates, "W. E. B. Du Bois and the Talented Tenth," in *The Future of the Race*, by Henry Louis Gates and Cornel West (New York, 1996), pp. 115–22.
4 W. E. B. Du Bois, *The Souls of Black Folk* (New York, 1995), p. 41.
5 See David Levering Lewis, *W. E. B. Du Bois: Biography of a Race, 1868–1919* (New York, 1993).
6 John Brueggemann, "A Century After 'The Philadelphia Negro': Reflections on Urban Ethnography and Race in America," *Journal of Contemporary Ethnography* 26 (October 1997), p. 364. See also W. E. B. Du Bois, *The Philadelphia Negro: A Social Study* (Philadelphia, 1899) and *The Souls of Black Folk*.
7 W. E. B. Du Bois, *Darkwater: Voices from Within the Veil* (New York, 1920), pp. 98–103.
8 Scott Herring, "Du Bois and the Minstrels," *Melus* 22 (summer 1997), pp. 3–4.
9 Du Bois, *The Souls of Black Folk*, pp. 112–15.
10 Ibid, p. 43. See also Gates, "W. E. B. Du Bois and the Talented Tenth," p. 84.
11 See Shamoon Zamir, *Dark Voices: W. E. B. Du Bois and American Thought* (Chicago, 1995), pp. 135–6.
12 W. E. B. Du Bois, *On Sociology and the Black Community*, ed. Dan Green and Edwin Driver (Chicago, 1978), pp. 244–5.
13 Ibid, p. 216.
14 Du Bois, *The Souls of Black Folk*, p. 265-8.
15 Ibid, p. 52.
16 Paul Gilroy, *The Black Atlantic: Modernity and Double Consciousness* (Cambridge, MA, 1993).
17 Du Bois, *Darkwater*, pp. 29–30.
18 Ibid, p. 30.
19 Ibid, p. 60.
20 See *Displacing Whiteness: Essays in Social and Cultural Criticism*, ed. Ruth Frankenberg (Durham, NC, 1997).
21 Du Bois, *Darkwater*, p. 73.

22 W. E. B. Du Bois, "The Talented Tenth" (1902), reprinted in *The Future of the Race*, pp. 133–4, 140.

23 Du Bois, *Darkwater*, p. 142.

24 Ibid, p. 135.

25 Ibid, p. 140.

26 See Du Bois, "The Talented Tenth," (1902). See also Ross Posnock, *Color and Culture: Black Writers and the Making of the Modern Intellectual* (Cambridge, MA, 1998).

27 Zamir, *Dark Voices*, pp. 114, 141–52.

28 Du Bois, *On Sociology and the Black Community*, p. 259.

29 Du Bois, *The Souls of Black Folk*, p. 119.

30 Du Bois, *Darkwater*, p. 49.

31 Ibid, p. 143.

32 Ibid, p. 183.

33 Du Bois, "The Talented Tenth" (1948), reprinted in *The Future of the Race*, by Henry Louis Gates and Cornel West (New York, 1996), p. 163

34 Du Bois, *Darkwater*, p. 71.

35 Ibid.

36 See the excellent biography of Perkins Gilman by Ann J. Lane, *To Herland and Beyond: The Life and Work of Charlotte Perkins Gilman* (New York, 1990).

37 Ibid, pp. 13–16; see also Robert Wiebe, *The Search for Order, 1877–1920* (New York, 1968).

38 See Lary May, *Screening Out the Past: The Birth of Mass Media and the Motion Picture Industry* (New York, 1980).

39 Charlotte Perkins Gilman, "Human Nature" (1890), in *Charlotte Perkins Gilman: A Nonfiction Reader*, ed. Larry Ceplair (New York, 1991), p. 45.

40 Charlotte Perkins Gilman, *Women and Economics* (Berkeley, CA, 1898; 1998), p. 146.

41 Ibid, p. 340.

42 Ibid, pp. 74–5; see also Charlotte Perkins Gilman, "The Labor Movement" (1892), in *Charlotte Perkins Gilman: A Nonfiction Reader*, ed. Larry Ceplair (New York, 1991), pp. 62–4.

43 Perkins Gilman, *Women and Economics*, p. 53; see also Lane, *To Herland and Beyond*, pp. 236–40.

44 Charlotte Perkins Gilman, "The Home" (1903), in *Charlotte Perkins Gilman: A Nonfiction Reader*, ed. Larry Ceplair (New York, 1991), p. 127.

45 Perkins Gilman, *Women and Economics*, p. 63.

46 Ibid, p. 338.

47 Ibid, p. 327.

48 Charlotte Perkins Gilman, "The Man-Made World" (1911), in *Charlotte Perkins Gilman: A Nonfiction Reader*, ed. Larry Ceplair (New York, 1991), pp. 210–12.

49 Charlotte Perkins Gilman, "His Religion and Hers" (1923), in *Charlotte Perkins Gilman: A Nonfiction Reader*, ed. Larry Ceplair (New York, 1991), pp. 296–301.

50 Perkins Gilman, *Women and Economics*, p. 211; see also Perkins Gilman, "The Home," p. 139.

51 Perkins Gilman, *Women and Economics*, p. 66.

52   Ibid, p. 157.
53   Ibid, p. 67.
54   Lane, *To Herland and Beyond*, p. 241.
55   Perkins Gilman, *Women and Economics*, pp. 182, 188-97.
56   Ibid, p. 291.
57   Perkins Gilman, "Why Cooperative Housekeeping Fails," p. 174.
58   Perkins Gilman, *Women and Economics*, p. 144.
59   Charlotte Perkins Gilman, "A New Generation of Women" (1923), in *Charlotte Perkins Gilman: A Nonfiction Reader*, ed. Larry Ceplair (New York, 1991), p. 286.
60   Charlotte Perkins Gilman, "Statements of Purpose" (1909 and 1916), in *Charlotte Perkins Gilman: A Nonfiction Reader*, ed. Larry Ceplair (New York, 1991), p. 197; see also Michael Kimmel and Amy Aronson, "Introduction to the 1998 Edition," in Charlotte Perkins Gilman, *Women and Economics* (Berkeley, CA, 1998), p. xliv.
61   Charlotte Perkins Gilman, "Our Place Today" (1891), p. 53; "Socialist Psychology" (1933), p. 311; "Human Work" (1904), pp. 145, 155, in *Charlotte Perkins Gilman: A Nonfiction Reader*, ed. Larry Ceplair (New York, 1991).
62   Kimmel and Aronson, "Introduction," p. lxiii.
63   Charlotte Perkins Gilman, "Is America Too Hospitable?" (1923), in *Charlotte Perkins Gilman: A Nonfiction Reader*, ed. Larry Ceplair (New York, 1991), p. 289.
64   Ibid, p. 292.

Conclusion

We live in an age distant in many ways from that of the classical social theorists. People in the West inhabit a fast-paced world, a global village made up of information super-highways and worldwide mass media. The nineteenth- and early twentieth-century industrial society of factory workers, a bourgeoisie whose wealth rested on manufacturing, the nuclear family, and a trust in science as a solution to problems has been replaced by a global post-industrial order characterized by the dominance of service work, information technologies, new types of blended families, and the ecological distrust of science. New social movements, such as feminism and gay and lesbian movements, and the decolonization of Africa and Asia throughout the second half of the twentieth century, have radically changed the social context of the twenty-first century compared to that of the nineteenth century. Issues of cultural identity, postcolonialism, and the relationship of reason to power help set the contemporary theoretical agenda.

These issues of late modernity raise new questions for social theory. Rather than concentrating on the nature of industrial society, individual and cultural identity, race, gender, and democracy are now fundamental topics that social theorists must address. These problems intersect with the widespread concern in the social sciences with understanding how language shapes social action and behaviors. In our mass-media age, power is exercised symbolically, through language and images, as well as through the material means of production. As Anthony Giddens states, modern philosophy has undergone a "linguistic turn," so that "personal experience is known to the self as a 'self' only via the public categories of language."[1] In the context of social theory, the study of language cannot be divorced from social power, so the linguistic turn places issues of cultural and symbolic power at the center of analysis. The particular ways in which people understand the world in a given society has enormous consequences for the configuration of social power in that society.

Many contemporary social theorists from Foucault to Touraine influenced by this linguistic approach have abandoned the ambition of achieving an overarching, universal theory that explains all societies and their histories, a goal which animated many of the classical thinkers we have studied. Many social theorists influenced by postmodernism are sensitive to the ways in which universalistic theories of society and social change based on rationalistic assumptions often marginalize or exclude other cultural knowledges which do not conform to their categories. Many feminists argue that such a notion of truth is inherently masculine, and reinforces the domination of men over women; queer theorists contend that it is tied to attempts to make heterosexuality seem natural and normal, thus dismissing the approaches developed by gays and lesbians; theorists of postcolonialism see this notion of a single reality as Orientalist, a way of stereotypically contrasting the West as the place of science and reason versus Eastern irrationality and exoticism, which justifies Western imperialism.

I have taken these questions as the background for my reading of the classical social theorists. I examined the classical sociological theory of Marx, Weber, Durkheim, Freud, Simmel, Mead, Du Bois, and Perkins Gilman through the lens of these new concerns, particularly the issues of colonialism, the paradox of rationalization, the possibilities for democracy tied to the public sphere, and the questions of individual and cultural identity. These issues demonstrate some of the weak spots of the classical social theorists. They sometimes equated the modern world with industrial society, focusing on economic processes to the exclusion of other dimensions of social life. They often did not recognize that many of the social categories that they took for granted, such as race and gender, were socially and historically constructed, their very content based on power relations. But these theorists also demonstrated surprising insights into these issues, providing theoretical resources for contemporary social thinkers.

In order to avoid simple and misleading criticisms of the classical social theorists, I have argued that they must be placed in their social and philosophical context in order to make sense of their thought. I have contended that the classical sociological theorists were engaged in understanding the new type of society that arose with capitalism and industrialism in nineteenth-century Europe, and which began to spread throughout the world. Theorists as disparate as Marx and Perkins Gilman attempted to comprehend the exceptional character of modernity: what was distinctive about modern Western societies? The answer to this question involved the exploration of the meaning of new political institutions such as the nation-state, and a new capitalist market-economic system. These theorists analyzed many new social phenomena, such as bureaucracy, democratic politics, a culture of secularism, money, and individualism, the new emphasis on art as a way of life, new types of social inequality based on social classes such as the bourgeoisie and the proletariat and colonialism, and demands by oppressed groups for the recognition of cultural identities, from workers to African-Americans to women. Classical sociological theorists offered up ideas such as capitalism (Marx), rationalization (Weber), and organic solidarity (Durkheim) to make sense of these social developments. The sheer scope and pace of social change encouraged them to see modernity as very different from the "traditional" societies which preceded them. They also viewed other cultures outside of the West as having these traditional characteristics, a perspective reinforced by European colonialism.

The classical writers tried to theoretically capture the nature of these common problems. They wrote in the wake of a crisis of European social and political representation. As democratic values slowly gained ground in Europe and monarchies faced opposition, questions about who had legitimate authority to rule in society became increasingly prominent. Individualism developed apace with new social institutions like unions, voluntary organizations, and the like, alongside a new capitalist economy that created social inequality and vast amounts of wealth. Hegel called this new arena civil society; the classical theorists recognized that many of the changes that they investigated originated in this new domain. Civil society mediated between the public and private spheres, between the state and the individual. Further, a new realm of debate, the public sphere, arose which guaranteed that any government had to be based on some measure, however limited, of popular sovereignty.

The classical social theorists did not just respond to social changes, however. They were also engaged in a philosophical and moral project, involving reflections on issues such as the meaning of freedom, the conditions whereby freedom could be exercised, and the nature of a good society. The decline of the feudal belief in a natural order of society ushered in new issues for political and social theorists. This dissolution of an overarching system of values coincided with problems of how to understand the social world: if God's plan did not inform society and nature, how could humankind comprehend the social and natural worlds? The answer to this question involved the supremacy of reason, demonstrated forcefully in the Enlightenment and the spread of rationality throughout Europe in the eighteenth and nineteenth centuries. Rational knowledge gave people the power to understand and control the world around them. The classical social theorists, too, thought that these philosophical issues could be addressed using the tools of rationality. They advocated a rationality that drew on the instrumental reason of the Enlightenment, but also went beyond it, and was sensitive to historical context. I have demonstrated the rich philosophical background influencing the classical social theorists, from the Enlightenment to Nietzschean philosophy, which informed their complex views of reason and science.

Moral visions of justice also motivated the thinkers we examined. Even when they consciously rejected ethical perspectives in favor of a scientific worldview, moral and philosophical issues remained dominant, from Marx's view of communism to Du Bois's analysis of African-American culture. Their commitment to science and empirical and historical study tempered their moral convictions, however. Much of the power of these theorists derives from their testing of their ideals through study of the real world. They took moral questions out of the realm of philosophical speculation and subjected them to empirical research. They argued in various ways that freedom invariably has a social component, and changing society provided the path to a better world.

But other factors also influenced the social and philosophical context of the classical social theorists, which are not usually included in narratives of the rise of their thought. Empire must be incorporated into an analysis of the historical era in which social theory developed. The West's relationship to its colonies invariably involved comparisons of European and non-Western cultures which were not just incidental to classical social theorists, but integral to their work. This emphasis on the interpretive moment in social theory involves rethinking the relationship of power and knowledge, which was often not theorized by the classical thinkers in a sophisticated way.

I discussed the rise of the disciplinary society in this context. Reason was a double-edged sword. Postmodernists such as Foucault argue that reason replaced God as a fundamental first principle of thinking and identity in the nineteenth century. The institutional use of rationality allowed social and governmental elites to regulate their populations, manifested in the rise of institutions such as prisons and asylums that legitimized the rule of experts. Foucault contends that these surveillance capacities were major components of the rise of the modern West. Knowledge was not disinterested, but tied to power. Elites tried to control those irrational aspects of social life that were outside of their province. Experts defined normal and abnormal behavior, often using rationality as the criteria to repress those behaviors that were not classified as typical. As Foucault states, the claim to universality on the part of rationality hides its historical origins. He demonstrates how people are shaped as individuals by the disciplinary society, and how reason and morality come to define a singular way of life as best.

While the classical social theorists sometimes shared this celebration of instrumental reason, I have argued that this does not capture the whole story of their thought. Their notions of rationality and science were influenced by Kant's reformulation of Enlightenment ideas of reason, and the various critiques of Kant advanced throughout the nineteenth century. The rationality of the classical social theorists was often sensitive to the intricacies and contradictions of particular social contexts. Unlike Foucault, they recognized that different types of community had differential effects for the rule of domination or freedom in the modern world, and that institutions influenced social life in multifarious and not always coherent ways. They saw people as active agents able to reshape their world, even though constrained by social circumstances.

Democracy was one such important institution examined by the classical theorists. They explored the nature and fate of democracy in European and American societies. Durkheim, Marx, Du Bois, and Mead, especially, had a participatory moment in their theoretical approaches, while Weber was interested in the problem of democratic citizenship. Each theorist drew in different ways on the republican tradition of active, public, and democratic participation in order to counter what they saw as the tendencies of contemporary society and economy to foster social inequality and privilege individualism over concern for the public good.

I argued that new theorists, including Simmel, Freud, Mead, Du Bois, and Perkins Gilman, must be integrated into the traditional sociological canon of Marx, Weber, and Durkheim. These theorists raise complex questions of individual and cultural identity not examined in detail by Marx, Weber, and Durkheim. They comprise a kind of second tradition of social theory, suspicious of all claims to absolute truth and sensitive to the incoherence and irrationality of everyday life. Freud, following Nietzsche, brings the body into social theory, demonstrating that sexuality and emotions must be studied by social theory. Mead, Simmel, and Du Bois demonstrate that a fluid, aesthetic sense of self is part of the modern condition. Much everyday social action is creative, akin to an art form. This dimension of experience calls for a flexible social science that can capture this aesthetic moment. Aesthetics is not opposed to rationality, but it is a different kind of rationality, based on thinking in terms of analogy rather than cause and effect. Finally, Du Bois and Perkins Gilman demonstrate that issues of race and gender inflect modern identity in subtle, often unrecognizable ways. The concerns of these theorists predate contemporary postmodern concerns – from multiculturalism, to the fragmentation of cultural identities, to the suspicion of all forms of community based on a single model of solidarity.

Some important lessons derive from my reading of the classics. Any philosophy of history based on a notion of inevitable rational progress must be rejected. However, I think that we should be cautious about ridding social science of notions such as the difference between tradition and modernity, as many postmodernists advocate. Rather, these ideas should be rethought. Abandoning this distinction can lead to a static

notion that nothing has changed in history, which underplays some key
dimensions of the specificity of modernity. The modern world is distinctive
because of the rise of capitalism and industrialism, its rapidly increased
scope and pace of change relative to other historical eras, and the emergence of new types of institutions, such as business corporations and a
state concerned with social welfare, which use rational knowledge such
as social statistics and econometric models of forecasting to understand
the social world and ensure their continued existence. Such considerations lead to a new sense of the meaning of rationalization and a more
complex view of the tradition–modernity distinction. The classical theorists, if read properly, grasped many of these dimensions of modernity.

Given my narrative of the classical social theorists, their value does not
reside in the accumulation of testable, reliable knowledge. The classical
theorists were not scientific precursors to contemporary quantitative sociology. In fact, their investment in a strong version of science often led
them astray. Though frequently sensitive to the singularity of social context, Marx, Weber, and Durkheim sometimes posited universal laws of
social development which did not take into account these cultural and
social particularities. These thinkers neglected issues of aesthetics and
cultural identity that were not amenable to positivistic scientific investigation. I demonstrated that Mead, Simmel, and Du Bois had a more flexible
version of science, which allowed them to capture a sense of the fluidity of
modern identity in ways that Marx, Weber, and Durkheim did not. These
reflections on the classical theorists call for a version of contemporary
social science that is open to moral, philosophical, and aesthetic questions.

The moral of this approach to the classical social theorists is that social
theory is tied to its context, but the best social theory illuminates that
context in a new way and develops themes which transcend it. It builds
on philosophical and social perspectives which precede it, refashioning
them in a new, creative manner and employing these ideas in empirical
and historical research. The passion for a better, more just society informed the writings of the theorists we explored, even with all their blind
spots to colonialism, gender, and the like. I think these arguments and
convictions should be heeded today. The best social theory explains the
social world and does not become solely concerned with abstract philosophical controversies. It explores theoretical questions in empirical and
historical context. We should be leery of making sweeping arguments
about social change and the supposed irrelevance of sociological and philosophical thinkers from other eras in our postmodern or late-modern age.
The best social theory draws on the insights of the past in a creative and
rich manner to help explain the present, highlighting what is socially,
culturally, and philosophically distinctive in the present, while sensitive to

historical continuities. The classical social theorists at their most insightful provide models for this "best" type of social theory, and provide resources for understanding our present epoch.

Note

1 Anthony Giddens, *In Defence of Sociology: Essays, Interpretations, and Rejoinders* (Cambridge, MA, 1996), p. 205.

Further Reading

The following list of suggested further reading comprises writings that I found particularly helpful, and it also includes influential interpretations of the prominent theorists. I have constructed the list around the major thinkers covered in the text.

Karl Marx

No one is neutral about Marx, so the reader should tackle Marx for herself. *The Communist Manifesto* is the logical starting point. I also recommend the "Economic and Philosophical Manuscripts of 1844," "The German Ideology," and "Wage Labor and Capital." There are numerous collections of Marx's work, but I have found most useful Robert Tucker's *Marx–Engels Reader* (New York: W. W. Norton, 1978). I developed my understanding of Marx early in my academic career, persuaded by the interpretations of Marx advanced by the Frankfurt School that view philosophical and cultural issues around alienation as central to his work. Influential studies include Jürgen Habermas, *Theory and Practice* (Boston: Beacon Press, 1973), Herbert Marcuse, *Studies in Critical Philosophy* (Boston: Beacon Press, 1973), Martin Jay, *Marxism and Totality* (Berkeley: University of California Press, 1984), and George Lichtheim, *Marxism: An Historical and Critical Study* (New York: Columbia University Press, 1982).

General analyses of Marx's work

Shlomo Avineri, *The Social and Political Thought of Karl Marx* (New York: Cambridge University Press, 1968).

Isaiah Berlin, *Karl Marx: His Life and Work* (New York: Oxford University Press, 1996).

Terrell Carver, ed., *The Cambridge Companion to Marx* (New York: Cambridge University Press, 1992).

G. A. Cohen, *Karl Marx's Theory of History* (Princeton, NJ: Princeton University Press, 2000).

Anthony Giddens, *A Contemporary Critique of Historical Materialism, vol. 1: Power, Property and the State* (Berkeley: University of California Press, 1981).
Anthony Giddens, *A Contemporary Critique of Historical Materialism, vol. 2: The Nation-State and Violence* (Berkeley: University of California Press, 1985).
David McLellan, *The Thought of Karl Marx: An Introduction* (New York: Harper and Row, 1972).
Bertell Ollman, *Alienation: Marx's Concept of Man in Capitalist Society* (New York: Cambridge University Press, 1977).
Cornel West, *The Ethical Dimensions of Marx's Thought* (New York: Monthly Review Press, 1991).

Philosophical aspects of Marx's thought

Louis Althusser, *For Marx* (New York: Verso, 1996).
Jacques Derrida, *Spectres of Marx* (New York: Routledge, 1994).
Leszek Kolakowski, *Main Currents in Marxism* (Oxford: Clarendon Press, 1978).
Henri Lefebvre, *The Sociology of Marx* (New York: Columbia University Press, 1982).

Marxist economics

Ernest Mandel, *The Formation of the Economic Thought of Karl Marx, 1843 to Capital* (New York: Monthly Review Press, 1971).
Fred Moseley, ed., *Marx's Method in Capital: A Reexamination* (Atlantic Highlands, NJ: Prometheus Books, 1993).
Paul Sweezy, *The Theory of Capitalist Development: Principles of Marxian Political Economy* (New York: Modern Reader Paperbacks, 1970).

Emile Durkheim

Most sociology students who study Durkheim read *The Division of Labor in Society* (New York: Free Press, 1984). Conventionally, anthropology students concentrated on his study of religion, *The Elementary Forms of the Religious Life* (New York: Free Press, 1995), but *The Elementary Forms* is a central work in the Durkheim corpus, and should be read alongside *The Division of Labor in Society*. The most complete study of Durkheim remains Stephen Lukes's *Emile Durkheim: His Life and Work* (New York: Harper and Row, 1972). I have been influenced by the interpretations of Durkheim that focus on the moral and democratic elements in his work. They include Mark Cladis, *A Communitarian Defense of Liberalism: Emile Durkheim and Contemporary Social Theory* (Stanford, CA: Stanford University Press, 1992) and Hans Joas's essay, "Durkheim and Pragmatism: The Psychology of Consciousness and the Social Constitution of Categories," in *Pragmatism and Social Theory* (Chicago: University of Chicago Press, 1993), pp. 55–78. Older studies I have found helpful include Jeffrey Alexander, *Theoretical Logic in Sociology, vol. 2: The Antinomies of Classical Thought: Marx and Durkheim* (Berkeley: University of California Press, 1982), and the introduction by Robert Bellah to his edited collection, *Emile Durkheim on Morality and Society* (Chicago: University of Chicago Press, 1973).

General analyses of Durkheim's work

Anthony Giddens, *Emile Durkheim* (New York: Viking Press, 1979).
Jennifer Lehmann, *Durkheim and Women* (Lincoln: University of Nebraska Press, 1994).
William Watts Miller, *Durkheim, Morals, and Modernity* (Montreal: McGill-Queens University Press, 1996).
Robert Nisbet, ed., *Emile Durkheim* (Englewood Cliffs, NJ: Prentice-Hall, 1965).
Frank Parkin, *Durkheim* (New York: Oxford University Press, 1992).
Frank Pearce, *The Radical Durkheim* (Boston: Unwin Hyman, 1989).
W. S. F. Pickering, ed., *Emile Durkheim: Critical Assessments*, 4 vols. (New York: Routledge, 2001).
Gianfrance Poggi, *Durkheim* (New York: Oxford University Press, 2000).
Stephen P. Turner, ed., *Emile Durkheim: Sociologist and Moralist* (New York: Routledge, 1993).

The philosophical dimensions of Durkheim's thought

Robert Alun Jones, *The Development of Durkheim's Social Realism* (New York: Cambridge University Press, 1999).
Dominick LaCapra, *Emile Durkheim: Sociologist and Philosopher* (Ithaca, NY: Cornell University Press, 1972).

Durkheim and religion

N. J. Allen, W. S. F. Pickering, and W. Watts Miller, eds., *On Durkheim's Elementary Forms of the Religious Life* (New York: Routledge, 1998).

Durkheim and the law

Roger Cotterell, *Emile Durkheim: Law in a Moral Domain* (Stanford, CA: Stanford University Press, 1999).

Max Weber

The literature on Weber is extensive. The best place to start is with Weber himself, especially his classic essay, *The Protestant Ethic and the Spirit of Capitalism* (New York: Routledge, 1992). A good collection of Weber's essays can also be found in the classic reader edited by H. H. Gerth and C. Wright Mills, *From Max Weber* (New York: Oxford University Press, 1958). Notable studies of Weber include Reinhard Bendix, *Max Weber: An Intellectual Portrait* (Berkeley: University of California Press, 1977), Julien Freund, *The Sociology of Max Weber* (New York: Pantheon Books, 1968), and the biography of Weber by his wife, Marianne Weber, *Max Weber* (New York: Wiley Press, 1974). Influential contemporary studies of Weber which I find helpful and that highlight his analysis of rationalization and modernity include Wolfgang Schluchter, *Paradoxes of Modernity: Culture and*

Conduct in the Theory of Max Weber (Stanford, CA: Stanford University Press, 1996), Bryan Turner, *Max Weber: From History to Modernity* (New York: Routledge, 1993), and the complex study of Weber by Jürgen Habermas in the first volume of his study *Theory of Communicative Action* (Boston: Beacon Press, 1984).

General analyses of Weber's work

John P. Diggins, *Max Weber: Politics and the Spirit of Tragedy* (New York: Basic Books, 1996).

William Hennis, *Max Weber: Essays in Reconstruction* (Boston: Allen and Unwin, 1988).

Stephen Kalberg, *Max Weber's Comparative-Historical Sociology* (Chicago: University of Chicago Press, 1994).

Lawrence A. Scaff, *Fleeing the Iron Cage: Culture, Politics and Modernity in the Thought of Max Weber* (Berkeley: University of California Press, 1989).

Alan Sica, *Weber, Irrationality, and Social Order* (Berkeley: University of California Press, 1988).

Bryan Turner, *For Weber: Essays on the Sociology of Fate* (London: Sage, 1995).

Stephen Turner, ed., *The Cambridge Companion to Weber* (New York: Cambridge University Press, 2000).

Weber on politics

David Beetham, *Max Weber and the Theory of Modern Politics* (New York: Polity Press, 1997).

Peter Breiner, *Max Weber and Democratic Politics* (Ithaca, NY: Cornell University Press, 1996).

Wolfgang Mommsen, *Max Weber and German Politics: 1890–1920* (Chicago: University of Chicago Press, 1992).

Weber on methodology

Fritz Ringer, *Max Weber's Methodology: The Unification of the Cultural and Social Sciences* (Cambridge, MA: Harvard University Press, 2000).

Weber on economics

Richard Swedberg, *Max Weber and the Idea of Economic Sociology* (Princeton, NJ: Princeton University Press, 2000).

Weber on religion

Toby Huff and Wolfgang Schluchter, eds., *Max Weber and Islam* (New Brunswick, NJ: Transaction Publishers, 1999).

Bryan Turner, *Weber and Islam* (New York: Routledge, 1974).

Sigmund Freud

The literature on Freud is immense, but much of it focuses on his work as a psychologist rather than as a social theorist. A clear presentation of psychoanalysis by the master himself is *A General Introduction to Psychoanalysis* (New York: Garden City Press, 1938). Freud's two most accessible works on society are *Civilization and Its Discontents* (New York: W. W. Norton, 1961) and *The Future of an Illusion* (New York: W. W. Norton, 1961). I have been influenced by the Frankfurt School interpretation of Freud that sees his work as culturally radical despite his political and social conservatism. These works include Herbert Marcuse, *Eros and Civilization: A Philosophical Inquiry into Freud* (New York: Vintage Books, 1962) and Russell Jacoby, *Social Amnesia* (Boston: Beacon Press, 1975). I have also found interesting the feminist interpretation of Freud by Nancy Chodorow, *The Reproduction of Mothering: Psychoanalysis and the Sociology of Gender* (Berkeley: University of California Press, 1978), and the feminist/postmodern approach of Judith Butler, *Gender Trouble: Feminism and the Subversion of Identity* (New York: Routledge, 1990).

Selected reading on or concerning Freud

Bruno Bettelheim, *Freud and Man's Soul* (New York: Alfred A. Knopf, 1983).
John Forrester, *The Seduction of Psychoanalysis: Freud, Lacan, and Derrida* (New York: Cambridge University Press, 1991).
Peter Gay, *Freud: A Life for Our Times* (New York: W. W. Norton, 1998).
Ernest Jones, *The Life and Work of Sigmund Freud* (New York: Basic Books, 1961).
Christopher Lasch, *The Culture of Narcissism* (New York: W. W. Norton, 1978).
Stephen A. Mitchell and Margaret J. Black, *Freud and Beyond: A History of Modern Psychoanalytic Thought* (New York: Basic Books, 1996).
Philip Rieff, *Freud: The Mind of a Moralist* (Chicago: University of Chicago Press, 1979).
Philip Rieff, *The Triumph of the Therapeutic: Uses of Faith After Freud* (Chicago: University of Chicago Press, 1987).
Richard Wollheim, *Sigmund Freud* (New York: Cambridge University Press, 1989).

Georg Simmel

Georg Simmel is only now beginning to find his rightful place in the sociological canon. His diverse writings are collected in various edited volumes. I found the most complete collection of his works in the older text by Simmel, *On Individuality and Social Forms*, edited by Donald Levine (Chicago: University of Chicago Press, 1971). A more recent text edited by David Frisby and Mike Featherstone gathers many of Simmel's writings on culture: see *Simmel on Culture: Selected Writings* (London: Sage, 1997). Simmel is best known for his book, *The Philosophy of Money* (New York: Routledge, 1990), which is interesting but difficult to read. I have found David Frisby's work among the best in deciphering Simmel. His books include *Sociological Impressionism: A Reassessment of Georg Simmel's Social Theory* (New York: Routledge, 1992) and *Fragments of Modernity: Theories of Modernity in the Work of Simmel, Kracauer, and Benjamin* (Cambridge, MA: MIT Press, 1988). Other works on Simmel include:

David Frisby, *Simmel and Since: Essays on Georg Simmel's Social Theory* (New York: Routledge, 1992).
David Frisby, ed., *Georg Simmel* (New York: Routledge, 1994).
Gary Jaworski, *Georg Simmel and the American Prospect* (Albany: State University of New York Press, 1997).
Gianfranco Poggi, *Money and the Modern Mind: Georg Simmel's Philosophy of Money* (Berkeley: University of California Press, 1993).
Denna Weinstein and Michael Weinstein, *Postmodern(ized) Simmel* (New York: Routledge, 1993).

George Herbert Mead

Despite his status as a founder of symbolic interactionism, Mead has not received his due as a social theorist. His major book is *Mind, Self, and Society from the Standpoint of a Social Behaviorist* (Chicago: University of Chicago Press, 1959), a collection of his lectures as noted by some of his students. Another important work by Mead is *The Philosophy of the Present* (Chicago: Open Court Publishing, 1932). Influential in my interpretation of Mead was his article on art, entitled "The Nature of Aesthetic Experience," *International Journal of Ethics* 36 (1925–6), pp. 382–93. In my view, Hans Joas is far and away the best interpreter of Mead's thought. His work includes *George Herbert Mead: A Contemporary Reexamination of His Thought* (Cambridge, MA: MIT Press, 1997), and *Pragmatism and Social Theory* (Chicago: University of Chicago Press, 1993). I also found Robert Dunn's interpretation of Mead very helpful. See *Identity Crises* (Minneapolis: University of Minnesota Press, 1998). Other works on Mead include:

Mitchell Aboulafia, *The Mediating Self: Mead, Sartre, and Self-Determination* (New Haven, CT: Yale University Press, 1986).
Mitchell Aboulafia, ed., *Philosophy, Social Theory, and the Thought of George Herbert Mead* (Albany: State University of New York Press, 1991).
Herbert Blumer, *Symbolic Interactionism: Perspective and Method* (Englewood Cliffs, NJ: Prentice-Hall, 1969).
Gary A. Cook, *George Herbert Mead: The Making of a Social Pragmatist* (Urbana: University of Illinois Press, 1993).
Norman Denzin, *Symbolic Interactionism and Cultural Studies: The Politics of Interpretation* (Cambridge, MA: Blackwell Publishers, 1992).

W. E. B. Du Bois

Du Bois's contributions to sociological theory are beginning to be recognized. Many sociologists now see his classic work, *The Souls of Black Folk* (New York: Penguin Books, 1995), as an important work of social theory as well as a literary masterpiece. Du Bois's other autobiographical study, *Darkwater: Voices from Within the Veil*

(New York: AMS Press, 1969), is also a central text for understanding his sociological perspective. A good collection of his sociological essays can be found in Dan Green and Edwin Driver, eds., *W. E. B. Du Bois on Sociology and the Black Community* (Chicago: University of Chicago Press, 1978). I have found recent cultural studies approaches that emphasize the philosophical and postmodern tendencies of Du Bois's work most helpful. In particular, see Paul Gilroy, *The Black Atlantic: Modernity and Double Consciousness* (Cambridge, MA: Harvard University Press, 1993), Henry Louis Gates and Cornel West, *The Future of the Race* (New York: Alfred A. Knopf, 1996), and Shamoon Zamir, *Dark Voices: W. E. B. Du Bois and American Thought* (Chicago: University of Chicago Press, 1995). Other studies of Du Bois include:

John Henrik Clarke, et al., *Black Titan: W. E. B. Du Bois* (Boston: Beacon Press, 1970).
Michael Katz and Thomas Sugrue, eds., *W. E. B. Du Bois, Race and the City: The Philadelphia Negro and Its Legacy* (Philadelphia: University of Pennsylvania Press, 1998).
David Levering Lewis, *W. E. B. Du Bois: Biography of a Race, 1868–1919* (New York: Henry Holt, 1993).
David Levering Lewis, *W. E. B. Du Bois: The Fight for Equality and the American Century, 1919–1963* (New York: Henry Holt, 2000).
Ross Posnock, *Color and Culture: Black Writers and the Making of the Modern Intellectual* (Cambridge, MA: Harvard University Press, 1998).
Adolph Reed, *W. E. B. Du Bois and American Political Thought: Fabianism and the Color Line* (New York: Oxford University Press, 1999).
Cary D. Wintz, eds., *African American Political Thought 1890–1930: Washington, Du Bois, Garvey, and Randolph* (Armonk, NY: M. E. Sharpe, 1996).

Charlotte Perkins Gilman

Perkins Gilman is known as much for her literary work as for her sociological studies. She wrote two classic feminist pieces, the short story "The Yellow Wallpaper" and the novel *Herland*. These writings can be found in Denise Knight, ed., *Herland, The Yellow Wall-paper, and Selected Writings* (New York: Penguin Books, 1999). Her most famous social scientific book is *Women and Economics* (Berkeley: University of California Press, 1998). A good collection of sociological pieces is in Larry Ceplair, ed., *Charlotte Perkins Gilman: A Nonfiction Reader* (New York: Columbia University Press, 1991). I found Ann J. Lane's excellent biography of Perkins Gilman most helpful; see *To Herland and Beyond: The Life and Work of Charlotte Perkins Gilman* (New York: Pantheon, 1990). Other works on Perkins Gilman include:

Polly Wynn Allen, *Building Domestic Liberty: Charlotte Perkins Gilman's Architectural Feminism* (Amherst: University of Massachusetts Press, 1988).
Catherine J. Golden and Joanna Schneider Zangrando, eds., *The Mixed Legacy of Charlotte Perkins Gilman* (Cranbury, NJ: Associated University Press, 2000).
Jill Rudd and Val Gough, eds., *Charlotte Perkins Gilman: Optimist Reformer* (Iowa City: University of Iowa Press, 1997).

Index

LaVergne, TN USA
25 April 2010
180322LV00012B/1/A